# Goat for Yahweh, Goat for Azazel

# Goat for Yahweh, Goat for Azazel

## The Impact of Yom Kippur on the Gospels

Hans M. Moscicke

LEXINGTON BOOKS/FORTRESS ACADEMIC

*Lanham • Boulder • New York • London*

Published by Lexington Books/Fortress Academic
Lexington Books is an imprint of The Rowman & Littlefield Publishing Group, Inc.
4501 Forbes Boulevard, Suite 200, Lanham, Maryland 20706
www.rowman.com

6 Tinworth Street, London SE11 5AL, United Kingdom

British Library Cataloguing in Publication Information Available

**Library of Congress Cataloging-in-Publication Data**

Names: Moscicke, Hans M., 1985- author.
Title: Goat for Yahweh, goat for Azazel : the impact of Yom Kippur on the gospels /
    Hans M. Moscicke.
Description: Lanham : Lexington Books/Fortress Academic, [2021] | Includes
    bibliographical references and index. | Summary: "This book explores the influence of
    the Day of Atonement on the Gospels. Hans M. Moscicke investigates how the gospel
    writers utilized the Yom Kippur traditions of the Second Temple period to craft
    Christological goat typologies and examines how scapegoat and Azazel traditions in
    first-century Judaism shaped the theology of the Gospels"—Provided by publisher.
Identifiers: LCCN 2021028126 (print) | LCCN 2021028127 (ebook) |
    ISBN 9781978712423 (cloth) | ISBN 9781978712430 (epub)
Subjects: LCSH: Bible. Gospels—Criticism, interpretation, etc. | Yom Kippur. |
    Scapegoat. | Azazel (Jewish mythology)
Classification: LCC BS2555.52 .M66 2021 (print) | LCC BS2555.52 (ebook) |
    DDC 226/.06dc23
LC record available at https://lccn.loc.gov/2021028126
LC ebook record available at https://lccn.loc.gov/2021028127

*To my parents, Mike and Carol Moscicke*

# Contents

# Acknowledgments

I have dedicated this book to my parents, Mike and Carol Moscicke, to whom I am most grateful for their loving support during my years of graduate school in Wheaton and Milwaukee. I attribute my initial interest in biblical literature and apocalypticism to my father, who encouraged my serious engagement with Scripture from a young age. My mother always encouraged me to pursue my own interests, and she truly believed I could do anything to which I set my mind. I am grateful to my parents for these things. I am also exceedingly grateful to Hugh and Judy Barlett, without whose help the writing of this book would not have been possible. I am blessed to have such wonderful parents-in-law who are practically supportive and exemplary models of godliness to me and my family.

# Introduction

In my earlier book, *The New Day of Atonement: A Matthean Typology*, I traced the First Evangelist's Yom Kippur typology of Jesus as the two goats of Leviticus 16 in Matthew 27, along with his other applications of Day of Atonement traditions in that same chapter.[1] I argue that Matthew remodels the Barabbas episode (Matt. 27:15–26) as a Yom Kippur lottery between two "goats." Pilate acts as high priest, designating Jesus as the immolated goat and Barabbas, along with the crowd, as a sin-bearing scapegoat. Matthew also casts Jesus as a scapegoat in the Roman-abuse scene (Matt. 27:27–31), in which he depicts Jesus as physically receiving the sins of the world. I suggest that Matthew, in his death-resurrection narrative (Matt. 27:50–54), arguably conceives Jesus as offering his life force to God as the sacrificial goat for Yahweh and descending to the realm of the dead as the goat for Azazel. That work, however, did not substantively consider the influence of Yom Kippur on other passages in the Gospel of Matthew. This work, in part, seeks to redress that particular weakness of my former book and advance our understanding of the Jewish evangelist's appropriation of Leviticus 16 and certain Day of Atonement traditions.

Such extensive thinking about the impact of Yom Kippur on the Gospel of Matthew raises the question of its influence on the other canonical gospels. Though commentators have conducted studies of individual passages, previous scholarship has generally neglected to consider the impact of Yom Kippur on the gospels as a whole. For example, Daniel Stökl Ben Ezra's magisterial and thorough work, *The Impact of Yom Kippur on Early Christianity*, investigates many New Testament passages in detail, but the only gospel text discussed in depth is Matthew's Barabbas account (Matt. 27:15–26).[2] The more recent volume, *The Day of Atonement: It Interpretations in Early Jewish and Christian Traditions*, edited by Thomas Hieke and Tobias Nicklas, dedicates

1

only one chapter to the gospels, and again only the Barabbas episode is discussed in detail.[3] The present volume seeks to redress this weakness in the current state of biblical scholarship as well.

Indeed, the Day of Atonement (*Yom ha-Kippurim*) was one of Israel's most important holy days on the liturgical calendar, and it remains so for the Jews to this day.

> Yom Kippur is the day for the purgation of the temple, a purgation eliminating
> everything which questions or disturbs human communication with the divine.
> It is also the day for the purgation of the people, the day the Israelites confess
> their iniquities and transgressions, and the day their sins are eliminated by way
> of an archaic ritual—sending the scapegoat into the wilderness.[4]

What significance did this very special occasion hold for the authors of the biblical gospels? The following work seeks to begin to provide an answer to that question.

This study does not set out to investigate every possible echo or allusion to Leviticus 16 and its associated traditions in the gospels. Rather, it identifies the passages that seem most likely to evince the influence of Leviticus 16 and Yom Kippur traditions and proceeds to analyze these passages in detail.

Chapter 1 comprises an analysis of the effect of Azazel and Yom Kippur traditions on Matthew's Final Judgment episode (Matt. 25:31–46), arguing that the evangelist portrays the expulsion of the unrighteous as a purgative event resembling the yearly expulsion of iniquity from the temple by means of the scapegoat. In chapter 2, I contend that Matthew constructs a goat-for-Yahweh typology in his baptism scene (Matt. 3:16–17) and a goat-for-Azazel typology in his temptation narrative (Matt. 4:1–11), foreshadowing the Christological goat typology in his passion narrative. I argue in chapter 3 that Luke's narrative regarding Jesus's visit to Nazareth (Luke 4:16–30) contains special material that has been shaped by Jubilee and Yom Kippur traditions. Jesus's scriptural citation of Isa. 58:6 and 61:1–2, and the townspeople's attempt to cast Jesus off a cliff, both recall Second Temple traditions pertaining to the Day of Atonement. Chapter 4 explores the impact of ancient elimination rituals and Azazel/scapegoat traditions on the Gerasene exorcism in the Gospel of Mark (Mark 5:1–20). I seek to understand how the Matthean and Lukan redactions develop these ritual tropes and trajectories (Matt. 8:28–34// Luke 8:26–40). Finally, chapter 5 investigates the influence of the Day of Atonement on John's resurrection narrative (John 20:11–23), especially his allusion to the cherubim and atonement slate in John 20:20. I raise the question of the significance of these Yom Kippur evocations for John's theology of atonement as a whole.

The methodology employed in this investigation largely consists of the traditional critical tools of source and redaction criticism, supplemented with literary and intertextual methods of analysis. Dale Allison's approach to discerning biblical typologies and Richard Hays's criteria of detecting scriptural echoes remain touchpoints in my analysis, though my use of these methods is implicit rather than explicit.[5] The approach of this monograph is in full agreement with Leroy Huizenga's insightful observation, that "Hays's criteria can help us listen for echoes not only to biblical texts but also to post-biblical *traditions* of interpretation attached to those texts."[6] That being said, detecting the effect of ancient traditions upon biblical literature can be, at times, quite difficult or seemingly futile. In some cases I argue for a deliberate biblical typology; in other cases I contend for the mere indirect influence of Yom Kippur traditions on a gospel text. In either case, the principal argument of this study is that the Day of Atonement has had a more profound impact on the gospels than has previously been recognized, especially those iconic figures in the Yom Kippur ritual known as "the goat for Yahweh" and "the goat for Azazel."

## NOTES

1. Hans M. Moscicke, *The New Day of Atonement: A Matthean Typology*, WUNT 2:517 (Tübingen: Mohr Siebeck, 2020).

2. Daniel Stökl Ben Ezra, *The Impact of Yom Kippur on Early Christianity: The Day of Atonement from Second Temple Judaism to the Fifth Century*, WUNT 1:163 (Tübingen: Mohr Siebeck, 2003).

3. Thomas Hieke and Tobias Nicklas, eds, *The Day of Atonement: Its Interpretation in Early Jewish and Christian Traditions*, TBN (Leiden: Brill, 2012).

4. Hieke and Nicklas, *The Day of Atonement*, vii. For an in-depth overview of Leviticus 16 and the scholarly critical issues regarding the biblical ritual, see Moscicke, *New Day of Atonement*, 55–65. For an in-depth overview of early Jewish Yom Kippur traditions, including those contained in the Book of Zechariah, the Book of Watchers, the Book of Jubilees, 4Q180–181, the Book of Giants, 11QMelchizedek, and the Apocalypse of Abraham, see ibid., 66–86.

5. Dale C. Allison, *The New Moses: A Matthean Typology* (Minneapolis: Fortress, 1993), 21–23; Richard B. Hays, *Echoes of Scripture in the Letters of Paul* (New Haven: Yale University Press, 1989), 29–32; idem, *The Conversion of the Imagination: Paul as Interpreter of Israel's Scripture* (Grand Rapids: Eerdmans, 2005), 34–45. This book's methodology closely follows that of Moscicke, *Day of Atonement*, 2–5.

6. Leroy A. Huizenga, *The New Isaac: Tradition and Intertextuality in the Gospel of Matthew*, NovTSup 131 (Leiden: Brill, 2009), 63 (emphasis mine).

# Chapter 1

# The Final Judgment as Ritual Purgation of Cosmos

## The Impact of Yom Kippur on "The Sheep and the Goats" (Matt. 25:31–46)

Arriving at the end of the gospel's fifth major discourse,[1] Matthew's final judgment scene (Matt. 25:31–46) depicts the Son of Man coming in glory with his angels, sitting upon "the throne of his glory" (v. 31), and judging all the nations gathered before him (v. 32a).[2] The Son of Man, like a shepherd, separates "the sheep" from "the goats," placing the sheep at his right hand and the goats at his left (vv. 32b–33). Now identified as a king (v. 34a), the Son of Man invites those sheep on his right side to inherit the kingdom prepared for them (v. 34b) and those goats on his left side to depart into the eternal fire prepared for the Devil and his angels (v. 41). Both judgments are issued on the basis of the treatment of "the least of these (my brothers)" (vv. 40, 45), in whom, to the surprise of all who are judged, the Son of Man was mysteriously present (vv. 35–39, 42–44).[3]

Given that scholars have yet to discover a satisfactory rationale for the negative valuation attributed to the "goats," and that, as Kathleen Weber observes, the "scapegoat that carries the sins of the people off into the desert in the ritual of the Day of Atonement (Lev 16:5–22) stands as a single negative exception that does not seem to have affected the consistently positive value accorded goats in OT poetic usage,"[4] it is surprising that there has hitherto been no investigation into the potential influence of Leviticus 16 and scapegoat traditions on the Matthean judgment account. Since both scenarios involve the expulsion of cursed goats, and since Matthew displays a keen interest in the Hebrew scriptures, it is prima facie quite plausible that early Jewish Yom Kippur traditions have influenced the imagery of Matt. 25:31–46. Such a theological underpinning to the climactic judgment scene would introduce into Matthew's eschatology a ritual element, wherein the final expulsion of all the unrighteous becomes a purgative event resembling the

5

yearly expulsion of iniquity from the earthly temple by means of the goat for Azazel (Lev. 16:21–22).[5]

In this chapter, I submit that Leviticus 16 and Second Temple Yom Kippur traditions have colored the portrayal of the sheep and especially the goats in Matt. 25:31–46.[6] While this underlying influence of the Day of Atonement is not the primary focus of the Matthean judgment episode, it sheds light on the scriptural background of the scene's imagery and brings to light a ritual component in the evangelist's eschatology. Having argued that Matt. 25:41 makes use of Azazel traditions attested in the Parables of Enoch, I propose five points of correspondence between Matt. 25:31–46 and early Jewish Yom Kippur traditions: (a) the imagery of goats, (b) the two opposing lots, (c) the expulsion of the goats, (d) the cursedness of the goats, and (e) the antithetical destination of the two animals. By mapping these tropes onto his account, Matthew colors the Son of Man's judgment as an eschatological ritual purgation of cosmos from human and angelic moral impurity.

## THE IMPACT OF AZAZEL TRADITIONS ON MATT. 25:31–46

In his important study, *The Son of Man in the Parables of Enoch and in Matthew*, Leslie Walck argues that the Parables of Enoch (1 Enoch 37–71) have influenced certain elements of Matt. 25:31–46, especially vv. 31–34, 41, 46.[7] While he cautiously eschews positing direct literary dependence on the Parables, Walck concludes that Matthew's unique material regarding the future Son of Man, particularly Matt. 13:37–43 and 25:31–46, "reveal[s] many characteristics of the Son of Man that are shared with the Parables. These two passages are unique to Matthew, containing the bulk of the traits attributed to the Son of Man. Of all the passages in Matthew containing 'Son of Man,' these two exhibit the most traits shared with the Parables, which suggests that Matthew's concept of the Son of Man was significantly influenced by the Parables."[8] David Catchpole had previously identified twelve points of correspondence between the Son of Man's judgment in Matt. 25:31–46 and 1 Enoch 62–63.[9] Building on Catchpole's catalog of similarities between these accounts, Walck demonstrates that Matt. 25:31–46 and the Parables of Enoch share several striking similarities. In short, these are: the Son of Man coming and sitting on "the throne of his glory" (Matt. 25:31; 1 En. 62.5; 69.27, 29; cf. 1 En. 47.3; 60.2; 62.2, 3; 71.7), the all-inclusive nature of the judgment (Matt. 25:32; 1 En. 48.5; 54.9–10; 62.3), the impossibility of reversing the verdicts of judgment (Matt. 25:34, 41; 1 En. 62.9–12, 13–16; 69.27), the hiddenness of the Son of Man to the righteous and the wicked (Matt. 25:40, 45; 1 En. 48.6–7; 62.5, 7), the criterion of judgment being the treatment of those with whom the Son of Man identifies (Matt. 25:40, 45; 1 En. 46.8; 47; 48.7; 62.11), the fiery fate of the unrighteous (Matt. 25:41; 1 En. 48.9; 54.1, 6), and the punishment prepared for the Devil/Satan, his angels, and the wicked of the earth (Matt. 25:41; 1 En. 54.5–6; 67.4–7, 12–13).[10] Summarizing his comparison between the Parables of Enoch and Matthew's future Son of Man sayings, Walck remarks, "The quantity and scope of these similarities together with the precise phrase 'the throne of glory' strongly suggests the influence of the Parables on Matthew's conception of the Son of Man."[11] While the question of the First Evangelist's literary dependence on the Parables remains a contentious issue, one may understand Walck's work as having satisfactorily demonstrated Matthew's knowledge of particular *traditions* associated with, and possibly deriving from, the Parables of Enoch.

The influence of the Parables of Enoch on Matt. 25:31–46 is significant for this study, since it opens up the possibility that the Azazel traditions attested in the Parables have impacted the judgment scene as well. Having narrated the king's dealings with the righteous "sheep," Matthew writes, "Then he will say to those at his left hand, 'Depart from me, cursed ones, into the eternal fire prepared for the Devil and his angels'" (Matt. 25:41). Walck draws attention to a parallel passage in 1 En. 54, where Enoch is shown a deep valley with burning fire, into which the kings and the mighty of the earth are thrown (1 En. 54.1–2).[12] The patriarch asks his *angelus interpres* about the great iron chains (1 En. 54.3–4), and the angel responds, "These are being prepared for the host of Azazel, that they might take them and throw them into the abyss of complete judgment" (1 En. 54.5).[13] A chapter later, Azazel's punishment is described in more detail: "Mighty kings who dwell on the earth, you will have to witness my Chosen One [=Son of Man], how he will *sit on the throne of glory* and *judge Azazel, and all his associates and all his host* in the name of the Lord of Spirits" (1 En. 55.4).[14] As Walck remarks, "The 'Devil and all his angels' (Mt. 25:41) bears a striking resemblance to 'Azazel and all his associates and all his host' (1 Enoch 55.4)."[15]

In fact, one detects a cluster of parallels between 1 En. 54.1–6; 55.4 and Matt. 25:41: (1) The place of eschatological punishment is fiery. In 1 En. 54.1, 6, it is described as "a deep valley with burning fire . . . the burning furnace." In Matt. 25:41, Matthew designates it as "the eternal fire." (2) The punishment is one that is specifically "prepared." Enoch asks the angel, "For whom are these chains being prepared?" (1 En. 54.4). The Son of Man identifies the eternal fire as "prepared for the Devil and his angels" (Matt. 25:41). (3) The punishment is for a malevolent spiritual leader. In 1 En. 55.4, the punishment is for Azazel. In Matt. 25:41, it is for the Devil. (4) The punishment is also for that leader's compatriots. It is for "the host of Azazel" in 1 En. 54.5. It is for "his angels" (the Devil's angels) in Matt. 25:41. (5) The earthly counterparts of these inimical powers suffer the same punishment. In 1 En. 54.2, "the kings and the mighty" are condemned alongside Azazel's host. In Matt. 25:42–45, the goats on the Son of Man's left side are judged alongside the Devil and his angels. (6) In both 1 En. 55.4 and Matt. 25:31, 41, the punishment of these malevolent powers occurs immediately after the Son of Man/Chosen One sits upon the "throne of glory." Noting just a few of these correspondences, Walck remarks, "These similarities are striking and extensive."[16]

Matthew's awareness of these Azazel traditions becomes almost certain in light of the fact that the redactional statement in Matt. 22:13 appears to be a verbal allusion to the Asael tradition of Greek 1 En. 10.4:[17] "Go, Raphael, and bind Asael hand and foot, and cast him into the darkness [δῆσον τὸν Ἀζαὴλ ποσὶν καὶ χερσίν, καὶ βάλε αὐτὸν εἰς τὸ σκότος]."[18] It is important to note that, in certain early Jewish apocalyptic circles, the fallen angel Asael came to be associated with Azazel of Leviticus 16 and conflated with the figure of the scapegoat.[19] In the Matthean parable, an intruder at the messianic banquet wearing garments of unrighteousness recapitulates the fate of this cosmic antagonist:[20] "Then the king said to his servants, 'Bind him hand and foot and cast him into the outer darkness' [δήσαντες αὐτοῦ πόδας καὶ χεῖρας ἐκβάλετε αὐτὸν εἰς τὸ σκότος τὸ ἐξώτερον]" (Matt. 22:13).[21] According to Ryszard Rubinkiewicz, Matthew draws upon the same vein of the scapegoat tradition attested in the Apocalypse of Abraham 13–14, where the patriarch's unclean garments symbolizing iniquity are given to Azazel, who is then banished to the nether regions of the earth.[22] This is a fascinating parallel, since the contexts of Matt. 22:13 and 25:41—two texts unique to the Gospel of Matthew— are essentially the same: at the eschatological judgment, a divine king banishes the unrighteous into perdition in a manner reminiscent of Asael/Azazel's expulsion.

It is therefore very likely that Matt. 25:31–46 has been influenced not only by the conception of the Son of Man as attested in the Parables of Enoch but also by the Azazel traditions attested within that same Enochic booklet. One need not posit direct literary dependence in this case, though this possibility cannot be ruled out. Rather, it will be safer to conclude that the same tradition concerning Azazel found in 1 En. 54:1–6; 55:4 appears to have influenced the composition of Matt. 25:41. This conclusion becomes even more certain, given Matthew's unique application of the Asael/Azazel tradition that is attested both in 1 En. 10:4 and in his Parable of the Wedding Feast (Matt. 22:13).

## THE INFLUENCE OF YOM KIPPUR ON MATT. 25:31–46

Turning to a broader analysis of Matt. 25:31–46, I propose five points of correspondence between the Matthean judgment account and early Jewish Yom

Kippur traditions: (a) the imagery of goats, (b) the two opposing lots, (c) the expulsion of the goats, (d) the cursedness of the goats, and (e) the antithetical destinations of the two animals. The mapping of these tropes associated with Israel's high holy day onto the judgment scene suffuses it with ritual undertones.

## The Imagery of Goats

Scholars remain perplexed about the origin and purpose of the imagery of the sheep and the "young goats,"[23] and about why it is that the goats are chosen to be the recipients of divine wrath in Matthew's judgment scene. Kathleen Weber's extensive research on the image of sheep and goats in Matt. 25:32–33 demonstrates that very little in Matthew's cultural milieu would suggest such a negative attitude toward goats.[24] She concludes that "the author of the Gospel according to Matthew expects his audience to have a basically positive attitude toward goats that will make the absolute condemnation of Matt. 24:31–46 surprising."[25] Noting that the Hebrew Bible portrays goats predominantly in a positive light, Weber makes the following important observation: "The scapegoat that carries the sins of the people off into the desert in the ritual of the Day of Atonement (Lev. 16:5–22) stands as a single negative exception that does not seem to have affected the consistently positive value accorded goats in OT poetic usage."[26] Students of Matthew have not considered whether early Jewish scapegoat traditions have contributed to the construction of the agricultural scene in Matt. 25:32–33. However, there might be a good explanation for this.

The LXX employs χίμαρος for "goat" (Lev. 16: 8, 9, 10, 15, 18, 20, 21, 22, 26, 27), not ἔριφος or ἐρίφιον, which are the terms used in Matt. 25:32–33. At first glance, this discrepancy in vocabulary seems like an insurmountable challenge to the thesis that the Matthean judgment scene draws upon scapegoat traditions. But upon closer inspection, this challenge loses its force. The term χίμαρος was not a *terminus technicus* for the goats of the Yom Kippur ritual. While the LXX uses χίμαρος, Philo, the Epistle to the Hebrews, and the Epistle of Barnabas employ τράγος (*Her.* 179; *Leg.* 2.52; Heb 9:12, 13; Barn. 7.4, 6, 8, 10). Josephus uses ἔριφος, the same term found in Matt. 25:32. Describing the customs of the Day of Atonement, he writes, "On the tenth of the same lunar month they fast until evening; on this day they sacrifice a bull, two rams, seven lambs, and a kid [ἔριφον] as sin-offering. But besides these they offer two kids [δύο ἐρίφους], of which one is sent alive into the wilderness beyond the frontiers, being intended to avert and serve as an expiation for the sins of the whole people."[27] The Book of Jubilees also affirms that the goats of Yom Kippur were young goats. In its second etiology of the high holy day, Jubilees grounds the Day of Atonement in the story of

Jacob's sons' betrayal of Joseph and their need for expiation. The pseude-pigraphon reads: "Jacob's sons slaughtered a *he-goat*, stained Joseph's cloth-ing by dipping it in its blood, and sent (it) to their father Jacob on the tenth of the seventh month . . . For this reason, it has been ordained regarding the Israelites that they should be distressed on the tenth of the seventh month . . . in order to make atonement for themselves on it *with a kid*."[28] In the LXX of Genesis 37, the biblical passage on which Jubilees bases its etiology, Jacob's sons stain Joseph's coat with the blood of an ἔριφος: "And having taken the coat of Joseph, they slew a kid of the goats [ἔριφον αἰγῶν; MT: שעיר עזים], and they stained the coat with blood" (Gen 37:31).

Weber attempts to explain the unexpected choice of goats in Matt. 25:31–46 by pointing to the apparent theme of surprise in all three eschatological discourses in Matthew 25.[29] The foolish virgins are surprised to find that the door is shut to the bridegroom's wedding banquet (Matt. 25:10–12). The lazy servant is surprised when his master confiscates his talent and gives it to another person (Matt. 25:26–29). The goats are surprised to learn that the Son of Man was mysteriously present in "the least of these" (Matt. 25:44–45). But even if one grants the presence of this theme in Matthew 25, the judgment of the goats still lacks a rationale that accords with the discourse's parabolic imagery, unlike the other two eschatological discourses. The rationale for the foolish virgins' punishment is their foolishness (Matt. 25:8–10), and the ratio-nale for the lazy servant's condemnation is his laziness (Matt. 25:18, 26–27), but there is no analogous rationale for the judgment of the goats.

In sum, some Second Temple traditions construe the two goats of the Yom Kippur ritual as young goats or "kids" (ἔριφοι), the same type of goats that appear in "the sheep and the goats" parable of Matt. 25:32–33. Very little in Matthew's Jewish milieu would suggest such a harshly negative attitude toward goats, except for the scapegoat of the Yom Kippur ritual. In this ritual, the goat designated "for Azazel" (Lev. 16:8, 10) inherited all of Israel's sins (Lev. 16:21) and was sent into the wilderness "to Azazel" (Lev. 16:10), to purge the nation's iniquity from the temple (Lev. 16:22). An association between the goats in Matt. 25:31–46 and the scapegoat provides a rationale for the negative appraisal of that lot of goats on the Son of Man's left side.

## The Two Opposing Lots

To explain why the shepherd would separate sheep from goats (Matt. 25:32–33), commentators often appeal to the alleged fact that Palestinian shepherds would customarily separate their mixed flocks at the end of the day, because sheep preferred the open air and goats were more susceptible to becoming cold, needing nightly shelter.[30] But Klaus Wengst has demonstrated that this notion has little factual basis in ancient Palestinian practice and actually derives from a misreading of a statement in Gustaf Dalman's *Arbeit und Sitte in Palästina* that has been perpetuated in modern scholarship.[31] Though other explanations have been proffered for the separation of the animals, these have proved less than satisfactory.[32] Luz remarks, "Why a shepherd should separate the goats from the sheep thus remains a puzzle."[33] The lack of an obvious agricultural explanation for the separation of the animals suggests that the separation is, at least in part, theologically motivated.[34]

Regardless of which agricultural verisimilitude the separating in Matt. 25:32–33 is intended to evoke, the outcome is the same: the shepherd generates two opposing lots, the sheep "at his right" (ἐκ δεξιῶν αὐτοῦ) and the goats "at his left" (ἐξ εὐωνύμων). This imagery continues implicitly throughout the judgment scene, as τοῖς ἐκ δεξιῶν αὐτοῦ (Matt. 25:34) recalls the image of the lot of sheep and τοῖς ἐξ εὐωνύμων (Matt. 25:41) recalls the image of the lot of goats. Such lot imagery brings to mind certain traditions associated with the Day of Atonement. In the Yom Kippur ritual, the high priest takes two goats, presents them before the Lord, and casts lots over them, "one lot for the Lord and one lot for Azazel" (Lev. 16:7–8).

Certain authors in the Second Temple period mapped the lot imagery of Lev. 16:8–10 onto antithetical social groups. Commenting on this phenomenon in the Dead Sea Scrolls, Stökl Ben Ezra writes that "the people from Qumran understood their own existence through the image of the two lots— they themselves are the people of God's lot in opposition to the lot of Belial led by the wicked priest."[35] Commenting on the notion that one could "cast his lot [יתן גורלו] among those who are cursed forever" by apostatizing from the sect (1QS II, 17), Miryam Brand remarks, "The manner in which *gwrl* is employed in II.17, and in fact throughout the entire passage of 1QS I.16– II.19, is drawn from the appearance of the term *gwrl* in the ceremony described in Lev. 16:7–10."[36]

Philo of Alexandria utilizes the imagery of the two lots to link those who seek after heavenly wisdom with the lot of the goat for Yahweh and those who seek after carnal things with the lot of the scapegoat:

> I am deeply impressed, too, by the contrast made between the two he-goats offered for atonement, and the difference of fate assigned to them . . . We see two ways of thinking; one whose concern is with things of divine virtue is consecrated and dedicated to God; the other whose aspirations turn to poor miserable humanity is assigned to creation the exile. For the lot which fell to creation is called by the oracles the lot of dismissal, because creation is a homeless wanderer, banished far away from wisdom.[37]

In the Apocalypse of Abraham, lots of humanity are associated both with Abraham, whom the author typologizes as the immolated goat, and with

Azazel, who is portrayed as a scapegoat. Consider the following passages in the Slavonic apocalypse:

> [He said:] "Stand up, Abraham, go boldly, be very joyful and rejoice! And I am with you, since an *honorable portion* has been prepared for you by the Eternal One" . . . And he said to him, "Reproach is on you, Azazel! Since Abraham's *portion* is in heaven, and *yours* is on earth" . . . "Since your *inheritance* are those who are with you, with men born with the stars and clouds. And *their portion* is you" . . . And he said to me, "As the number of the stars and their host, so shall I make your seed into a company of nations, set apart for me in *my lot* with Azazel."[38]

According to Andrei Orlov, "The transference of this imagery of the two lots onto humankind is significant here, as the cultic functions of the lots are assigned not merely to eschatological or human characters, but to the social bodies themselves."[39]

Origen also applies a sociological interpretation of the lot imagery. In his *Homilies on Leviticus*, Origen sets out a programmatic understanding of the Yom Kippur lot imagery:

> If all the people of God were holy and all were blessed, there would not be two lots for the he-goats, one lot to be sent "into the wilderness," the other offered to God, but there would be one lot and one offering to the Lord alone. But now since in the multitude of them who approach the Lord, some are of the Lord but others are those who ought to be sent "into the wilderness," that is, who are worthy to be cast out and separated from the offering of the Lord . . . a lot falls upon both.[40]

Origen designates Lazarus as a member of the lot of Yahweh and the rich man as an affiliate of the lot of the scapegoat:

> Do you want me to show you clearly how these two lots always are operative and each of us becomes either "the lot of the Lord" or "the lot of the scapegoat" or of "the wilderness"? Consider in the Gospels that "rich man" living "splendidly" and luxuriously and "Lazarus lying at his door full of sores and wanting to be filled with the crumbs which were falling from the table of the rich man." The end of each one is described. It says, "Lazarus died and was carried by the angels into the bosom of Abraham. But likewise the rich man also died and was carried into the place of torment." You notice clearly the different places of each lot.[41]

Origen then typologies the faithful criminal crucified with Jesus as a constituent of the lot of Yahweh and the criminal who reviled Jesus as a participant in the scapegoat's lot.

But do you still want to see another form of the two lots? Consider those two "robbers" who at the time of his crucifixion "were suspended one at his right hand and one at his left." See that the one who confessed the Lord was made "a lot of the Lord" and was taken without delay "to paradise." But that other one who "reviled" him was made "the lot of the scapegoat" that was sent "into the wilderness" of Hell.[42]

The two lots of Yom Kippur also became associated with the right and the left sides in early rabbinic Judaism. The Mishnah describes the lot-casting custom as involving the high priest raising his right or left hands as the lots were cast:

He shook the casket and took up the two lots. On one was written "For the Lord," and on the other was written "For Azazel." The Prefect was on his right and the chief of the father's house on his left. If the lot bearing the Name came up in his right hand the Prefect would say to him, "My lord High Priest, raise thy right hand"; and if it came up in his left hand the chief of the father's house would say to him, "My lord High Priest, raise thy left hand." He put them on the two he-goats and said, "A Sin-offering to the Lord."[43]

In the Babylonian Talmud, the immolated goat is associated with the right side during times of divine favor:

Our Rabbis taught: Throughout the forty years that Simeon the Righteous ministered, the lot ["For the Lord"] would always come up in the right hand; from that time on, it would come up now in the right hand, now in the left . . . Our Rabbis taught: During the last forty years before the destruction of the Temple the lot ["For the Lord"] did not come up in the right hand.[44]

Targum Pseudo-Jonathan connects the high priest's right hand with the goat for Yahweh and his left hand with the goat for Azazel, instructing the high priest to sprinkle the blood of the immolated goat with his right hand, but then to lay only his left hand directly upon the scapegoat: "And he shall take some of the blood of the bull and of the blood of the goat . . . And he shall sprinkle some of the blood upon it seven times with the finger of his *right hand* . . . Aaron shall lay both his hands on the head of the live goat, *in this fashion: his right hand upon his left.*"[45] The two eschatological lots of Abraham and Azazel in the Apocalypse of Abraham also possess right and left imagery, though these sections of the Slavonic pseudepigraphon may contain Bogomil influence.[46]

In short, the imagery of two opposing lots in Matthew's judgment scene (Matt. 25:32–34, 41) is congruous with the way other Second Temple authors interpreted the "lot for Yahweh" and the "lot for Azazel" (Lev. 16:8–10), mapping each lot onto antithetical social groups. The imagery of the right and left side also parallels the way the lot motif was interpreted in later Judaism, the right side being associated with the lot for Yahweh and the left side with the lot for Azazel. Given the lack of an otherwise satisfactory explanation for the separation of the animals into two opposing lots, this separation is plausibly motivated by an underlying Yom Kippur typology.[47]

## The Expulsion of the Goats

Commenting on the violent expulsion of the lot of goats in the Matthean judgment scene (Matt. 25:41), Kathleen Weber remarks, "Certainly, the audience of Matthew's own time could point to certain blemishes on the reputation of goats as animals . . . but not with negative qualities extreme enough to merit this expulsion."[48] However, if the goats in Matthew's judgment scene are intended to evoke to the sin-bearing scapegoat that was banished from Jerusalem and sent to the nefarious desert-dwelling deity Azazel (="The Devil and his angels"), then their expulsion in Matt. 25:41 is entirely fitting.

Once he deposited Israel's sins upon the scapegoat, the high priests banished the goat for Azazel into the wilderness, where those sins could pose no further threat: "The goat shall bear all their iniquity to a remote area, and he shall release the goat into the wilderness" (Lev. 16:22).[49] This became a memorable trope in early Jewish thought. Philo reports that the scapegoat "was to be sent out into a trackless and desolate wilderness."[50] He allegorizes the Septuagint's term for the scapegoat, ἀποπομπαῖος (Lev. 16:8, 10), underlining that the goat "is removed, caused to live apart, and driven away."[51] According to Josephus, the scapegoat "is sent alive into the wilderness beyond the frontiers."[52] In apocalyptic appropriations of the scapegoat ritual, the celestial scapegoat Asael/Azazel is cast into the cosmic wilderness. Raphael is told to "bind Asael hand and foot, and cast him into the darkness; and make an opening in the wilderness that is in Doudael. Throw him there."[53] In the Apocalypse of Abraham, Azazel becomes "the firebrand of the furnace of the earth" and is banished "into the untrodden parts of the earth," that is to say, into the cosmic wilderness.[54]

While one wishes for a verbal parallel between Matthew's πορεύεσθε ἀπ' ἐμοῦ (Matt. 25:41) and a term for the scapegoat's "sending" in Lev. 16:10, 21–22, 26 LXX (ἀποστέλλω, ἀφίημι, ἐξαποστέλλω), the conceptual parallel between the goats' expulsion in Matt. 25:41 and the scapegoat's expulsion in early Judaism is quite strong. The correspondence between Matthew's judgment scene and apocalyptic applications of the scapegoat ritual is more striking, since in both scenarios the banished subjects are personified scapegoats and grave perpetrators of evil.

## The Cursedness of the Goats

The presence of the Matthean *hapax legomenon* καταράομαι (Matt. 25:41) has puzzled some scholars, since this word occurs in a verse that otherwise bears the mark of the evangelist's editorial hand. Yet it is perfectly fitting that "those at his left hand," that is, the lot of goats, should be identified as "cursed," since the scapegoat was also an inheritor of curses in early Jewish traditions.

Philo reports that the scapegoat was sent into the wilderness "bearing on itself the curses [τὰς ἀράς] for those who have erred."[55] The Epistle of Barnabas's halakhic source employs a close cognate to Matthew's καταράομαι to call the scapegoat "cursed": "Pay attention: 'The one they take to the altar, but the other is cursed [ἐπικατάρατον],' and the one that is cursed [τὸν ἐπικατάρατον] is crowned."[56] Tertullian similarly writes that the scapegoat was "surrounded with scarlet, *cursed* and spit upon."[57] The Mishnah reports that the scapegoat was effectively the recipient of verbal cursing: "And they made a causeway for it because of the Babylonians who used to pull its hair, crying to it, 'Bear [our sins] and be gone! Bear [our sins] and be gone'!"[58] Yahoel similarly curses Azazel in the Slavonic apocalypse: "This is iniquity, this is Azazel! . . . Reproach is on you, Azazel! Since Abraham's portion is in heaven, and yours is on earth."[59]

The goats of Matt. 25:31–46 suffer a similar cursed status as the goat for Azazel. Such cursedness was a natural extension of the notion that the scapegoat bore upon itself the sins of the people (Lev. 16:21–22). One may rightfully object that the goats in Matthew's judgment scene do not bear the sins or curses of others, but neither does Asael/Azazel obviously bear others' iniquity in the Enochic tradition—he appears to be punished primarily for his own transgressions.[60] This is an important transformation in the scapegoat tradition, which seems to have allowed Matthew to map a scapegoat typology onto the goats of Matt. 25:31–46.

## The Antithetical Destinations of the Two Animals

The destinations of the sheep and goats are antithetical, the righteous entering into the Father's kingdom and the wicked being cast into eternal punishment: "Then the king will say to those at his right hand, 'Come, you that are blessed by my Father, inherit the kingdom prepared for you from the foundation of the world' . . . Then he will say to those at his left hand, 'You that are accursed, depart from me into the eternal fire prepared for the devil and his angels' . . . And these will go away into eternal punishment, but the righteous into eternal life" (Matt. 25:34, 41, 46). Such stark antithetical destinations evoke the spatial movement of the high priest and the two goats on Yom Kippur.

Lev. 16:8 commands that Aaron "cast lots on the two goats, one lot for the Lord, and one lot for Azazel." The parallelism in the phrase גורל אחד ליהוה וגורל אחד לעזאזל, highlighted by the preposition ל, suggests the contrary movements of the two animals: one will go "to the Lord" beyond the inner veil, and the other will go "to Azazel" in the wilderness. This notion is confirmed by Lev. 16:10, which states that the scapegoat is to be "sent away into the wilderness *to Azazel* [לעזאזל]." Summarizing this phenomenon, Stökl Ben Ezra writes:

> This Temple ritual consisted of two antagonistic movements, which I call centripetal and centrifugal: the entrance of the High Priest into the Holy of Holies and the expulsion of the scapegoat. As the first movement, the holiest person, the High Priest, entered the most sacred place, the Holy of Holies of the Jerusalem Temple [with the blood of the goat for Yahweh] ... As a second movement, the scapegoat burdened with the sins of the people was sent with an escort to the desert.[61]

The halakhic material utilized in the Epistle of Barnabas alludes to the antithetical destinations of the two animals: "The one they take to the altar, but the other is cursed."[62]

This antithetical-destination motif seems to be reflected in the apocalyptic *imaginaire* of Yom Kippur as well. In the Book of Watchers, Asael is banished like a scapegoat into an abyss in 1 Enoch 10, and then Enoch experiences the opposite cosmic movement, ascending into the heavenly temple in 1 Enoch 14. Orlov summarizes:

> It is intriguing that, while the main antagonist of the Book of Watchers is envisioned as the eschatological scapegoat, the main protagonist of the story—the patriarch Enoch—appears to be understood as the high priestly figure who is destined to enter into the celestial Holy of Holies. This dynamic once again mimics the peculiar processions of the protagonist and the antagonist on the Day of Atonement, wherein the high priest enters the divine presence, and the scapegoat is exiled into the wilderness. The Book of Watchers reflects the same cultic pattern as its hero, Enoch, progresses in the opposite direction of his antagonistic counterpart Asael.[63]

This pattern is also reflected in the Animal Apocalypse. Enoch experiences an ascent into a high tower symbolic of the heavenly sanctuary:[64] "And those three who came after took hold of me by my hand and raised me from the generations of the earth, and lifted me onto a high place, and they showed me a tower high above the earth, and all the hills were smaller."[65] Immediately after this, Enoch witnesses the judgment of Azazel: "And I saw one of those four who had come before; he seized that first star that had fallen from heaven, and he bound it by its hands and feet and threw it into an abyss, and that abyss was narrow and deep and desolate and dark."[66]

The Apocalypse of Abraham employs the antithetical paradigm of the Yom Kippur goats as well. Azazel is to undergo a cosmic descent (Apoc. Ab. 14.5–6), but Abraham will ascend into the celestial sanctuary (Apoc. Ab. 15–32) and become a sacrifice to God.[67] Orlov remarks:

> In a manner similar to Enoch in the Book of Watchers, in the Abrahamic pseudepigraphon, the hero progresses in the opposite direction of his negative counterpart. Abraham ascends into heaven, while his infamous fallen counterpart descends into the lower realms. In both texts, then, there are mirroring themes of ascent and descent. The apocalyptic drama of the Slavonic pseudepigraphon can thus be seen as a reenactment of the two spatial dynamics which are also reflected in the Yom Kippur ritual: there is both an entrance into the upper realm and an exile into the underworld.[68]

In sum, Matthew appears to map the antithetical destinations of the two goats of Yom Kippur onto the two lots of humanity in the judgment scene as other Jewish writers of his time had done. As with the apocalyptic Yom Kippur traditions, the respective movements of both entities become cosmic and acquire eschatological significance.

## MATT. 25:31–46 IN LIGHT OF MATTHEW'S CONCEPT OF SIN AND ATONEMENT

Matthew's repeated use of the scapegoat-Azazel motif raises the broader question of his conception of sin and atonement in the gospel. While space cannot afford a thorough consideration of these matters here, several comments are in order. Scholars have posited a Christological immolated goat typology in the Barabbas episode (Matt. 27:15–26) and a Christological scapegoat typology in the Roman-abuse narrative (Matt. 27:27–31).[69] The latter betrays the same notion of banishing iniquity that is present in Matt. 22:13 and 25:41. Only in Matthew's abuse narrative is Jesus adorned with a *scarlet* garment (Matt. 27:28), which is likely intended to recall the scarlet ribbon tied around the scapegoat, symbolizing the sins placed upon it.[70] Jesus is then led outside the city, like the scapegoat carrying away Israel's iniquity (Matt. 27:31; cf. Lev. 16:21–22). This ritual drama is apparently part of what it means for Jesus's death to be εἰς ἄφεσιν ἁμαρτιῶν (Matt. 26:28). Noting that Lev. 16:26 constitutes the only occurrence of εἰς ἄφεσιν in the Septuagint, which speaks of the release of the scapegoat (and the sins it bore) into the wilderness, Hamilton intriguingly suggests that, in his saying over the cup (Matt. 26:28), "Matthew's terminology—περί, ἁμαρτία, ἄφεσις—is that of Leviticus 16, where . . . the sending away of sin (through the scapegoat) is part of a rite of atonement."[71]

But Matthew's mapping of a scapegoat typology on both the wicked at the final judgment (Matt. 22:13; 25:41) and Jesus in the passion narrative (Matt. 26:28; 27:28, 31) leads to a paradox: How could the righteous and the unrighteous both fulfill the function of the goat for Azazel? First, as noted earlier, the scapegoat tradition undergoes a transformation in Enochic literature, so that Asael/Azazel as scapegoat now primarily bears his own iniquity. This disjunction explains one difference in how the scapegoat typology is mapped onto Jesus and the unrighteous, as Jesus bears the sins of others, while the unrighteous, who are co-conspirators with the Devil/Azazel (Matt. 22:13; 25:41), only bear their own iniquity.

Second, Matthew's variegated application of the scapegoat typology is constituent of what appears to be a prevailing concept of sin in the First Gospel, namely, sin as an object in need of physical removal or elimination.[72] Matthew employs this notion primarily in eschatological contexts.[73] John the Baptist proclaims, "Every tree that does not bear good fruit is cut down and thrown into the fire" (Matt. 3:10; cf. 3:12). Disciples who lose their saltiness are "thrown out and trampled underfoot" (Matt. 5:13). The right eye or hand that causes one to sin should be "torn out and thrown away" (Matt. 5:29–30; 18:8–9). They are commanded to "remove the log" (major sin) from their eyes before they "remove the speck" (minor sin) from their neighbor's eye (Matt. 7:3–5). The unfruitful tree "is cut down and thrown into the fire" (Matt. 7:19). Evildoers are told, "I never knew you. Go away from me" (Matt. 7:23). The weeds sowed in the field are "collected and bound in bundles to be burned" (Matt. 13:30). The Son of Man will gather all σκάνδαλα and workers of lawlessness and "cast them into a fiery furnace" (Matt. 13:41–42). The eschatological harvestmen "throw out" the bad fish "into the furnace of fire" (Matt. 13:48, 50). Every plant that the heavenly Father has not planted "will be uprooted" (Matt. 15:13). When Satan becomes a σκάνδολον to Jesus, he is told to "depart" (Matt. 16:23). Those who scandalize young disciples would justly be "drowned in the depths of the sea" (Matt. 18:6). Jesus himself becomes a σκάνδολον (Matt. 11:6; 13:37) to be discarded as "the stone that the builders rejected" (Matt. 21:42; cf. 21:39). The man dressed in garments of unrighteousness is bound and "hurled into the outer darkness" (Matt. 22:13). Noah's wicked generation is "swept away" by the Flood (Matt. 24:39). The unfaithful steward is "cut in pieces and placed with the hypocrites" (Matt. 24:51). The lot of unrighteous goats are told, "Depart from me into the eternal fire" (Matt. 25:41; cf. 25:46).

Such statements assume a metaphor of sin, whether abstractly or as embodied in sinners, as an object in need of physical removal or elimination.[74] This is the same notion of sin that is operative in Leviticus 16 and early Jewish scapegoat traditions.

## CONCLUSION

Based on the foregoing analysis, it is highly probable that Leviticus 16 and Second Temple Yom Kippur traditions have influenced the composition of Matt. 25:31–46, suffusing it with ritual undertones. There are at least five points of correspondence between the Matthean account and early Jewish Yom Kippur traditions: (a) the imagery of goats, (b) the two opposing lots, (c) the expulsion of the goats, (d) the cursedness of the goats, and (e) the antithetical destinations of the two animals. The noticeable effect of the Azazel traditions attested in the Parables of Enoch (1 En. 54.1–6; 55.4) on the evangelist's climactic episode, especially on Matt. 25:41, lends compelling support to this thesis.[75]

What Lester Grabbe claims regarding the conflation of Azazel and Satan traditions in the description of the dragon's punishment in Revelation 20 seems to hold true for Matt. 25:41:

> Whatever the original significance of the Azazel goat, it became a demonological figure in Judaism. To many Jews in the last century or so before the fall of the Second Temple, the mention of the name Azazel was likely to evoke this entire developed demonic tradition. A reference to Satan did not necessarily suggest the Day of Atonement ceremony, yet it was always available in the background and its symbolism could be called on when needed . . . Thus, the punishment of Satan has been assimilated to the Asael tradition of 1 Enoch.[76]

That is to say, Matthew has apparently assimilated aspects of Asael/Azazel's profile to that of the Devil in Matt. 25:41. Scholars should further investigate the impact of Enochic demonological traditions on the Gospel of Matthew.

The ritual shading that Matt. 25:31–46 acquires in light of its use of Yom Kippur imagery fits exceptionally well into Matthew's overarching interest in moral purity. As Anders Runesson observes, "Matthew operates fully within a Jewish interpretive paradigm in which both ritual and especially moral purity concerns are active and affect how the story is being told."[77] The logical conclusion to the drama of moral impurity in Matthew's theological imagination involves the Son of Man's eschatological purgation of iniquity from the cosmos in a manner reminiscent of the yearly expulsion of moral impurity from Israel's temple by means of the scapegoat ritual.

## NOTES

1. The five major discourses in Matthew are (1) Matt. 5:1–7:27, (2) Matt. 9:36–10:42, (3) Matt. 13:1–52, (4) Matt. 17:22–18:35, and (5) Matt. 23:1–25:46. The Parable of the Sheep and the Goats (Matt. 25:31–46) follows three parables concerning eschatological judgment (Matt. 24:45–51; 25:1–13, 14–30), concludes Jesus's Olivet discourse begun in Matt. 24:3, and is Jesus's last saying before the ensuing events of the passion narration.

2. Interpreters have understood πάντα τὰ ἔθνη to mean (1) all human beings, (2) only Christians, (3) all non-Christians, or (4) all non-Jews. In his comprehensive history of interpretation, Sherman W. Gray concludes that, of those who discuss the meaning of the phrase, the majority of commentators in every historical era take a universalist interpretation, that is to say, option one (*The Least of My Brothers, Matthew 25:31–46: A History of Interpretation*, SBLDS 114 [Atlanta: Scholars, 1989], 348; see also Ulrich Luz, *Matthew: A Commentary*, trans. James E. Crouch, 3 vols., Hermeneia [Minneapolis: Fortress, 2001–2007], 3:267–74; idem, "The Final Judgment [Matt. 25:31–46]: An Exercise in 'History of Influence' Exegesis," in *Treasures New and Old: Contributions to Matthean Studies*, ed. David R. Bauer and Mark Allen Powell [Atlanta: Scholars Press, 1996], 271–310). The second most common reading is option two. The last two readings did not emerge until the modern era, and even then, they are minority interpretations (Gray, *Least of My Brothers*, 349). The standard universalist interpretation seems most likely, given that (a) πάντα τὰ ἔθνη elsewhere includes non-Christians (Matt. 24:9, 14; 28:19), ruling out option two, (b) "one expects here a solemn appeal to those within the church . . . [given that] the passage belongs to a long section which is full of paraenesis for believers [Matt. 24:36–25:30]" (W. D. Davies and Dale C. Allison, *The Gospel According to Matthew*, ICC, 3 vols. [Edinburgh: T&T Clark, 1988–1997], 3:422), which makes option three unlikely, and (c) Jews are the object of (eschatological) judgment throughout the gospel (Matt. 3:7–10; 5:20; 12:34–37, 41–42; 21:41–45; 23:1–39), casting doubt on option four. In further support of option one, (d) the righteous and unrighteous are judged simultaneously in the redactional Parable of the Wheat and the Tares (Matt. 13:31–43), (e) though ἔθνη (plural) usually refers to pagan Gentiles in the First Gospel (Matt. 4:15; 6:32; 10:5, 18; 12:18; 20:19, 25; 21), ἔθνη embraces Christians in Matt. 12:21, and ἔθνος (singular) indicates Christians in Matt. 21:43, and (f) πάντα τὰ ἔθνη seems to include Christians in Acts 15:17; Rom. 15:11; 16:26; Rev. 12:5. Space cannot afford a more in-depth discussion on this topic.

3. The phrase εἷς τούτων (τῶν ἀδελφῶν μου) τῶν ἐλαχίστων (Matt. 25:40, 45) has historically been understood as (1) people in general or (2) Christians only (or some subset thereof, such as Christian missionaries). According to Gray, the particularist reading (option two), when compared to the universalist reading (option one), occurs at a ratio of about two to one throughout the history of interpretation (*Least of My Brothers*, 349–50). However, the number of interpreters, ancient and modern, who are neutral with regard to "the least of these," when compared to the particularist reading, occurs at a ratio of about three to two (ibid.). It is unclear whether such neutrality should be construed as affirming a universalist reading. From a literary

perspective, a particularist reading of "the least of these" (Matt. 25:40, 45) seems most probable, since Matthew uses a similar phrase, εἷς/ἓν τῶν μικρῶν τούτων, in reference to Jesus's disciples in Matt. 10:42; 18:6, 10, 14 (see also Matt. 11:11; cf. Mark 9:37–42) (Graham Stanton, *A Gospel for a New People: Studies in Matthew* [Edinburgh: T&T Clark, 1992], 214–18). Matt. 10:42 is a particularly striking parallel, since, (a) not only is ἕνα τῶν μικρῶν τούτων similar to εἷς τούτων τῶν ἐλαχίστων (Matt. 25:45), but (b) there is also an act of mercy resulting in a reward, as in Matt. 25:34–36, and (c) two verses earlier in Matt. 10:40, Jesus explicitly identifies himself with his disciples in a manner similar to Matt. 25:40, 45 (cf. Jan Lambrecht, *Out of the Treasure: The Parables in the Gospel of Matthew* [Louvain: Peeters, 1991], 278–79). Space does not allow for a more thorough analysis of this subject.

4. Kathleen Weber, "The Image of the Sheep and the Goats in Matthew 25:31–46," *CBQ* 59 (1997): 657–78, at 670. See further below.

5. Scholars typically propose one of several possibilities with regard to the origin and tradition history of "Azazel" (Lev. 16:8, 10, and 26) in ancient Israel: (1) "Azazel" was the name of a supernatural deity, (2) "Azazel" was the name or description of the (type of) place where the scapegoat was sent, (3) "Azazel" was an abstract noun indicating the sacerdotal function of the scapegoat, or (4) "Azazel" denoted the act of sending away the scapegoat. For a recent summary of these viewpoints, see Aron Pinker, "A Goat to Go to Azazel," *JHebS* 7 (2007): 2–25, at 4–13; see also Bernd Janowski and Gernot Wilhelm, "Der Bock, der die Sünden hinausträgt," in *Religionsgeschichtliche Beziehungen zwischen Kleinasien, Nordsyrien und dem Alten Testament*, ed. Bernd Janowski et al., OBO 129 (Freiburg: Vandenhoeck & Ruprecht, 1993), 109–69, at 119–29, 134–58; Bernd Janowski, "Azazel," in *Dictionary of Deities and Demons in the Bible*, ed. Karel van der Toorn, Bob Becking, and Pieter W. van der Horst, 2nd ed. (Leiden: Brill, 1999), 128–31, at 128–29. Most scholars affirm the supernatural identity of Azazel at some point in Israel's history. Jacob Milgrom, whom most scholars follow on this point, argues that Azazel was originally conceived as a wilderness deity but was later eviscerated of his supernatural identity in the Priestly redaction of the Pentateuch (*Leviticus: A New Translation with Introduction and Commentary*, AB, 3 vols. [New York: Doubleday, 1991–2001], 1:1021). David P. Wright agrees with Milgrom, adding that in Leviticus 16 the scapegoat "does not appear to be a propitiary offering to Azazel, but only serves as a vehicle for transporting the sins" (*The Disposal of Impurity: Elimination Rites in the Bible and in Hittite and Mesopotamian Literature*, SBLDS 101 [Atlanta: Scholars, 1986], 21–25, 30). Janowski reverses the position of Milgrom and Wright, arguing that Azazel only came to possess a celestial identity in post-exilic Judaism ("Der Bock," 130). Pinker proposes that Azazel was originally a name for the pre-Temple desert-dwelling God of Israel (i.e., Yahweh), whose identity was transformed to a deity when the Temple was constructed ("Goat to Go to Azazel," 19–25).

6. The quest to determine precisely which elements of Matt. 25:31–46 comprise tradition and which consist of redaction remains largely inconclusive. We certainly know that this episode occurs in no gospel besides Matthew. Beyond this, opinions widely diverge, some taking Matt. 25:31–46 to be mostly traditional. For example, on the basis of similar lists of moral good-doing in Jewish literature and the supposed

lack of distinct Christian characteristics in Matt. 25:31–46, Rudolf Bultmann writes, "Thus it is impossible to avoid thinking that Matt. 25:31–46 derives from Jewish tradition. Perhaps, when it was taken up by the Christian Church the name of God was replaced by the title Son of Man" (*The History of the Synoptic Tradition*, trans. John Marsh [New York: Harper & Row, 1963 (1921)], 123–24). After an extensive linguistic analysis, Johannes Friedrich concludes that only συνάγω (v. 32), πάντα τὰ ἔθνη (v. 32), μὲν-δε (v. 33), τοῦ πατρός μου (v. 34), and κύριος are probably redactional, stating, "Von diesen wenigen Worten aus, die eine matt Red nahelegen und den zusätzlichen, bei denen eine solche möglich ist, kann man eine matt Sprachfärbung . . . nicht bestätigen" (ibid., 46) (*Gott im Bruder?*, CTM 7 [Germany: Calwer Verlag Stuttgart, 1977], 45–46). On the contrary, Robert H. Gundry posits that Matthew's "characteristic diction and parallelistic style appear everywhere in the passage" (*Matthew: A Commentary on His Handbook for a Mixed Church under Persecution*, 2nd ed. [Grand Rapids: Eerdmans, 1994], 511). According to Lambrecht, "Matt 25:31–46 is rightly called a grandiose Matthean construction" (*Out of the Treasure*, 275). Indeed, the evangelist is most likely responsible for Matt. 25:31–32a. As Luz observes, "Verses 31 and 32a contain many Mattheanisms and furthermore are reminiscent of biblical language. In addition, not only does this introduction take up the thread of 24:30–31; it also is reminiscent of 13:40–43, 49–50, of 16:27, and especially of 19:28" (*Matthew*, 3:265). His hand is evident in Matt. 25:32b–46 as well, though to a lesser degree, as is evidenced by the presence of Matthean parallelisms (v. 34//v. 41, vv. 35–36//vv. 42–43, vv. 37–39//v. 44, v. 40//v. 45) and vocabulary, such as τότε (vv. 31, 34, 37, 41, 44, 45), πατήρ μου (v. 34), δίκαιος (vv. 37, 46), and perhaps ἀμὴν λέγω ὑμῖν (vv. 40, 45) (Lambrecht, *Out of the Treasure*, 268; Davies and Allison, *Matthew*, 3:418; Luz, *Matthew*, 3:265 n. 20; Leslie W. Walck, *The Son of Man in the Parables of Enoch and in Matthew* [London: T&T Clark, 2011], 198). Yet, several Matthean *hapax legomena*—ἔριφος (v. 32), ἐρίφιον (v. 33), γυμνός (vv. 36, 38, 43, 44), ἐπισκέπτομαι (vv. 36, 43), καταράομαι (v. 41), and κόλασις (v. 46)—possibly betray the traditional material that the gospel writer has adapted. Scholars have proposed various editorial seams in an attempt to recover the original form of the tradition that Matthew has inherited: (a) the switch from ὁ υἱὸς τοῦ ἀνθρώπου (v. 31) to ὁ βασιλεύς (v. 34), (b) the change from the neuter πάντα τὰ ἔθνη (v. 32) to the masculine αὐτούς (v. 32), (c) the transition from shepherd/animals (vv. 32–33) to king/people (vv. 34–45), and (d) the shift from nations (v. 32) to individuals (vv. 34–45). However, none of these proposals have proved satisfactory. Lambrecht concludes, "The discrepancies mentioned above—shepherd and king, Son of Man and king, nations and individuals (see pp. 265–66)—are really much too slight to postulate a source text" (*Out of the Treasure*, 274). Having extensively surveyed these options, Walck remarks, "The attempt to locate the redactional seam precisely has thus proved futile. None of the possible locations has proved feasible" *Son of Man*, 195–97. It therefore seems prudent to affirm what Ulrich Luz deems the majority position regarding the Matt. 25:31–46 complex, namely, "that the evangelist took it over from his special material tradition and reworked it with varying degrees of intensity" (*Matthew*, 3:264). However, given the unique position of these verses within Matthew's discourse structure, John Nolland's conclusion may be more likely: "Probably the level of Matthean intervention here is unusually high since Matthew uses this final piece to provide a climax for and to draw together not just the Eschatological Discourse but the whole set of five linked discourses" (*The Gospel of Matthew: A Commentary on the Greek Text*, NIGTC [Grand Rapids: Eerdmans, 2005], 1023).

7. Walck, *Son of Man*, 194–225. Similarly, see Heinz Eduard Tödt, *The Son of Man in the Synoptic Tradition*, trans. Dorothea M. Barton (London: SCM, 1965); Johannes Theisohn, *Der auserwählte Richter*, SUNT 12 (Göttingen: Vandenhoeck & Ruprecht, 1975), 149–201. Against Matthew's dependence on the Parables, see Maurice Casey, *Son of Man: The Interpretation and Influence of Daniel 7* (London: SPCK, 1979); Douglas R. A. Hare, *The Son of Man Tradition* (Minneapolis: Fortress, 1991); idem, *The Solution to the "Son of Man" Problem* (London: T&T Clark International, 2007), 91–111. On the dating of the Parables of Enoch, see R. H. Charles, *The Book of Enoch or I Enoch* (Oxford: Clarendon, 1912), liv–lv; J. C. Hindley, "Towards a Date for the Similitudes of Enoch," *NTS* 14 (1968): 551–65; J. T. Milik, *The Books of Enoch: Aramaic Fragments of Qumrân Cave 4* (Oxford: Clarendon, 1976), 89–107; Jonas C. Greenfield, and Michael E. Stone, "The Enochic Pentateuch and the Date of the Similitudes," *HTR* 70 (1977): 51–65; Michael A. Knibb, "The Date of the Parables of Enoch: A Critical Review," *NTS* 25 (1978–1979): 344–59; Christopher L. Mearns, "Dating the Similitudes of Enoch," *NTS* 25 (1978–1979): 360–69; John J. Collins, *The Apocalyptic Imagination*, 2nd ed. (New York: Crossroad, 1998), 177–78; the articles by David W. Suter, Michael E. Stone, James H. Charlesworth, Darrell D. Hannah, Luca Arcari, Hanan Eshel, and Daniel C. Olson in *Enoch and the Messiah Son of Man*, ed. Gabriele Boccaccini (Grand Rapids: Eerdmans, 2007), 415–98; Walck, *Son of Man*, 15–23. Paolo Sacchi, by way of summarizing the results of the Third Enochic Seminar in 2005, states: "[W]e may observe those scholars who have directly addressed the problem of dating the Parables all agree on a date around the time of Herod . . . given the impressive amount of evidence gathered in support of a pre-Christian origin of the document. The burden of proof has now shifted to those who disagree with the Herodian date. It is now their responsibility to provide evidence that would reopen the discussion" ("The 2005 Camaldoli Seminar on the Parables of Enoch," in *Enoch and the Messiah Son of Man*, 499–512, at 510–11). James H. Charlesworth remarks that "dating the Parables of Enoch to the time of Herod the Great and the Herodians has become conclusive," noting that "this conclusion was shared by almost every leading specialist on 1En or Second Temple Judaism" in the present colloquium, except for Michael A. Knibb ("The Date and Provenience of the Parables of Enoch," in *Parables of Enoch: A Paradigm Shift*, ed. James H. Charlesworth and Darrell L. Bock [London: Bloomsberry, 2013], 37–57, at 56, 56 n. 47).

8. Leslie W. Walck, "The Son of Man in the Parables of Enoch and the Gospels," in *Enoch and the Messiah Son of Man*, 299–337, at 330. According to Adela Yarbro Collins, "Walck rightly concludes that most of the Son of Man sayings in the Gospels are not dependent on the Parables. He has made a good case, however, for the conclusion that there is a relationship of literary dependence between the Matthean redactions of certain Son of Man sayings from the Synoptic sayings source (Q) and the Parables. It is more likely that the author of Matthew is dependent on the Parables

than vice versa. The link between the epithet 'Son of Man' and the precise phrase 'the throne of his glory' in Matt. 19:28 and 25:31 probably derives from 1 En. 62.5, 69.27, and/or 69.29" ("The Secret Son of Man in the Parables of Enoch and the Gospel of Mark: A Response to Leslie Walck," in *Enoch and the Messiah Son of Man*, 338–51, at 339). Actually, Walck seems to equivocate on the question of literary dependence with regard to the First Gospel. While he writes that "literary dependence may not be claimed" (Walck, *Son of Man*, 249), he then remarks, "Because so many features Matthew has incorporated do not appear in other contemporary literature, it is likely that he knew and used *Par. En.* in particular, along with his other sources for the story of Jesus" (ibid., 250).

9. David R. Catchpole, "The Poor on Earth and the Son of Man in Heaven: A Re-appraisal of Matthew 25:31–46," *BJRL* 61 (1979): 378–83, at 380–81. In summary, these are: (1) the Son of Man sits upon the "throne of his glory" (ἐπὶ θρόνου δόξης αὐτοῦ) in Matt. 25:31, as he does in 1 En. 62.5: "They will see that Son of Man sitting on the throne of his glory" (see also 1 En. 62.2, 3). (2) Judgment coincides with the Son of Man's enthronement in Matt. 25:32–33 and 1 En. 62.1–2 (the "Chosen One" is another title for the "Son of Man" in the Parables of Enoch; e.g., 1 En. 62.5, 7, 9, 14; 71.14). (3) The judgment is far-reaching in scope, as it is directed toward πάντα τὰ ἔθνη in Matt. 25:32 and "the kings and mighty ones" in 1 En. 62.1, 3, 6, 9–12. (4) Those who are judged are divided into two groups in Matt. 25:32–33 and 1 En. 62.9–12, 13–16. (5) Those who are judged are eternally separated from each other in Matt. 25:34, 41 and 1 En. 62.13; 63.11. (6) The righteous enjoy the Son of Man's heavenly presence in Matt. 25:34, 46 and 1 En. 62.14. (7) The Son of Man is the agent of judgment in Matt. 25:31 and 1 En. 62.5, 7, 9, 14; 63.11. (8) Yet God is still the ultimate judge, as suggested by "my father" and the passive verbs in Matt. 25:34, 41 and 1 En. 62.10; 63.2–10. (9) Angels are involved in the Son of Man's judicial activity in Matt. 25:31 and 1 En. 62.11; 63.1. (10) The motif of recognition is operative in Matt. 25:37–39, 44 and 1 En. 62.1, 3, 5. (11) There is solidarity between the one who judges and those who suffer in Matt. 25:40, 45 and 1 En. 62.11. (12) The criterion of judgment is the treatment of those in solidarity with the judge in Matt. 25:40, 45 and 1 En. 62.11. Several of these points are slightly redundant, namely, points (4) and (5), (7) and (8), and (11) and (12). In my estimation, the strongest similarities in Catchpole's list are (1), (2), (4), (5), (7), (9), (10), (11), and (12). On the theme of recognition in both texts, see Catchpole, "Poor on Earth," 381–82; G. W. E. Nickelsburg, *Resurrection, Immortality and Eternal Life in Intertestamental Judaism* (Cambridge: 1972), 72.

10. Walck, *Son of Man*, 216–19; idem, "Son of Man," 329–30.

11. Walck, "Son of Man," 330.

12. Walck, *Son of Man*, 219.

13. G. W. E. Nickelsburg and James C. VanderKam, eds, *1 Enoch: The Hermeneia Translation* (Minneapolis: Fortress, 2012), 68.

14. Nickelsburg and VanderKam, *1 Enoch*, 69 (emphasis mine).

15. Walck, *Son of Man*, 219.

16. Ibid.

17. Ryszard Rubinkiewicz, *Die Eschatologie von Henoch 9–11 und das Neue Testament*, trans. Herbert Ulrich, ÖBS 6 (Klosterneuburg: Österreichisches Katholisches Bibelwerk, 1984), 98–100; David C. Sim, "Matthew 22.13a and 1

Enoch 10.4a: A Case of Literary Dependence?" *JSNT* 47 (1992): 3–19, at 6–13; Davies and Allison, *Matthew*, 3:206; G. W. E. Nickelsburg, *1 Enoch 1: A Commentary on the Book of 1 Enoch, Chapters 1–36; 81–108*, Hermeneia (Minneapolis: Fortress, 2001), 84; Catherine Sider Hamilton, *The Death of Jesus in Matthew: Innocent Blood*, SNTSMS 167 (Cambridge: Cambridge University Press, 2017), 171–72.

 18. Nickelsburg and VanderKam, *1 Enoch*, 28. Thus reads Codex Panopolitanus. Syncellus reads slightly differently. See Matthew Black and Albert-Marie Denis, eds, *Apocalypsis Henochi Graece*, FPQSG (Leiden: Brill, 1970), 24–25.

 19. While the influence of the Yom Kippur ritual on 1 Enoch 10 is debated, there is wide scholarly support for this position (for a bibliography, see Andrei A. Orlov, *Divine Scapegoats: Demonic Mimesis in Early Jewish Mysticism* [Albany, NY: SUNY, 2015], 202 n. 87). Daniel Stökl Ben Ezra provides a compelling argument for the influence of scapegoat traditions on 1 Enoch 10, concluding that the "elements of Yom Kippur are so numerous and central in this chapter that the Yom Kippur background could be recognized even without exact identity of the names [Asael and Azazel]" ("Yom Kippur in the Apocalyptic Imaginaire and the Roots of Jesus's High Priesthood," in *Transformations of the Inner Self in Ancient Religions*, ed. Jan Assmann and Guy Stroumsa [Leiden: Brill, 1999], 349–66, 353). For the influence of the Day of Atonement on 4Q180 1 7–10 and 4Q203 7 I, 5–7, see Stökl Ben Ezra, *Impact of Yom Kippur*, 87; Andrei A. Orlov, *The Atoning Dyad: The Two Goats of Yom Kippur in the Apocalypse of Abraham*, Studia Judaeoslavica (Leiden: Brill, 2016), 87–88. On the Yom Kippur typology in the Apocalypse of Abraham, see Rubinkiewicz, *Die Eschatologie von Henoch 9–11*, 101; Lester Grabbe, "The Scapegoat Tradition: A Study in Early Jewish Interpretation," *JSJ* 18 [1987]: 152–67, at 156–58; Orlov, *Divine Scapegoats*; idem, *Atoning Dyad*, 81–160.

 20. On the garment imagery, see John P. Meier, *Matthew*, NTM 3 (Wilmington, DE: Michael Glazier, 1981), 248; Rubinkiewicz, *Die Eschatologie von Hen 9–10*, 109.

 21. Davies and Allison suspect that Matt. 22:11–14 is a free Matthean composition (*Matthew*, 3:194).

 22. Rubinkiewicz, *Die Eschatologie von Hen 9–10*, 97–113.

 23. The term ἔριφος (Matt. 25:32b; ἐρίφιον in 25:33) means "kid" (LSJ, 689) and not "he-goat" (Klaus Wengst, "Wie aus Böcken Ziegen wurden [Mt 25, 32–33]," *EvT* 54 [1994]: 491–501, at 497–98; cf. BDAG, 392). Ἔριφος is used 26 times in the LXX, usually translating the Hebrew גדי ("kid") and almost always referring to a kid of a "goat" (עז, שעיר): Gen. 27:9, 16; 37:31; 38:17, 20, 23; Exod. 12:5; Lev. 1:10; Judg. 6:19; 13:15, 19; 15:1; 1 Sam. 16:20; 2 Chr. 35:7, 8; Jer. 51:40 (in reference to עתוד); Ezek. 43:22, 25; 45:23. Genesis 27:9 is a pertinent example: "And go to the flock [πρόβατα] and take for me thence two young goats [ἐρίφους; MT: שני גדיי עזים]." Here the term ἔριφοι is used with no modifiers (such as αἰγῶν) but clearly refers to goat-kids, and the ἔριφοι are taken directly from Isaac's πρόβατα. The word ἔριφος is used with reference to a different animal species only once in the LXX (Amos 6:4, which translates כר, "lamb"). Ἔριφος occurs without reference to an animal species only in Judg. 14:6; Song 1:8; Isa. 11:6. Luz notes, "For ἔριφοι (young sheep) there is not a single source [in the LXX]; however, the frequent appearance together of ἄρνες and ἔριφοι in the Bible and in Greek probably shows that the latter could not be

lambs. Thus ὁ/ἡ ἔριφος also means not 'young animal,' as Wengst ('Böcken,' 498) surmises, but 'young goat'" (*Matthew*, 3:277). Given the LXX's usage, "young goat" is the best rendering of ἔριφος in Matt. 25:32–33.

24. Weber, "The Image of the Sheep and the Goats," 657–78. Weber carefully considers evidence from four distinct cultural milieus. In her examination of modern twentieth-century Greece, Weber indicates that goats have a very negative connotation among the Greek Sarakatsan transhumant pastoralists, but beyond this social group, attitudes toward goats in the modern Mediterranean basin vary widely (ibid., 662–64). In the ancient Greco-Roman world, while sheep were generally deemed more valuable than goats, and while goats often symbolized sexual promiscuity, "they would still be surprised at the contrast of sheep with goats in Matt. 25:31–46, because nothing in the Greco-Roman symbolic repertoire makes goats the plausible target of the extreme animus exhibited by the divine judge" (ibid., 665–67, at 667). In terms of twentieth-century Palestine, Weber finds no negative valuation of goats, noting that their rambunctious personality and lesser value than sheep provide no grounds for such vitriol against them (ibid., 667–69). With regard to first-century Jewish Syria and Palestine, Weber observes that (a) many animals, but never goats, are contrasted with sheep or symbolize evil (Jer. 2:24; Hos. 8:9; Sir. 26:25; 1 En. 83–90), (b) the Hebrew Bible consistently portrays goats in a positive light (Gen. 15:9; 32:14–15; Num. 7:12–88; Deut. 32:14; Judg. 13:15; 15:1; 1 Sam. 25:2; Isa. 11:6; Song 4:1; 5:1; 6:5), and (c) Ezek. 34:17 probably bears little relationship to Matt. 25:32–33 (ibid., 669–73).

25. Weber, "Image of the Sheep and the Goats," 673. She adds a notable caveat: "Certainly, the audience of Matthew's own time could point to certain blemishes on the reputation of goats as animals, less valuable and more demanding than others, and possibly (if Hellenistic attitudes had their influence) as animals closely associated with sexual excess, but not with negative qualities extreme enough to merit this expulsion" (ibid.).

26. Ibid., 670. On the positive portrayal of goats in the Old Testament, see note above.

27. *Ant.* 3.240–41 (Thackeray).

28. Jub. 34.12, 18 (James C. VanderKam, *The Book of Jubilees: Translated*, CSCO 511 [Louvain: Peeters, 1989], 228–29) (emphasis mine). While in this typology, the slaughtered kid most obviously corresponds to the immolated goat, whose blood is manipulated by the priests (Lev. 16:15–19), Stökl Ben Ezra observes a parallel to the scapegoat as well, as the garment dipped in the kid's blood is *sent* to Jacob, as the scapegoat is *sent* to Azazel (Lev. 16:21–22) (*Impact of Yom Kippur*, 96). More importantly, since in Second Temple tradition the two goats of Yom Kippur were required to be similar in appearance (m. Yoma 6:1; Barn. 7.6, 10; Justin, *Dial.* 40.4–5; Tertullian, *Marc.* 3.7.7; *Adv. Jud.* 14.9–10), it is implied that the scapegoat was also a young goat, even if the kid in Jubilees only corresponds to the immolated goat.

29. Weber, "Image of the Sheep and the Goats," 658–59, 673–75.

30. Joachim Jeremias, *The Parables of Jesus* (New York: Charles Scribner's Sons, 1972), 206; Gundry, *Matthew*, 512; Donald Senior, *Matthew*, ANTC (Nashville: Abingdon, 1998), 281; Davies and Allison, *Matthew*, 3:423; Craig S. Keener, *A*

*Commentary on the Gospel of Matthew* (Grand Rapids: Eerdmans, 1999), 603; Weber, "The Image of the Sheep and the Goats," 670. Weber observes that, in ancient and modern times, a cultural boundary lies between Greece and Syria, wherein "West of this line, sheep and goats are kept in separate herds. . . East of this line, sheep and goats are kept in mixed herds" ("Image of the Sheep and the Goats," 673).

31. Wengst, "Böcken," 491–501. Gustaf Dalmn's infamous statement, based on contemporary, not ancient, Palestinian customs, is as follows: "Die Schafe wollen frische Luft haben, die Ziegen sollten wärmer stehen, weil Kälte ihnen schadet. Nach dem Sprichwort gilt von ihnen" (*Arbeit und Sitte in Palästina: Band VI* [Hildesheim: Georg Olms Verlagsbuchhandlung, 1964 [1939], 276).

32. One theory is that ἔριφοι means "bucks," which are separated from the females, so that the latter may be milked (Lambrecht, *Out of the Treasure*, 261). But Luz notes that ἔριφος rarely means "buck," despite BAGD's incorrect gloss (ibid., 3:276–77). Nolland adds that "LXX usage offers no encouragement . . . to this alternative" (*Matthew*, 1025). Following Wengst ("Böcken," 499–500), Luz proposes that the young goats are separated to be slaughtered, since "[i]n almost all texts where ἔριφοι appear, they are slaughtered, eaten, or sacrificed" (ibid., 3:277). Yet, this suggestion faces three difficulties. First, Luz overstates his case, as ἔριφοι are not slaughtered nor sacrificed in Gen. 38:17, 20, 23; Judg. 15:1; 1 Sam. 16:20; Isa. 11:6; Song 1:8; 1 Esd. 1:7; Sir. 47:3. Second, in many instances where ἔριφοι are slaughtered, they are done so in sacrifice to God (e.g., Lev. 1:10; Judg. 13:19; Ezek. 43:22, 25, 45:23), which carries a positive, not negative, connotation. Third, as Nolland notes, Luz's proposal "would be more attractive if the text had 'the kids' being separated from 'the flock' and not the reverse, and if the diminutive form ἐρίφιον had been used in Mt. 25:32 and not only later" (*Matthew*, 1026).

33. Luz, *Matthew*, 3:276.

34. I say, "at least in part," because the phrase ὥσπερ ὁ ποιμὴν ἀφορίζει τὰ πρόβατα ἀπὸ τῶν ἐρίφων (Matt. 25:320 suggests that the evangelist is assuming the plausibility of such an agricultural custom. Admittedly, this phrase makes the interpretation set forth in this chapter more difficult to accept. Yet, it is not an insurmountable challenge. Matthew possibly retains this agricultural verisimilitude because it derives from his special source, or perhaps his community was already familiar with the image of a shepherd separating sheep from goats by means of an earlier Christian tradition. This plausible scenario would explain why Matthew preserves this image and yet blends it with imagery from the Yom Kippur ritual.

35. Stökl Ben Ezra, *Impact of Yom Kippur*, 98. There may be a hint in 4Q418 81 4–5 that such "lot" imagery bore a direct relationship to the Yom Kippur ritual: "he has placed you as a holy of holies [over all] the earth, and among all the [g]o[ds] he has cast your lot [גורלכה הפיל]" (Florentino García Martínez and Eibert J. C. Tigchelaar, eds, *The Dead Sea Scrolls Study Edition*, 2 vols. [Leiden: Brill, 1997–1998], 2:871–72). Among the "lot" imagery used in the Dead Sea Scrolls is the following: the lot of God (1QM XIII, 5; XV, 1; XVII, 7), the lot of the holy ones (1QS XI, 7–8), the lot of light (1QM XIII, 9; CD XIII, 12; 4Q267 9 IV, 9), the lot of your truth (1QM XIII, 2; 4Q284 4 3), the lot of the King of Kings (4Q381 76–77 7), the lot of the people of his throne (4Q511 2 I, 10), the lot of Melchizedek (11Q13 II, 8),

the lot of Belial (1QS II, 5; 1QM I, 15; IV, 2; XIII, 2, 4, 12; 1Q177 IV, 16; 4Q256 II, 12–13; 4Q257 II, 1; 4Q286 7 II, 1; 5Q11 1 I, 3; 11Q13 II, 12, 13), the lot of the sons of darkness (1QM I, 1), the lot of darkness (1QM I, 11; XIII, 5; 1Q177 III, 8), the lot of wickedness (4Q510 2 1).

36. Miryam T. Brand, *Evil Within and Without: The Source of Sin and Its Nature as Portrayed in Second Temple Literature*, JAJS 9 (Göttingen: Vandenhoeck & Ruprecht, 2013), 247.

37. Philo, *Her.* 179 (Colson and Whitaker). See also Philo, *Leg.* 2.52; *Post.* 70.

38. Apoc. Ab. 10.15; 13:7; 14.6; 20:5 (Alexander Kulik, *Retroverting Slavonic Pseudepigrapha: Toward the Original of the Apocalypse of Abraham* [Leiden: Brill, 2005], 18, 20–21, 25) (Apoc. Ab. 20:5 may be a Bogomil interpolation). Orlov notes that "it is certainly significant that the Slavonic term for 'lot' (часть) found in the *Apocalypse of Abraham* appears to be connected to the Hebrew גורל, a notion prominent in many of the cultic descriptions found in biblical and rabbinic accounts, as well as in the eschatological developments attested by the Qumran materials" (*Atoning Dyad*, 92–93).

39. Orlov, *Atoning Dyad*, 91.

40. Origen, *Hom. Lev.* 9.3.2 (Gary Wayne Barkley, *Origen: Homilies on Leviticus 1–16*, FC 83 [Washington DC: Catholic University of America Press, 1990], 181).

41. Origen, *Hom. Lev.* 9.4.2 (Barkley, *Origen*, 182).

42. Origen, *Hom. Lev.* 9.5.2 (Barkley, *Origen*, 184).

43. M. Yoma 4:1 (Herbert Danby, *The Mishnah: Translated from the Hebrew with Introduction and Brief Explanatory Notes* [Oxford: Oxford University Press, 1933, 166]).

44. B. Yoma 39a–b (Isidore Epstein, ed., *The Babylonian Talmud*, [London: Soncino, 1935–1952]).

45. Tg. Ps.-J. Lev. 16:18–19, 21 (Martin McNamara, Robert Hayward, and Michael Maher, trans., *Targum Neofiti 1: Leviticus. Targum Pseudo-Jonathan: Leviticus*, ArBib 3 [Collegeville, MN: Liturgical, 1994], 168) (emphasis original).

46. Apoc. Ab. 22:4–5; 27:1–2; 29:11. See Orlov, *Divine Scapegoats*, 103–26; idem, *Atoning Dyad*, 133–35.

47. One might reasonably object that, if a Yom Kippur typology underlies the imagery of the two opposing lots in Matt. 25:32–33, then the righteous lot ought also to be a lot of (righteous) *goats* to match the two goats of the Day of Atonement ritual. Three points can be made in response: (1) The evangelist may have been stubbornly attracted to the image of sheep, since "sheep" (πρόβατα) is a common metaphor for God's people (e.g., Jer. 23:1–2; 27:6, 17 LXX; Ezek 34 LXX; Zech 11 LXX; Matt. 9:36; 10:6; 15:24; 18:12; 26:31; John 10). (2) He may have reckoned the characteristics of sheep and goats as "close enough" to apply Yom Kippur imagery to both. As Nolland remarks, "The dominant impression created by a survey of OT uses of 'sheep' and 'goat' is the degree to which they are interchangeable . . . However important the difference between them might have been for certain purposes . . . the animals are first and foremost thought of together. In their normal dirty state, it might even have been considered wise to leave it to the skilled shepherd to distinguish with confidence the sheep from the goats" (*Matthew*, 1026). (3) In a late medieval

collection of older midrashic traditions, one ram (viz., an uncastrated male sheep) is sacrificed to God as the Yom Kippur sin-offering for the people, and one ram is sent to Azazel, instead of goats (Yalqut Shim'oni 1:44) (see Stökl Ben Ezra, *Impact of Yom Kippur*, 128). (4) According to Num. 29:8, one ram and seven male lambs are offered as burnt-offerings on Yom Kippur (Lev. 16:3, 5 has two rams).

48. Weber, "Sheep and Goats," 673.

49. Wright, *Disposal of Impurity*, 29–30.

50. Philo, *Spec.* 1.188 (Colson).

51. Philo, *Her.* 179 (Colson and Whitaker).

52. *Ant.* 3.241 (Thackeray).

53. 1 En. 10.4–5 (Nickelsburg and VanderKam, *1 Enoch*, 28).

54. Apoc. Ab. 14.5–6 (Kulik, *Slavonic Pseudepigrapha*, 21).

55. Philo, *Spec.* 1.188.

56. Barn. 7.9 (Ehrman); see also Tertullian, *Marc.* 3.7.7.

57. Tertuallian, *Marc.* 3.7 (Ernest Evans, *Tertullian: Adversus Marcionem: Books 1–3* [Oxford: Clarendon, 1972], 191).

58. M. Yoma 6:4 (Danby, *Mishnah*, 169).

59. Apoc. Ab. 13.7 (Kulik, *Slavonic Pseudepigrapha*, 20).

60. It is not clear as to whose sins are "written upon Asael" in 1 En. 10.8—the sins of Asael himself, the Watchers, the Giants, humanity, or some combination of the above? There is a similar ambiguity in 4Q180 1 7–9 and 4Q203 7 I, 5–7.

61. Daniel Stökl Ben Ezra, "The Biblical Yom Kippur: The Jewish Fast of the Day of Atonement and the Church Fathers," *SP* 34 (2002): 493–502, at 494.

62. Barn. 7.9 (Ehrman). See also Philo, *Her.* 179; Origen, *Hom. Lev.* 9.4.2; 9.5.2.

63. Orlov, *Atoning Dyad*, 55.

64. James C. VanderKam, *Enoch: A Man for all Generations* (Columbia, SC: University of South Carolina Press, 1995), 171.

65. 1 En. 87.3 (Nickelsburg and VanderKam, *1 Enoch*, 121).

66. 1 En. 88.1 (ibid).

67. Orlov, *Atoning Dyad*, 128–57.

68. Orlov, *Atoning Dyad*, 145.

69. On the former, see Albert Henry Wratislaw, *Notes and Dissertations: Principally on Difficulties in the Scriptures of the New Covenant* (London: Bell and Daldy, 1863), 12–23; idem, "The Scapegoat-Barabbas," *ExpTim* 3 (1891): 400–03; Stökl Ben Ezra, *Impact of Yom Kippur*, 165–71; Jennifer K. Berenson Maclean, "Barabbas, the Scapegoat Ritual, and the Development of the Passion Narrative," *HTR* 100 (2007): 309–34, at 324–30; Stökl Ben Ezra, "Fasting with Jews, Thinking with Scapegoats: Some Remarks on Yom Kippur in Early Judaism and Christianity, in Particular, 4Q541, Barnabas 7, Matthew 27 and Acts 27," in Hieke and Nicklas, *Day of Atonement*, 165–88, at 179–84. On the latter, see John Dominic Crossan, *The Cross that Spoke: The Origins of the Passion Narrative* (San Francisco: Harper & Row, 1988), 114–59; Helmut Koester, *Ancient Christian Gospels: Their History and Development* (London: SCM, 1990), 220–30; Stökl Ben Ezra, *Impact of Yom Kippur*, 170; Berenson Maclean, "Barabbas, the Scapegoat Ritual," 332–33; Orlov, *Atoning Dyad*, 63–64.

70. Barn. 7.8, 11; m. Yoma 4:2; 6:6; m. Šabb. 9:3; Tertullian, *Marc.* 3.7; Hippolytus, *Frag.* 75. So Koester, *Gospels*, 225; Stökl Ben Ezra, *Impact of Yom Kippur*, 170; idem, "Fasting with Jews," 183; Christian A. Eberhart, "To Atone or Not to Atone: Remarks on the Day of Atonement Rituals According to Leviticus 16 and the Meaning of Atonement," in *Sacrifice, Cult, and Atonement in Early Judaism and Christianity*, ed. Henrietta L. Wiley and Christian A. Eberhart (Atlanta: SBL, 2017), 197–231, at 230–31.

71. Hamilton, *Death of Jesus*, 221. Similarly, Davies and Allison write, "There is no parallel in the other Last Supper accounts to this clause [εἰς ἄφεσιν ἁμαρτιῶν] . . . It appears only here in Matthew and never in the LXX (where ἄφεσις is linked only once to 'sin,' in Lev 16:26)."

72. Indeed, Matthew also utilizes the metaphor of sin as a debt (Matt. 6:12; 18:23–35), as argued by Nathan Eubank, *Wages of Cross-Bearing and Debt of Sin: The Economy of Heaven in Matthew's Gospel*, BZNW 196 (Berlin: De Gruyter, 2013). However, despite his deft analysis, Eubank focuses on the debt metaphor to the exclusion of other metaphors of sin and atonement in the Gospel of Matthew, as indicated by Rikard Roitto, "The Two Cognitive Frames of Forgiveness in the Synoptic Gospels," *NovT* 57 (2015): 136–58, at 143; Marius J. Nel, "The Conceptualisation of Sin in the Gospel of Matthew," *In die Skriflig/In LuceVerbi* 51 (2017): 1–8.

73. Of the passages discussed, the following occur only in Matthew: Matt. 7:19 (cf. 3:10; Luke 3:9); 13:30, 41–42, 48; 15:13; 22:13; 25:41, 46; the saying in Matt. 5:29–30 is also uniquely repeated in Matt. 18:8–9.

74. Apocalyptic traditions have certainly influenced the vision of eschatological judgment in the First Gospel. David C. Sim argues that Matthew, more than nearly all early Jewish and Christian writers, emphasizes the fiery eschatological punishment of sinners (*Apocalyptic Eschatology in the Gospel of Matthew*, SNTMS 88 [Cambridge: Cambridge University Press, 1996], 129–40).

75. One weakness of this reading is that the early church fathers do not appear to have commonly linked Matt. 25:31–46 and Leviticus 16. The earliest Christian witness to connect these two passages, of which I am aware, is Cyril of Alexandria in *Letter* 41.8: "Accordingly, the goat, or the he-goat, or the kid was the sacrifice for sin according to the decision of the law, for the divinely inspired Scripture in very many places compares the just to sheep and the lover of iniquity to a goat . . . For this reason, also, our Lord Jesus Christ says, 'But when the Son of Man will sit on the throne of his glory; and he will set the sheep on his right hand, but the goats on his left'" (John I. McEnerney, *St. Cyril of Alexandria: Letters 1–50*, FC 76 [Washington, DC: Catholic University of America Press, 1987], 173).

76. Grabbe, "The Scapegoat Tradition," 166.

77. Anders Runesson, "Purity, Holiness, and the Kingdom of Heaven in Matthew's Narrative World," in *Purity and Holiness in Judaism and Christianity: Essays in Memory of Susan Haber*, ed. Carl Ehrlich, Anders Runesson, and Eileen Schuller (Tübingen: Mohr Siebeck, 2013), 144–80, at 157.

## Chapter 2

# Jesus as Goat for Yahweh and Goat for Azazel in Matthew's Baptism-Temptation Narrative (Matt. 3:16–4:11)

Ever since the publication of Daniel Stökl Ben Ezra's monograph *The Impact of Yom Kippur on Early Christianity*, and Jennifer K. Berenson Maclean's article in *Harvard Theological Review*, "Barabbas, the Scapegoat Ritual, and the Development of the Passion Narrative," a growing number of scholars have acknowledged the presence of a Day of Atonement typology in Matthew's passion narrative.[1] The evangelist casts Jesus as the goat for Yahweh that is chosen to be slaughtered as a sacrifice in the Barabbas episode (Matt. 27:15–26), and as the goat for Azazel that bears the sins of many in the Roman-abuse scene (Matt. 27:27–31).[2] One weakness of this reading, however, is its apparent failure to meet the criterion of recurrence.[3] As Dale Allison notes, the probability of a typological allusion "will be enhanced if it can be shown (on other grounds) that a passage's proposed subtext belongs to a book or tradition which held some significance for its authors."[4] That is to say, if a Christological goat typology can be independently demonstrated in Matthew's passion narrative and his baptism-temptation account, then the likelihood of each typology increases significantly.

This chapter argues, independently of the Yom Kippur typology in Matthew 27, that the First Evangelist has constructed a Day of Atonement typology in his baptism-temptation narrative (Matt. 3:16–4:11), whereby Jesus is portrayed as both the goat for Yahweh and the goat for Azazel. While I do not think that the presentation of Jesus as both goats is the evangelist's primary motive in narrating the baptism and temptation stories, it is a significant aspect of the author's redactional agenda that deserves closer attention.[5] Namely, Matthew employs the template of Leviticus 16 and early Yom Kippur traditions to suggest Jesus's roles as the immolated goat at his baptism and as the scapegoat during his wilderness ordeal. In an atmosphere where all of Israel's sins are being confessed (Matt. 3:5–6), Jesus's sacrificial vocation is evoked by the voice of the deity (3:17), who reveals himself to Jesus behind the heavenly veil (3:16b). Having identified with the sinful people by means of the priestly baptizer's rite of elimination (3:16a), Jesus is sent into the wilderness (4:1a), where he encounters a nefarious deity (4:1b). There, Jesus engages in a prolonged fast (4:2) and recapitulates Israel's desert afflictions (4:3–4).

As I submit below, each of these points finds resonance in Leviticus 16 or Second Temple traditions regarding the Day of Atonement. When considered as a conceptual cluster, the accumulative strength of these parallels is impressive enough to posit a Yom Kippur typology in the Matthean account, though this typology is secondary to the prevailing Israel and Moses typologies in the same narrative segment.[6] The argument is bolstered by many Matthean redactions that appear to accentuate the correspondences between Jesus's experiences at the Jordan River and in the Judean wilderness, and that of the two goats of Yom Kippur.

## GOAT FOR YAHWEH, GOAT FOR AZAZEL

Barring the detailed argument for a goat typology that follows below, the first notable parallel between Matthew's baptism-temptation narrative and Leviticus 16 is the structural correspondence between the gospel story and the sequence of events in the ritual of the two goats. Recalling the antagonistic spatial movements of the two animals, Stökl Ben Ezra remarks, "As the first movement, the holiest person, the High Priest, entered the most sacred place, the Holy of Holies of the Jerusalem Temple [with the blood of the immolated goat] . . . As a second movement, the scapegoat burdened with the sins of the people was sent with an escort to the desert."[7] Christian Eberhart notes this characteristic of Yom Kippur as well: "While sacrificial rituals feature dynamics toward the sanctuary [i.e., Lev. 16:15–19], the scapegoat ritual moves in the opposite direction: it leads away from the sanctuary into the wilderness."[8] We observed in the previous chapter that the opposing movement of the high priest/goat for Yahweh and the goat for Azazel became a literary trope in early Jewish writings. Without relaying those passages in detail, one recalls that this trope seems to have made an impression on the Book of Watchers (1 En. 10; 14), the Animal Apocalypse (1 En. 87.3; 88.1), Philo (*Her.* 179), the Apocalypse of Abraham (Apoc. Ab. 14.5–6; 15–32), the Epistle of Barnabas (7.9), and Origen (*Hom. Lev.* 9.4.2; 9.5.2).

Now, Matthew preserves the tight sequence derived from his Markan *Vorlage* (Mark 1:10–12), which describes Jesus's baptism by John (Matt. 3:16–17) and immediately transitions to his wilderness ordeal (Matt. 4:1–11). On the contrary, Luke disrupts this sequence by sandwiching Jesus's genealogy between his baptism and temptation (Luke 3:23–38), thereby obfuscating the potential correspondence between the rite of the two goats (Lev. 16:15–19, 20–22), and Jesus's baptism and temptation. The First Evangelist's conservation of this sequence is significant, since it will highlight Jesus's function as both goats of Leviticus 16. During his baptism, the heavens are opened, Jesus encounters God, and his sacrificial vocation is evoked (Matt. 3:16–17), which parallels Aaron's penetration of the innermost temple veil with the blood of the goat for Yahweh (Lev. 16:15–19). Jesus is then sent into the desert, where he encounters a diabolical power (Matt. 4:1–11), which parallels the goat for Azazel's journey into the Judean wilderness (Lev. 16:20–22). These points will be explored in greater detail below.

## CONFESSION OF SINS

In contrast to the Gospel of Luke, Matthew follows his Markan *Vorlage* in narrating that the inhabitants of Jerusalem, Judea (and the region along the Jordan) traveled to John to be baptized by him, "confessing their sins" (ἐξομολογούμενοι τὰς ἁμαρτίας αὐτῶν) (Matt. 3:5–6//Mark 1:5). The First Evangelist's choice to retain mention of "all" the nation's confession of sins may be motivated, in part, by a broader Yom Kippur typology underlying his baptism-temptation narrative. On the Jewish holy day, Aaron is instructed to bring forth the scapegoat and confess over it all Israel's iniquities, transgressions, and sins: "Aaron shall lay his hands on the head of the living goat, and he shall confess [ἐξαγορεύσει] over it all the iniquity of the children of Israel, and all their unrighteousness, and all their sins [πάσας τὰς ἁμαρτίας αὐτῶν], and he shall place them on the head of the living goat, and he shall send it away into the desert by the hand of a prepared man" (Lev. 16:21 LXX). This hand-leaning rite, in conjunction with Aaron's confession, was the means by which the high priest transferred Israel's moral impurities onto the scapegoat.[9] The priest's verbal confession was thought to "release" Israel's defiant sins and enable their transference onto the Azazel goat.[10]

Though the difference in vocabulary between Lev. 16:21 LXX and Matt. 3:6 is too stark to posit an allusion to this verse,[11] the evangelist leaves in place a crucial detail that could easily be interpreted in conjunction with the Yom Kippur typology that arguably follows in his baptism-temptation narrative. Not only does the biblical witness command Israel to "afflict themselves" on the Day of Atonement (תענו את־נפשתיכם, Lev. 16:29, 31; 23:27–32; Num. 29:7), the practice of communal self-abasement became a hallmark of the holy day according to Second Temple sources. Philo reports that there was no food, drink, entertainment, alcohol, festive decorations, merriment, dancing nor music played on Yom Kippur.[12] The Mishnah prohibits eating, drinking, washing, anointing, putting on sandals, and marital intercourse.[13] According to the Book of Jubilees, Jacob's great mourning over Joseph's alleged death becomes the origin of the Day of Atonement.[14] Other penitential deeds were performed as well: "Some may wear sackcloth and place ashes on the head; they abstain from sleep, induce tears and cry, stand for long hours during the prayer, or suffer more extreme afflictions."[15]

Matthew's decision to narrate that great swaths of individuals were voyaging to John to confess their sins and be baptized recalls the infamous confession of Israel's collective sins and the solemnity of the self-denial performed annually on the Yom Kippur. As An observes, "John the Baptist's call for 'baptism of repentance' by which the people from 'all Judea' and 'all areas along the Jordan' gathered to confess their sins (Matt. 3:5) parallels Israel's nationwide convocation for self-negation on the Day of Atonement (Lev. 16:29, 31)."[16]

## SACRIFICE TO YAHWEH

Since Matthew has largely followed Mark's baptism account, except for the addition of Matt. 3:14–15, one cannot easily determine which aspects of the episode are related to the evangelist's immolated goat typology. However, there may be a hint of Jesus's role as the goat for Yahweh in the baptismal scene. According to An, "After Jesus's baptism, Jesus emerges as God's chosen one who bears all the people's confessed sins at the Jordan River and beyond."[17]

Davies and Allison summarize the majority view regarding the scriptural background of the heavenly voice, οὗτός ἐστιν ὁ υἱός μου ὁ ἀγαπητός, ἐν ᾧ εὐδόκησα (Matt. 3:17):[18] "[T]he first line of our text is from or has been influenced by Ps 2.7 (LXX?) while the next two lines are derived from a non-LXX version of Isa 42.1."[19] Leroy Huizenga has challenged this consensus, arguing that "we have no reason to be as confident as Davies and Allison that the empirical author of Matthew 'saw' and 'heard' Ps 2:7 and Isa 42:1 in the voice at the baptism."[20] While his contention that the phrase μου ὁ ἀγαπητός should be attributed to an Isaac typology is plausible (cf. Gen. 22:2, 12, 16 LXX), Huizenga has not mounted a compelling case against an allusion to Isaiah 42 in the baptismal episode.

Only Matthew quotes Isa. 42:1 in his lengthy citation of Isa. 42:1–4 (Matt. 12:18–21), indicating that the passage was significant to him. Additionally, the verbal parallels between Matt. 12:18 (freely rendered from the Hebrew of Isa. 42:1) and Matt. 3:17 are quite strong: (a) Matthew's unique addition of ἰδού at the beginning of Matt. 3:17 matches ἰδού at the beginning of Matt.

12:18//Isa. 42:1, (b) ὁ ἀγαπητός (Matt. 3:17) parallels ὁ ἀγαπητός μου (Matt. 12:18//Isa. 42:1), (c) ἐν ᾧ εὐδόκησα (Matt. 3:17) closely matches εἰς ὃν εὐδόκησεν (Matt. 12:18//Isa. 42:1), and (d) the Spirit's descent in Matt. 3:16 strikingly corresponds conceptually to Isa. 42:1: "I have placed my spirit upon him."[21]

Since the figures of the Suffering Servant and, perhaps, Isaac, are likely in view in Matthew's account of the heavenly voice, the evangelist probably conceives an adumbration of Jesus's role as sacrificial offering in the event of Jesus's baptism. Though some scholars have recently challenged the traditional view that the figure of the Isaianic Servant has informed Matthew's understanding of Jesus's death,[22] the evangelist's allusion to Isa. 50:6 in his scene of Jesus's abuse by the Sanhedrin (Matt. 26:67),[23] his unique citations of Isa. 42:1–4 and Isa. 53:4,[24] and his emphasis on the cultic dimension of the Isaiah 53 allusion in his saying over the cup (Matt. 26:28),[25] all suggest that the figure of the Servant, whose role involves becoming a sacrifice on behalf of the people (Isa. 53:10, 12), has made at least a minimal impact on the evangelist's interpretation of Jesus's death. If Huizenga's contention that the title ὁ υἱός μου ὁ ἀγαπητός (Matt. 3:17) alludes to the figure of Isaac is valid,[26] then it is all the more likely that the heavenly voice evokes the notion of sacrifice, since the Akedah is reckoned as sacrificial in Genesis 22 and extra-biblical traditions.[27] The conclusion of R. T. France therefore appears to be sound:

> The link with the descent of the Spirit certainly makes an echo of Isa 42:1 strongly plausible, so that Matthew's readers would learn to see Jesus in the role of the "servant of Yahweh" who would die for the sins of the people . . . It is also possible, though less likely, that some readers who knew the Genesis story well might have noticed the echo of the phrase "beloved son, whom you love" and reflected that God was now going to give up his own son to death just as he had once asked Abraham to do.[28]

Thus, Jesus's death, and probably his role as a sacrifice to God—a unique emphasis in the First Gospel (Matt. 26:28)—seem to be intimated in Matthew's baptism scene.[29]

While the principal scriptural background of Matt. 3:17 resides in Psalm 2, Isaiah 42, and/or Genesis 22, Leviticus 16 should be considered as having influenced Matthew's baptismal account as well. First of all, we have established that the notion of sacrifice is probably subtly suggested in the content of the heavenly voice (Matt. 3:17). As Jerry Shepherd remarks, "As he submits himself to be baptized, his [Jesus's] role as sacrifice for sin is highlighted."[30] Moreover, whereas Mark writes τὸ πνεῦμα (Mark 1:10), and Luke has τὸ πνεῦμα τὸ ἅγιον σωματικῷ εἴδει (Luke 3:22), only Matthew adds that "the Spirit *of God*" (τὸ πνεῦμα τοῦ θεοῦ) descended upon Jesus during his baptism (Matt. 3:16). The addition of "God" fits well with an immolated goat typology, since the lot of the sacrificial goat was specifically designated "for Yahweh" (ליהוה), while the lot of the scapegoat was "for Azazel" (לעזאזל) (Lev. 16:8–10).[31]

Additionally, the opening of the heavens and the subsequent theophany (Matt. 3:16–17) recall the high priest's distinguished entrance into the Holy of Holies on Yom Kippur (Lev. 16:2–4, 11–17).[32] Although this point is most salient in the Gospel of Mark, where the "splitting" (σχίζω) of the heavens (Mark 1:10) forms an *inclusio* with the "splitting" (σχίζω) of the sanctuary veil in the passion narrative (Mark 15:38), Matthew has left Mark's broader *inclusio* between the baptism and death scenes intact, in contrast to his Lukan counterpart.[33] The effect of this *inclusio* in the First Gospel's baptismal episode would be to foreshadow Jesus's sacrificial death, the expiatory effect of which will reach beyond the sanctuary curtain (Matt. 27:51) and procure the divine Presence, or "God with us" (cf. Matt. 1:23; 18:20; 27:54; 28:20)—the *raison d'être* of the Day of Atonement.[34] The evangelist's possible allusion to Ezekiel 1 by changing Mark's σχιζομένους τοὺς οὐρανοὺς (Mark 1:10) to ἠνεῴχθησαν οἱ οὐρανοί (Matt. 3:16) fits well within this sacerdotal context,[35] since the prophet's vision of the *Kavod* by the river Chebar becomes the foundation of later heavenly ascent traditions also associated with Yom Kippur.[36]

Finally, before his famed approach toward the divine Presence, the high priest was required to bathe his entire body in water (Lev. 16:4). According to Jacob Milgrom, this is an anomalous rite, as nowhere else in Scripture is the priest required to bathe his whole body except on the Day of Atonement.[37] Shepherd notices that Jesus's "baptism by John is one in which he 'washes' by water, even as did the high priest on the Day of Atonement."[38] In fact, the sequence of the high priest's bathing before his approach toward the deity matches the sequence of Matt. 3:16–17, where Jesus is washed in water immediately before receiving his theophanic vision. Thus, Matthew has possibly conflated an immolated goat typology with a high priestly typology, though this connection should probably not be pressed.[39]

To sum up, it seems likely that Leviticus 16 has had some impact on Matthew's baptism scene. Not only does the evangelist's scriptural intertexts evoke the notion of sacrifice, he also retains the tight *inclusio* between Jesus's baptism (Matt. 3:16–17) and his death (27:51), which in the First Gospel is explicitly "for the forgiveness of sins" (26:28). The sequence of a bodily cleansing (Matt. 3:16), followed by an encounter with the deity (3:17), brings to mind the distinctive rites of the high priest's bathing and entrance into the Holy of Holies on the Day of Atonement.

## THE PRIESTLY TRANSFERENCE OF SINS

By means of his editorial addition in Matt. 3:14–15, Matthew indicates the redundancy of John's baptism of repentance from sins with regard to Jesus. The function of Jesus's baptism, rather, is "to fulfill all righteousness" (Matt. 3:15). Though the meaning of the phrase πληρῶσαι πᾶσαν δικαιοσύνην has provoked a large body of scholarship that cannot be discussed here,[40] it is a relatively uncontroversial position that, for Matthew, Jesus's baptism grants him corporate solidarity with the sinners he is destined to save (Matt. 1:21).[41] As Jeffrey Gibbs remarks, "Though without personal need of baptism, Jesus receives John's baptism and thus identifies himself, son of God, with sinful Israel. He quite literally stands with sinners."[42] This aspect of Jesus's baptism is further betrayed in the typology of Jesus as Israel, who goes down to Egypt (Matt. 2:13–15), passes through the Jordan waters (Matt. 3:13–17), and is tempted in the wilderness for forty days (Matt. 4:1–11).[43] As discussed earlier, the heavenly voice in Matt. 3:17 likely alludes to Isa. 42:1, thereby associating Jesus with the Suffering Servant, who is frequently identified corporally as "Israel" in Deutero-Isaiah.[44] It therefore seems to be the case that his baptism, at least in part, serves to symbolize Jesus's corporate solidarity with *sinful* Israel in the Gospel of Matthew.

An interesting parallel to the scapegoat ritual emerges. As noted earlier, the high priest, having gathered Israel's defiant sins from the adytum of the temple (Lev. 16:15–16), transferred those sins onto the scapegoat by placing his hands upon the head of the animal and verbally confessing those sins over the goat (Lev. 16:21). According to An, "we can detect a formal correspondence between the hand-leaning rite on the head of the scapegoat by Aaron and Jesus's baptism by John, who was also of the Aaronic priestly line (Luke 1:5). Just as Aaron's placement of the hands on the live goat officially transferred all of Israel's sins upon its head, John's 'baptism of repentance' led to the public disclosure of Jesus as God's sacrificial provision, or the 'scapegoat,' which carries away humanity's sins."[45]

Though An overstates the degree to which Matthew's baptismal scene visibly foreshadows Jesus's role as cultic offering, her observation regarding the correspondence between the two priestly rites deserves elaboration. To state it more precisely, the parallel is between the scapegoat's association with Israel's sins by means of the high priest's transference rite, and Jesus's association with sinful Israel by means of the priestly baptizer's rite. We already observed that both scenarios involve the confession of sins (Lev. 16:21; Matt. 3:5–6). Both are rites of elimination as well. By means of the scapegoat, Israel's sins were literally banished from the temple and eliminated in the desert (Lev. 16:22). By means of John's baptism, the sins of individuals were symbolically reckoned as having been washed downstream and eliminated.[46]

To summarize, the sins of all Israel having being confessed, a priestly officiant performs an elimination ritual that associates Jesus with the sinful people. This conceptual cluster evokes the high priest's confession of Israel's sins and his transference of those sins onto the goat for Azazel in the elimination ritual of Yom Kippur. If this typology holds, then one would expect Jesus, like the scapegoat, to be led immediately into the wilderness.

## INTO THE WILDERNESS

Having gained solidarity with sinful Israel by means of the priestly baptizer's rite of symbolic elimination, Jesus is immediately led "into the wilderness," which recalls the sin-bearing scapegoat's journey into the Judaean desert:[47] "Then Jesus was led into the desert [εἰς τὴν ἔρημον] by the Spirit" (Matt. 4:1; cf. Mark 1:12).[48] Unlike his Lukan counterpart, who writes ἐν τῇ ἐρήμῳ (Luke 4:1), Matthew employs εἰς τὴν ἔρημον, a phrase that appears three times in Leviticus 16 LXX:

> He shall release it [the scapegoat] into the desert [εἰς τὴν ἔρημον] . . . And he shall lay them [the sins] upon the head of the living goat, and shall send it by the hand of a ready man into the wilderness [εἰς τὴν ἔρημον]. And the goat shall bear their unrighteousness upon itself into a desolate land. And Aaron shall send away the goat into the wilderness [εἰς τὴν ἔρημον].[49]

Matthew's decision to retain εἰς τὴν ἔρημον is surprising, given that the form ἐν τῇ ἐρήμῳ occurs in Deut. 6:4; 8:2, 16, that is to say, in the two chapters from which Jesus quotes Scripture in the temptation narrative (Deut. 8:3 in Matt. 4:4//Luke 4:4; Deut. 6:16 in Matt. 4:7//Luke 4:12; Deut. 6:13 in Matt. 4:10//Luke 4:8).[50] While this fact may have motivated Luke's change to ἐν τῇ ἐρήμῳ (cf. Mark 1:13), one wonders why Matthew, who is usually quick to demonstrate Jesus's fulfillment of Torah, retains εἰς τὴν ἔρημον, especially since he freely diverges from the remainder of his Markan source (cf. Mark 1:12–13).[51] This change is all the more puzzling, given that ἐν τῇ ἐρήμῳ may be the evangelist's preferred phrase, as he writes it three times (Matt. 3:1, 3; 24:26) and εἰς τὴν ἔρημον just one other time (Matt. 11:7). A deliberate connection to Leviticus 16 seems more probable in light of these redactions.

The parallel between the scapegoat and Jesus's journey "into the desert," where both figures encounter a diabolical entity (see below), has caused Fleming Rutledge, Hannah An, John Kleinig, and Jerry Shepherd to perceive a link to the figure of the scapegoat in this gospel episode.[52] While the term for Jesus's "sending" differs from that used for the scapegoat in Lev. 16:10, 21–22, 26 LXX (ἀποστέλλω, ἀφίημι, ἐξαποστέλλω), the verb ἀνάγω, which Matthew utilizes to describe Jesus's being "led up" by the Spirit into the wilderness (Matt. 4:1), is a cognate of the verb ἄγω, which the author of the Epistle of Barnabas uses to describe the handler's "leading" the scapegoat into the wilderness:[53] "And when it happens thus, the one who carries away the goat leads it into the wilderness [ἄγει . . . εἰς τὴν ἔρημον]" (Barn. 7.8).[54] Thus, Matthew's vocabulary is consistent with contemporaneous descriptions of the scapegoat's journey into the desert,[55] and his choice to retain εἰς τὴν ἔρημον, contrary to Luke, recalls the language of Leviticus 16 LXX.

## TO AZAZEL

Not only is Jesus led into the wilderness, but there he encounters a nefarious deity, which makes the case for an allusion to Leviticus 16 particularly compelling. For not only was the scapegoat sent into the desert, but it was sent into the desert "for/to Azazel" (לעזאזל, Lev. 16:8, 10, 26), a sinister deity of the Judean wilderness,[56] whom some Jewish communities in the Second Temple period identified as Asael of the Watcher's tradition.[57] As Shepherd remarks, "There [in the wilderness], even as the scapegoat encountered Azazel, Jesus now encounters Satan."[58]

The fact that Matthew elsewhere appears to conflate the figures of the Devil, Satan, and Azazel makes it probable that here too in the temptation narrative the Devil acquires Azazel's persona. In the previous chapter, I argued that Matthew appropriates Asael/Azazel traditions in his portrayal of the Devil in Matt. 25:41, highlighting the similarity between "the eternal fire prepared for the Devil and his angels" (Matt. 25:41) and the "prepared" judgment of "Azazel, and all his associates and all his host" (1 En. 54.4; 55.4), both at the behest of the Son of Man/Elect One seated on a "throne of glory" (Matt. 25:31; 1 En. 55.4).[59] This proposal was confirmed by the parallel scene of eschatological expulsion described in Matt. 22:13, the language of which almost certainly appropriates Asael/Azazel traditions.[60]

Yet, there may be more evidence that Asael/Azazel traditions have colored Matthew's conception of the chief cosmic antagonist. Crispin Fletcher-Louis has suggested that Jesus's rebuke of Peter at Caesarea Philippi, "Get behind me, Satan" (ὕπαγε ὀπίσω μου σατανᾶ, Matt. 16:23; Mark 8:33), evokes the enigmatic desert figure:

[This verse] may put Peter in the position not just of Satan, but of the demon Azazel. According to the Mishnah the people dispatch the scapegoat on the Day of Atonement with the words "Take (our sins) and go forth" (*m. Yoma* 6:4). In

*Apocalypse of Abraham* 13:12 the angel guiding Abraham through his mystical
ascent wards off the Azazel bird with the words "Depart from this man." A little
later Abraham himself rebukes Azazel: "Therefore through your own destruction may you have disappeared from me!." (14:7)[61]

The clause that follows Jesus's rebuke of Peter/Satan, "For you are setting
your mind not on divine things but on human things" (Matt. 16:23; Mark
8:33), makes the impact of the scapegoat-Azazel complex on this gospel tradition more probable since the statement aptly summarizes the nature of the
transgression of the Watchers, who literally set their minds on human things
by illicitly comingling with the human race (cf. 1 En. 6–11).[62]

In light of the connection to the scapegoat-Azazel complex in the statement, ὕπαγε ὀπίσω μου σατανᾶ (Matt. 16:23; Mark 8:33), it is remarkable
that only Matthew inserts a similar phrase at the end of his temptation narrative, "Depart, Satan" (ὕπαγε, σατανᾶ, Matt. 4:10; cf. Luke 4:8, 13), especially
since the switch to σατανᾶς disrupts his use of διάβολος throughout the narrative (Matt. 4:1, 5, 8, 11). That is to say, since Matt. 4:10 and 16:23 are
tightly linked from a redactional and literary point of view,[63] the likelihood
that Jesus's command, "Depart, Satan" (Matt. 4:10), also intimates the tradition of Asael/Azazel's eschatological expulsion, which was inspired in part
by the scapegoat's banishment in the temple ritual of Yom Kippur, is quite
plausible.

## THE FAST

As Luz observes, "Matthew puts special emphasis on Jesus's fasting,"[64]
uniquely writing, unlike his Markan and Lukan counterparts, that Jesus
"fasted" while he was in the desert, not only for forty days but also for "forty
nights": "And having fasted [νηστεύσας] forty days and forty nights, after-
ward he was hungry" (Matt. 4:2).[65] Dale Allison argues that a Moses typology
has motivated the evangelist's additions of "fasted" and "forty nights" in this
verse, since the Pentateuch repeatedly mentions Moses's journey to the top of
Mount Horeb for "forty days and forty nights," where he went without food
and drink (Exod. 24:18; 34:28; Deut. 9:9, 11, 18, 25; 10:10).[66] While Allison's
argument for a Moses typology in the temptation narrative is convincing on
the whole, there are reasons to doubt that only Mosaic traditions exercised
influence on Matthew's redaction of the account. For one, the term νηστεύω
or νηστεία never occurs in the aforementioned Pentateuchal passages describing Moses's journey on Mount Sinai. Moreover, the LXX always employs the
exact wording, τεσσαράκοντα ἡμέρας καὶ τεσσαράκοντα νύκτας, instead of
Matthew's ἡμέρας τεσσεράκοντα καὶ νύκτας τεσσεράκοντα.[67] And while

Jesus's transportation to a high mountain possibly recalls Moses's alpine expedition (Matt. 4:8), Jesus engages in fasting not when he is on the mountain but while he is in the desert (Matt. 4:2). There is room, therefore, to posit the effect of other Jewish traditions upon Matthew's account.

Remarkably, scholars have rarely considered the Day of Atonement as background to Jesus's "fasting" in Matt. 4:2, as no other occasion on the Jewish calendar was more associated with fasting in the Second Temple period than Yom Kippur. In fact, most ancient sources that directly address the Day of Atonement make some reference to the practice of fasting. Abstaining from food and drink became such a prominent feature of this high holy day that both early Jews and Christians widely referred to Yom Kippur as "the Fast" (ἡ νηστεία).

Isa. 1:13–14 LXX may be the earliest witness to this tradition: "Your new moons, and sabbaths, and great day I cannot endure. Fasting [νηστείαν], and rest, and your new moons, and your feasts my soul hates."[68] Describing the Qumran community's persecution by "the Wicked Priest," Pesher Habakkuk reports that, "during the rest of the Day of Atonement, he appeared to them, to consume them and make them fall on the day of fasting [ביום צום], the sabbath of their rest."[69] The Psalms of Solomon also attest to the custom of fasting on the Day of Atonement: "The righteous constantly searches his house, to remove his unintentional sins. He atones for (sins of) ignorance by fasting [νηστείᾳ] and humbling his soul, and the Lord will cleanse every devout person and his house."[70] Philo of Alexandria repeatedly refers to Yom Kippur as a day of fasting.[71] In *On the Special Laws*, he writes, "On the tenth day is the Fast [ἡ νηστεία], which is carefully observed not only by the zealous for piety and holiness but also by those who never act religiously in the rest of their life. For all stand in awe, overcome by the sanctity of the day, and for the moment the worse vie with the better in self-denial and virtue."[72] In *On the Life of Moses*, Philo states, "Again, who does not every year shew awe and reverence for the Fast, as it is called [τὴν λεγομένην νηστείαν], which is kept more strictly and solemnly than the 'holy month' of the Greeks?"[73] Josephus describes Yom Kippur as "the day on which it was the universal custom to keep fast [νηστεύειν] to God."[74] Elsewhere, he writes, "On the tenth of the same lunar month they fast [διανηστεύοντες] until evening."[75] In Pseudo-Philo's Biblical Antiquities, God commands Moses regarding the Day of Atonement, "A fast of mercy you will fast for me for your own souls, so that the promises made to your fathers may be fulfilled."[76] In the Apocalypse of Abraham, the patriarch fasts for forty days and nights before his encounter with Azazel.[77] According to Mishnah Yoma, "On the Day of Atonement, eating, drinking, washing, anointing, putting on sandals, and marital intercourse are forbidden."[78] Tg. Ps.-J. Lev. 16:29 states, "In the seventh month, *that is, the month of Tishri*, on the tenth *day* of the month, you shall mortify

yourselves (abstaining) *from food and drink, from the enjoyment of the baths
and of anointing (from wearing) shoes, and from marital intercourse.*"[79]

Fasting characterizes the Day of Atonement in early Christian literature as
well. Luke makes a passing reference to Yom Kippur in Acts 27:9: "Since
much time had been lost and sailing was now dangerous, because even the
Fast [τὴν νηστείαν] had already gone by, Paul advised them."[80] The Epistle
of Barnabas relays a version of Lev. 23:29 that interprets the command to
practice humiliation on the Day of Atonement as a command to fast:
"Whoever does not keep the fast [νηστεύσῃ τὴν νηστείαν] must surely die."[81]
Justin Martyr also employs the appellation, "the Fast," for Yom Kippur:
"Likewise, the two identical goats which had to be offered during the fast [τῇ
νηστείᾳ] . . . were an announcement of the two comings of Christ . . . You
also know very well that the offering of the two goats, which had to take place
during the fast [νηστείᾳ], could not take place anywhere else except
Jerusalem."[82] Justin reads Isa. 58:6 as a reference to the fasting of the holy
day: "[In] that same place of Jerusalem you shall recognize him whom you
had subjected to shame, and who was a sacrificial offering for all sinners who
are willing to repent and to comply with that fast which Isaiah prescribed
when he said [νηστευόντων ἣν καταλέγει Ἡσαΐας νηστείαν], *loosing the
strangle of violent contracts*, and to observe likewise all the other precepts
laid down by him."[83] Tertullian knows the Day of Atonement as "the Fast" as
well: "If also I am to submit an interpretation of the two goats which were
offered at the Fast, are not these also figures of Christ's two activities?"[84] In
his Homilies on Jeremiah, Origen refers to "keeping the Jewish fast" on Yom
Kippur.[85] Finally, Eusebius writes that "all the Jews still perform their fast"
on the Day of Atonement.[86]

Although fasting is not mandated in the biblical ordinances of Yom
Kippur, the extant textual witnesses suggest that fasting was perhaps the most
commonly noted feature of the Day of Atonement in the Second Temple
period. Most ancient authors who refer to Yom Kippur make some reference
to the fasting that was customarily performed on the holy day. The very
strong association of the Day of Atonement with fasting makes Matthew's
explicit mention of Jesus's "fasting" both day and night likely to evoke the
hallmark practice of abstinence from food and drink on Israel's high holy
day.[87]

## MANNA AND DESERT AFFLICTIONS

When the Devil tempts Jesus to transform stones into bread, Jesus retorts by
quoting from Deut. 8:3, "Man shall not live by bread alone." This tradition
derives from Q (Matt. 4:4//Luke4:4), and its shorter form as contained in

Luke likely reflects the extent of the citation in Q.[88] Matthew, however, lengthens the quotation with the following: "Man shall not live by bread alone, *but by every word that comes forth from the mouth of God*" (Matt. 4:4). Since the First Evangelist does not elongate either of the other two scriptural citations in the temptation narrative (cf. Matt. 4:7//Luke 4:12; Matt. 4:10// Luke 4:8), the lengthened quotation of Deut. 8:3 suggests Matthew's special interest in this verse, the context of which refers to God leading Israel into the wilderness for forty years to be tested (Deut. 8:2).[89] Significantly, Yom Kippur became associated with Israel's wilderness wanderings and the tradition concerning manna in early Judaism.

Most strikingly, Philo draws a correspondence between Israel's trials in the desert and the command to practice self-affliction on the Day of Atonement (Lev. 16:29, 31; 23:27–32; Num. 29:7), citing Deut. 8:3 to make his point. In *Allegorical Interpretation*, Philo writes:

> He says in Deuteronomy also: "And He afflicted thee and made thee weak by hunger, and fed thee with mana, which thy fathers knew not, that He might proclaim to thee, that not on bread alone shall man live, but on every word that goeth forth through the mouth of God" (Deut viii. 3). This affliction is propitiation; for on the tenth day also by afflicting our souls He makes propitiation (Lev xvi. 30). For when we are being deprived of pleasant things, we think we are being afflicted, but in reality, thereby we have God propitious to us.[90]

For Philo, Israel's reliance upon manna during the wilderness afflictions symbolizes the self-abasement that the Jewish people performed on Yom Kippur in anticipation of receiving divine mercy.

In *On the Special Laws*, Philo recounts a prayer made on the Day of Atonement for those who had just gathered their autumnal harvest. In this petition, God's provision of manna for the Israelites during their forty years of desert wanderings is reckoned as an example of the divine provision that the people expected during the fast of Yom Kippur. Philo reports:

> We have gladly received and are storing the boons of nature, yet we do not ascribe our preservation to any corruptible thing, but to God the Parent and Father and Saviour of the world and all that is therein, Who has the power and the right to nourish and sustain us by means of these or without these. See, for example, how the many thousands of our forefathers as they traversed the trackless and all-barren desert, were for forty years, the life of a generation, nourished by Him as in a land of richest and most fertile soil; how He opened fountains unknown before to give them abundance of drink for their use; how He rained food from heaven, neither more nor less than what sufficed for each day, that they might consume what they needed without hoarding, nor barter for the

prospect of soulless stores their hopes of His goodness, but taking little thought of the bounties received rather reverence and worship the bountiful Giver and honour Him with the hymns and benedictions that are His due.[91]

The motif of manna is central in this Yom Kippur prayer. Additionally, the prayer's description of "the trackless and all-barren desert" of the nation's wandering recalls the "barren region" where the goat for Azazel was sent (Lev. 16:22).

A rewritten version of Deuteronomy, 1QWords of Moses (1Q22) sets forth an exhortation to the children of Israel to obey God's laws concerning the sabbatical years and the Day of Atonement.[92] As Barthélemy and Milik point out, this scroll attributes the origins of Yom Kippur to the end of the Israelite's wilderness wanderings.[93] A portion of the fragmentary text reads as follows:

> [Go]d [will bless you, forgiving you your] sin[s . . .] . . . [. . .] in the year [. . .] of the month of [. . .] . . . [. . .] on this day [. . . For] your [father]s wandered [in the wilderness] until the [te]nth day of the month {the [. . . on the te]nth [day] of the month} [You shall] refrain [from all work.] And on the te[nth] day [of the] month, atonement shall be made [. . .] of the month [. . . and] they shall take.[94]

Again, Israel's lengthy period of desert trials seems to be interpreted in light of the command to "afflict yourselves" on Yom Kippur, and the conclusion of the wilderness wanderings comes to symbolize the expiatory miracle of the high holy day.

A Festival Prayer found at Qumran appears to maintain the association between Yom Kippur and the tradition concerning manna.[95] Though the text is highly fragmentary, a few lines of it read: "in the lot of the righ[te]ous but for the wicked the l[o]t . . . in their bones a disgrace to all flesh; but the righteous . . . fat by the clouds of heaven and the produce of the earth, to distinguish [between the righ]teous and the wicked. And you give the wicked (for) our [r]ansom, and/but the tr[eacher]ous ones . . . the extermination of all our oppressors."[96] According to Stökl Ben Ezra, "the phrase 'fat by the clouds of heaven' clearly refers to the heavenly manna" in this prayer designated for Yom Kippur.[97] Lastly, it is noteworthy that the Babylonian Talmud connects Yom Kippur to the manna tradition as well.[98]

In summary, the evangelist's decision in Matt. 4:4 to lengthen the quotation of Deut. 8:3 has the effect of highlighting the motifs of heavenly manna and Israel's desert afflictions, which are linked to Yom Kippur in certain Second Temple traditions. Philo utilizes Deut. 8:3 to draw a parallel between the afflictions of Israel's desert trials and the self-afflictions performed on

Yom Kippur (*Leg.* 3.174). Two liturgical prayers incorporate the manna motif into their petitions made on the Day of Atonement (Philo, *Spec.* 2.198–99; 1Q34 3 I, 1–8//4Q508 1 1–3; cf. b. Yoma 74b). And the end of Israel's wilderness wanderings becomes the historical etiology for Yom Kippur in 1QWords of Moses. This evidence further suggests that traditions pertaining to the Day of Atonement have made an impact on Matthew's temptation narrative.

## CONCLUSION

To reiterate, I have argued the multiple points in this chapter: (a) Matthew, as opposed to his Lukan counterpart, preserves the structural parallel between the rite of the two goats (Lev. 16:7–10, 15–22) and the baptism-temptation narrative (Matt. 3:16–17; 4:1–11). (b) In contrast to Luke, Matthew follows his Markan *Vorlage* by situating the baptism in a context where all of Israel's sins are being confessed (Matt. 3:5–6), which recalls the hallmark confession of all the sins of Israel on Yom Kippur (Lev. 16:21). (c) The scriptural inter-texts in the heavenly voice (Matt. 3:17), namely, Isaiah 42 and possibly Genesis 22, evoke Jesus's sacrificial vocation. Moreover, the sequence of a bodily cleansing (Matt. 3:16), followed by an encounter with the deity (3:17), plus the Matthean addition of the word "God" (θεός, 3:16), brings to mind the distinctive rites of the high priest's bathing (Lev. 16:4) and entrance into the Holy of Holies with the blood of the goat for Yahweh (Lev. 16:15–17). (d) In light of the redactional verses of Matt. 3:14–15, the priestly baptizer's elimi-nation ritual symbolically associates Jesus with the sinful people in the First Gospel, which parallels how the high priest caused the goat for Azazel to inherit Israel's sins in the context of an elimination ritual (Lev. 16:21). (e) Jesus is sent "into the wilderness" (Matt. 4:1) like the scapegoat on the Day of Atonement (Lev. 16:10, 21–22). Contrary to Luke, Matthew's decision to retain the form εἰς τὴν ἔρημον recalls Leviticus 16 LXX, where that phrase occurs three times with regard to the scapegoat. (f) Like the goat for Azazel on Yom Kippur (Lev. 16:8, 10, 26), Jesus encounters a nefarious deity in the desert (Matt. 4:1–11). Moreover, the First Evangelist uniquely conflates the Devil and possibly Satan with the figure of Azazel elsewhere in the gospel (Matt. 16:23; 25:41). (g) Only Matthew employs the term "to fast" (νηστεύω) in his temptation account (Matt. 4:2), which evokes the distinctive feature of abstaining from food and drink on Yom Kippur, as well as the holy day's famous moniker, "the Fast" (ἡ νηστεία). (h) Matthew's choice to lengthen Jesus's quotation of Deut. 8:3 (Matt. 4:4) highlights the motifs of heavenly manna and Israel's desert afflictions, which are linked to the Day of Atonement in certain Second Temple traditions.

Though varying in strength individually, these eight points of correspondence, when evaluated as a whole, are impressive enough to conclude that Matthew has deliberately associated Jesus with the goat for Yahweh and the goat for Azazel in his baptism-temptation narrative.[99] Since five of these parallels are present in Mark (a, b, c, e, f), and only two are present in Luke (c, f),[100] it is reasonable to posit that the Yom Kippur typology is original to Mark or a pre-Markan source and was absent from Q. If Mark is responsible, he appears to suppress the goat typology, possibly in an attempt to remove the allusions to the esoteric Jewish ritual for his more Gentile-oriented audience.

Finally, having established the likelihood of a Christological goat typology in Matthew's baptism-temptation narrative, the goat typology in Matthew 27 is substantially strengthened by virtue of the criterion of recurrence. It thus seems highly probable that the First Evangelist has intended Jesus's association with the goat for Yahweh and the goat for Azazel in the baptism and temptation stories to foreshadow Jesus's typological designation as both goats in the Barabbas and Roman-abuse episodes (Matt. 27:15–26, 27–31). As Huizenga observes, "relatively little of a comprehensive character seems to have been written pertaining to the mechanics of Jesus's sacrificial death in the Gospel of Matthew; the issue is not a central concern of major Matthean scholars."[101] Hopefully, students of Matthew will now additionally look to Leviticus 16 and the Day of Atonement ritual to understand what it means for Jesus's death to be "for the release of sins" (Matt. 26:28) in the First Gospel.

## NOTES

1. Stökl Ben Ezra, *Impact of Yom Kippur*, 165–71; Berenson Maclean, "Barabbas, the Scapegoat Ritual, 324–30. See also Wratislaw, *Notes and Dissertations*, 12–23; idem, "The Scapegoat-Barabbas," 400–03; Koester, *Ancient Christian Gospels*, 220–30; Stökl Ben Ezra, "Fasting with Jews," 179–84. For a bibliography of scholars who support this interpretation in Matthew or Mark, see Moscicke, *New Day of Atonement*, 100 n. 4, 140 n. 4.

2. For a detailed argument on this score, see Hans M. Moscicke, "Jesus, Barabbas, and the Crowd as Figures in Matthew's Day of Atonement Typology (Matt. 27:15–26)," *JBL* 139 (2020): 125–53; idem, "Jesus as Scapegoat in Matthew's Roman-abuse Scene (Matt. 27:27–31)," *NovT* 62 (2020): 229–56; idem, *New Day of Atonement*, 99–180.

3. See Hays, *Echoes of Scripture*, 30; idem, *Conversion of the Imagination*, 37–38.

4. Allison, *New Moses*, 21–22.

5. Hannah S. An has recently argued that "the ritual prescriptions of the Day of Atonement, particularly those found in Leviticus 16:20–22, decisively inform our

interpretation of the Matthean witness of Jesus's baptism and temptation (Matt. 3:5–4:1)" ("Reading Matthew's Account of the Baptism and Temptation of Jesus [Matt. 3:5–4:1] with the Scapegoat Rite on the Day of Atonement [Lev. 16:20–22]," *Canon & Culture* 12 [2018]: 5–31). While I do not agree with all of her conclusions (see below), An's interpretive intuition may be correct. Prior to An, Fleming Rutledge had made the following note: "I have not been able to find anyone other than myself who sees a glancing reference to the scapegoat imagery in Mark 1:12 ("The Spirit immediately drove [Jesus] out into the wilderness," where he contended with Satan)" (*The Crucifixion: Understanding the Death of Jesus* [Grand Rapids: Eerdmans, 2015], 248 n. 32). In fact, John Kleinig (*Leviticus*, ConC [Saint Louis: Concordia, 2003], 347–48, n. 35) and Richard N. Boyce (*Leviticus and Numbers* [Louisville, KY: Westminster John Knox Press, 2008], 57) had already perceived a connection between the baptism-temptation narrative and Leviticus 16. Now, Jerry Shepherd joins them (*Leviticus*, SGBC, ed. Tremper Longman III and Scot McKnight [Grand Rapids: Zondervan, forthcoming]). Though I have yet to discover any ancient attestation for this interpretation of the gospel episodes, David Dawson has pointed to three seventeenth-century commentators (Thomas Jackson, John Trapp, and Peter Heylyn) who advanced the typological correspondence between Jesus and the scapegoat in the temptation narrative (*Flesh Becomes Word: A Lexicography of the Scapegoat or, the History of an Idea* [East Lansing, MI: Michigan State University Press, 2013], 157–58 n. 47).

6. As Allison persuasively argues, the evangelist overlays an existing Moses typology with an Israel typology in Matthew 2, and that he overlays an existing Israel typology with a Moses typology in Matthew 4 (ibid., 166).

7. Stökl Ben Ezra, "Biblical Yom Kippur," 494.

8. Eberhart, "To Atone or Not to Atone," 223.

9. Wright, *Disposal of Impurity*, 17; Milgrom, *Leviticus*, 1:1041–43; Roy Gane, *Cult and Character: Purification Offerings, Day of Atonement, and Theodicy* (Winona Lake, IN: Eisenbrauns, 2005), 245. According to Milgrom, the one-handed hand-leaning rite (e.g., Lev. 1:4; 3:2; 4:4, 24) symbolizes ownership of the sacrificial animal (*Leviticus*, 1:152; so also Wright, *Disposal of Impurity*, 17 n. 6).

10. Milgrom, *Leviticus*, 1:1042–43; Baruch Schwartz, "The Bearing of Sin in the Priestly Literature," in *Pomegranates and Golden Bells: Studies in Biblical, Jewish, and Near Eastern Ritual, Law, and Literature in Honor of Jacob Milgrom*, ed. David P. Wright, David Noel Freedman, and Avi Hurvitz (Winona Lake, IN: Eisenbrauns, 1995), 3–22, at 17; cf. Baruch A. Levine, *Leviticus*, JPSTC (Philadelphia: Jewish Publication Society, 1989), xx. Apparently, for Schwartz the חטאת blood "removes" the deliberate sins from the adytum, but the blood cannot ultimately purge them; they must be transferred onto the scapegoat ("The Bearing of Sin," 20). Thus, Israel's deliberate sins seem to "hang in suspension" between the rites of the immolated goat and the scapegoat.

11. Lev. 16:21 LXX uses ἐξαγορεύω, while Matt. 3:6 uses ἐξομολογέω. Πᾶς accompanies the list of moral evils in Lev. 16:21 LXX (i.e., πάσας τὰς ἁμαρτίας αὐτῶν), while Matthew only has τὰς ἁμαρτίας αὐτῶν. An suggests that the term πᾶς in the phrase πᾶσαν δικαιοσύνην (Matt. 3:15) evokes the repeated use of πᾶς in Lev. 16:16, 21 (An, "Baptism and Temptation," 11–13). But this is doubtful, since, if this

were the case, then Matthew most likely would have included πᾶς in the phrase ἐξομολογούμενοι τὰς ἁμαρτίας αὐτῶν (Matt. 3:6), to evoke the phrases πασῶν τῶν ἁμαρτιῶν αὐτῶν and ἐξαγορεύσει . . . πάσας τὰς ἁμαρτίας αὐτῶν in Lev. 16:16, 21 LXX.

12. Philo, Spec. 2.193; cf. 2.196.

13. M. Yoma 8:1.

14. Jub. 34.12, 17–19.

15. Stökl Ben Ezra, Impact of Yom Kippur, 34.

16. An, "Baptism and Temptation," 24.

17. Ibid., 12.

18. Mark 1:11: σὺ εἶ ὁ υἱός μου ὁ ἀγαπητός, ἐν σοὶ εὐδόκησα. Luke 3:22: σὺ εἶ ὁ υἱός μου ὁ ἀγαπητός, ἐν σοὶ εὐδόκησα. John 1:34: οὗτός ἐστιν ὁ υἱὸς τοῦ θεοῦ.

19. Davies and Allison, Matthew, 1:338.

20. Huizenga, New Isaac, 156–66.

21. Huizenga claims that the discrepancy between ἐν ᾧ εὐδόκησα (Matt. 3:17) and εἰς ὃν εὐδόκησεν (Matt. 12:18) is the "Achilles' heel" of the consensus view, since Matthew could have easily assimilated these phrases (New Isaac, 163). But the form in Matt. 3:17 can be explained by the evangelist's attempt to leave untouched the phrasing of the undoubtedly important tradition of the heavenly voice (Mark 1:11//Matt. 3:17//Luke 3:22; cf. John 1:33–34), while adapting it from the second to third person. And the form of Matt. 12:18 can be accounted for as Matthew's preferred wording, which probably has some precedent in earlier Greek versions, as both Theodotion and Symmachus translate the phrase ον ευδοκησεν (Joseph Ziegler, ed., Isaias, 3rd ed., Septuaginta, VTG 14 [Göttingen: Vandenhoeck & Ruprecht, 1983], 276).

22. E.g., Morna Hooker, Jesus and the Servant: Influence of the Servant Concept of Deutero-Isaiah in the New Testament (London: SPCK, 1959), esp. 1–102; eadem, "Did the Use of Isaiah 53 to Interpret his Mission Begin with Jesus?" in Jesus and the Suffering Servant: Isaiah 53 and Christian Origins, ed. W. H. Bellinger and William R. Farmer (Harrisburg, PA: Trinity Press International, 1998), 88–103; eadem, "Response to Mikael Parsons," in ibid., 120–24; Huizenga, New Isaac, 189–208; Richard B. Hays, Echoes of Scripture in the Gospels (Waco: Baylor University Press, 2016), 160–61.

23. Mark 14:65 and Matt. 26:67 employ three words (ἐμπτύω, πρόσωπον, ῥάπισμα/ῥαπίζω) that echo Isa. 50:6 LXX: "I gave my back to scourges and my cheeks to blows [ῥαπίσματα]; I did not turn my face [πρόσωπόν] away from the shame of a spitting [ἐμπτυσμάτων]" (Ziegler, Isaias, 311). Yet, the First Evangelist's redaction seems to emphasize the allusion (Davies and Allison, Matthew, 3:536), making it perhaps the strongest allusion to the Servant Songs in Matthew's passion narrative.

24. On the connection between Matthew's use of these Isaianic texts and Jesus's passion, see Otto Betz, "Jesus and Isaiah 53," in Bellinger and Farmer, Suffering Servant, 70–87, at 81; Donald A. Carson, "Matthew," in The Expositor's Bible Commentary, ed. F. E. Gaebelein, vol. 8 (Grand Rapids: Zondervan, 1984), 205–7; Donald A. Hagner, Matthew, 2 vols., WBC 33A–B (Dallas: Thomas Nelson, 1995),

1:210–11; Senior, *Matthew*, 100. Some scholars deny that Matthew's use of Isa. 42:1–4 or 53:4 has any bearing on the meaning of Jesus's death in the First Gospel (e.g., Luz, *Matthew*, 2:14; Huizenga, *New Isaac*, 200).

25. Scholars often claim that the ὑπὲρ πολλῶν phrase in Mark 14:24 (parr.) alludes to Isaiah 53 (Joachim Jeremias, *The Eucharistic Words of Jesus*, 3rd ed., trans. Norman Perrin [New York: Charles Scribner's Sons, 1966], 227–29; Martin Hengel, *The Atonement: The Origins and the Doctrine in the New Testament* [Philadelphia: Fortress, 1981], 72–73; Adela Yarbro Collins, "Finding Meaning in the Death of Jesus," *JR* 78 [1998]: 175–96, at 176–78; cf. Hooker, "Isaiah 53," 94–95; Luz, *Matthew*, 3:381). By changing ὑπέρ to περί, a word frequently used in reference to sacrifice in the LXX (cf. Isa. 53:10 LXX; Gundry, *Matthew*, 528), and by stylistically sandwiching περὶ πολλῶν between τό and ἐκχυννόμενον, "a sacrificial word which connotes a violent death" (Davies and Allison, *Matthew*, 3: 474), Matthew highlights the cultic flavor of the probable Isa. 53:12 allusion. On the cultic imagery in Isaiah 53, see Yarbro Collins, "Finding Meaning," 176–78; KyeSang Ha, "Cultic Allusions in the Suffering Servant Poem (Isaiah 52:13–53:12)" (PhD diss., Andrews University, 2009); cf. Bernd Janowski, "He Bore Our Sins: Isaiah 53 and the Drama of Taking Another's Place," in *The Suffering Servant: Isaiah 53 in Jewish and Christian Sources*, ed. Bernd Janowski and Peter Stuhlmacher, trans. Daniel P. Bailey (Grand Rapids: Eerdmans, 2004), 48–74.

26. Huizinga summarily remarks, "Thus, not only does Matt. 3:17 have ὁ υἱός μου ὁ ἀγαπητός in common with Gen. 22:2, 12 and 16; both Matt. 3:17 and Gen. 22:11 and 15 share the phrase ἐκ τῶν οὐρανῶν/ἐκ τοῦ οὐρανοῦ as well. Further, the Matthean heavenly voice parallels the angel calling to Abraham. In short, the Matthean baptism of Jesus and the biblical Akedah share conspicuously similar language" (*New Isaac*, 154). Davies and Allison attribute the epithet ὁ ἀγαπητός to Isa. 44:2 LXX, which speaks of the Servant (*Matthew*, 1:337); cf. Huizinga, *New Isaac*, 164–65.

27. See Gen 22:2, 3, 6, 13, where Isaac assumes the role of a burnt offering (עלה/ὁλοκάρπωσις). On the sacrificial and possibly expiatory aspects of the Akedah in early Jewish and Christian traditions, see Huizinga, *New Isaac*, 75–128. According to An, "it is apparent that the Spirit's anointing on Jesus exposed the salvific provision of God's own sacrifice, already foreshadowed in the near-sacrifice of Isaac (Gen. 22:7)" ("Baptism and Temptation," 17).

28. R. T. France, *The Gospel of Matthew*, NICNT (Grand Rapids: Eerdmans, 2007), 123–24.

29. Contra Luz, who writes, "In particular the interpretation of our text in terms of the passion is a widespread eisegesis of the text" (*Matthew*, 143).

30. Shepherd, *Leviticus*, forthcoming.

31. See Milgrom, *Leviticus*, 1:1019–24.

32. Andrei A. Orlov, *The Glory of the Invisible God: Two Powers in Heaven Traditions and Early Christology*, JCTCRS 31 (London: T&T Clark, 2019), 164.

33. On the Markan *inclusio*, see David Ulansey, "The Heavenly Veil Torn: Mark's Cosmic *Inclusio*," *JBL* 110 (1991): 123–25. Ulansey draws upon the analysis of Stephen Motyer, who noticed additional parallels between the baptism and death

narratives in Mark ("The Rending of the Veil: A Markan Pentecost," *NTS* 33 [1987]: 155–57). Summarizing these points, Ulansey notes that "(1) at both moments a *voice* is heard declaring Jesus to be the *Son of God* (at the baptism it is the voice of God, whereas at the death it is the voice of the centurion); (2) at both moments something is said to *descend* (at the baptism it is the spirit-dove, whereas at the death it is the tear in the temple veil, which Mark explicitly describes as moving *downward*); (3) at both moments the figure of *Elijah* is symbolically present (at the baptism Elijah is present in the form of John the Baptist, whereas at Jesus's death the onlookers think that Jesus is calling to Elijah); (4) the *spirit* (πνεῦμα) which descends on Jesus at his baptism is recalled at his death by Mark's repeated use of the verb ἐκπνέω (expire), a cognate of πνεῦμα" ("Heavenly Veil," 123). Interestingly, Matthew retains all of these parallels and even enhances some of them, while Luke omits most of them: (1) a voice declares Jesus as God's Son (Matt. 3:17; 27:54; cf. Luke 23:47); (2) the Spirit descends (Matt. 3:16), and the veil is torn from top to bottom (27:51; cf. Luke 23:45); (3) changing Mark's ελωι ελωι (Mark 15:34) to ηλι ηλι (Matt. 27:46), Matthew clarifies that Jesus is calling to Elijah, whom only the First Evangelist explicitly identifies as John the Baptist (11:14; cf. Luke 23:44–45); (4) Matthew changes Mark's ἐξέπνευσεν (Mark 15:37) to ἀφῆκεν τὸ πνεῦμα (Matt. 27:50; cf. Luke 23:46), which more closely parallels mention of τὸ πνεῦμα in the baptism scene (Mark 1:10//Matt. 3:16//Luke 3:22).

34. Schwartz, "Bearing of Sin," 21; Jacob Milgrom, "Israel's Sanctuary: The Priestly 'Picture of Dorian Gray'," *RB* 83 (1976): 390–99, at 398–99. For a recent analysis of the meaning of the torn veil in Matt. 27:51, see Daniel M. Gurtner, *The Torn Veil: Matthew's Exposition of the Death of Jesus*, SNTSMS 139 (Cambridge: Cambridge University Press, 2007).

35. Ezek. 1:1 LXX: ἠνοίχθησαν οἱ οὐρανοί, καὶ εἶδον ὁράσεις θεοῦ. According to Davies and Allison, Matthew's "modifications probably signal assimilation to Ezek 1:1" (*Matthew*, 1:329). For further parallels between Ezek. 1:1–4 and Matt. 3:16, see Luz, *Matthew*, 1:143 n. 28.

36. E.g. 1 En. 14.8–25; 87.3–4 T. Levi 2–5; Apoc. Ab. 9–32; 2 En. 18.8–9; 22.6–9. See Martha Himmelfarb, *Ascent to Heaven in Jewish and Christian Apocalypses* (New York: Oxford University Press, 1993), 9–46; Stökl Ben Ezra, *Impact of Yom Kippur*, 80–85.

37. Cf. Exod. 30:19. Milgrom, *Leviticus*, 1:1017.

38. Shepherd, *Leviticus*, forthcoming.

39. Boyce suggests that Jesus's baptism prepares him for his sacrificial work in a manner similar to the high priest's bathing on Yom Kippur (*Leviticus and Numbers*, 57).

40. See the range of interpretive options relayed in Davies and Allison, *Matthew*, 321–23.

41. Meier, *Matthew*, 26; Hagner, *Matthew*, 1:57; Jeffrey A. Gibbs, "Israel Standing with Israel: The Baptism of Jesus in Matthew's Gospel (Matt. 3:13–17)," *CBQ* 64 (2002): 511–26, at 521; France, *Matthew*, 120.

42. Gibbs, "Israel Standing with Israel," 521.

43. Ibid., 525–26. Though, as Allison points out, the typology of Jesus as Israel wandering in the wilderness for forty years while being tested derives from Q (cf. Luke 4:1–13) (*New Moses*, 165).

44. Isa. 41:8; 42:1 LXX; 44:1; 44:2 LXX; 44:21; 45:4.

45. An, "Baptism and Temptation," 13. Shepherd similarly gestures toward this point (*Leviticus*, forthcoming).

46. According to Jonathan Klawans, John the Baptist steered a course between the Qumran sectarians, who held sin to be ritually defiling and therefore required sinners to undergo ritual purification, and the Tannaim, who kept moral and ritual impurity entirely separate (*Impurity and Sin in Ancient Judaism* [Oxford: Oxford University Press, 2000], 138–43). John's baptism was effective not for ritual purification but for moral purification; that is, it atoned for sins (ibid., 139). But since water rituals were generally not used for moral purification in the Hebrew Bible, John's baptism is best explained as a concretization of the metaphor one finds in passages such as Isa. 1:16–17, Jer. 2:22, Ezek. 36:16–22, and Psa. 51:7–9, which use the image of ritual purification in the context of atonement for moral impurity (ibid., 142–43).

47. Indeed, as many commentators observe, Jesus's venture into the wilderness also evokes the journey of Israel—also God's son—in the wilderness (Meier, *Matthew*, 29; Davies and Allison, *Matthew*, 1:354; Gibbs, "Israel Standing with Israel," 526; France, *Matthew*, 128). The Israel and scapegoat typologies are not mutually exclusive.

48. Summarizing the question of the source of Matt. 4:1–2//Luke 4:1–2, Davies and Allison write, "In these two verses there are five points of agreement between Matthew and Luke against Mark: the naming of Jesus, the use of διάβολος rather than σατανᾶς, the remark that Jesus fasted or did not eat anything, the placement of 'forty' before (instead of after) 'days,' and the word, ἐπείνασεν. From this, it may be inferred, Q's introduction to the temptation related how Jesus fasted forty days, became hungry, and encountered the devil. Probably further details were also mentioned, but the Markan/Q overlap prevents their discovery" (*Matthew*, 1:353).

49. Lev. 16:10, 21–22 LXX (Greek of Leviticus LXX is from John William Wevers, ed., *Leviticus*, Septuaginta, VTG 2:2 [Göttingen: Vandenhoeck & Ruprecht, 1986], here at 186, 191).

50. The phrase ἐν τῇ ἐρήμῳ occurs in Deut. 1:1, 31; 4:43, 45; 6:4; 8:2, 16; 9:7, 28; 11:5; 29:4; 32:51. The phrase εἰς τὴν ἔρημον occurs only in Deut. 1:40; 2:1.

51. Matthew replaces καὶ εὐθύς with τότε, changes ἐκβάλλει to ἀνήχθη, moves πειράζω ahead in word order, includes the name Ἰησοῦς (following Q; cf. Luke 4:1), and changes σατανᾶ to διαβόλου (again, following Q; cf. Luke 4:2).

52. Routledge, *The Crucifixion*, 248 n. 32; Kleinig, *Leviticus*, 347–48, n. 35; An, "Baptism and Temptation," 18–23; Shepherd, *Leviticus*, forthcoming.

53. As Davies and Allison suggest, it is relatively uncertain whether Matthew's ἀνάγω derives from Q (*Matthew*, 1:354). Luke's ἤγετο more closely matches Barn. 7.8, but his decision to write ἐν τῇ ἐρήμῳ makes it unlikely that Luke 4:1 alludes to the scapegoat figure.

54. Philo employs προσάγω with regard to the presentation of the two goats (*Leg.* 5.52; cf. Lev. 16:7 LXX), and Josephus uses ἄγω with regard to the purported disposal of the immolated goat's carcass outside of Jerusalem (*Ant.* 3.240).

55. On the many terms employed to describe the "sending" of the scapegoat into the wilderness, see chapter 4. There appears to have been no *terminus technicus* for this event.

56. See note on the demonic identity of Azazel in chapter 1. David P. Wright summarizes the four major interpretations of the word עזאז in Leviticus 16: "(a) It is the name of a demon . . . (b) It is a geographical designation meaning something like 'precipitous place' or 'rugged cliff' . . . (c) It is an abstract noun meaning 'destruction' or 'entire removal' . . . (d) It is made up of the terms *'ēz 'ōzēl* 'goat that goes (away)' and is a description of the dispatched goat" (*ABD* 1:536–37). The evidence for the first option, which Wright also finds most probable, is at least fivefold: (1) The words יהוה and עזאזל are set in direct parallelism in Lev. 16:8, suggesting that "Azazel," like "Yahweh," is a divine name: "And Aaron shall casts lots over the two goats, one lot for Yahweh and one lot for Azazel" (Wright, *Disposal of Impurity*, 21–22; Levine, *Leviticus*, 102; Milgrom, *Leviticus*, 1:1020; Janowski, "Azazel," 128). (2) The wilderness was the abode of evil spirits, including goat demons (שעיר) (cf. Isa. 13:21; 34:14; 2 Chr. 11:15). Just several verses after Leviticus 16, Lev. 17:7 prohibits sacrificing to goat demons, suggesting that the Israelites had been doing this: "And they shall no longer offer their sacrifices to goat demons [שעירם], after whom they whore" (Wright, *Disposal of Impurity*, 22; Levine, *Leviticus*, 102, 251–53; Milgrom, *Leviticus*, 1:1020; Janowski, "Azazel," 129). (3) A good case can be made that עזאזל is a metathesized form of עזזאל, meaning "fierce god" or "angry god" (Hayim Tawil, "Azazel, Prince of the Steepe: A Comparative Study," *ZAW* 92 [1980], 43–59, at 57–59; Wright, *Disposal of Impurity*, 22; Milgrom, *Leviticus*, 1:1020). (4) Many analogous expulsion rites involving wilderness deities have been identified in ancient Near Eastern religions, some of which share striking resemblances to the scapegoat ritual (Tawil, "Azazel," 47–52; Wright, *Disposal of Impurity*, 31–74; Milgrom, *Leviticus*, 1:1071–79). (5) The reception history of the term reveals that some Jews in the Second Temple period understood Azazel to be identical to Asael of the Watchers traditions (Tawil, "Azazel," 53–55; Wright, *Disposal of Impurity*, 22; Milgrom, *Leviticus*, 1:1020–21; Janowski, "Azazel," 130–31).

57. See note on the conflation of Asael and Azazel in Chapter One; 1 Enoch 10; 4Q180 1 7–10; 4Q203 7 I, 5–7; Apoc. Ab. 13–14.

58. Shepherd, *Leviticus*, forthcoming.

59. See Chapter One. On the conflation of the Devil with Satan, Azazel, Belial, and other such figures, see G. J. Riley, "The Devil," in *Dictionary of Deities and Demons in the Bible*, 244–49, at 246–47.

60. Again, see Chapter One; 1 En. 10.4.

61. Crispin H. T. Fletcher-Louis, "The Revelation of the Sacral Son of Man: The Genre, History of Religions Context and the Meaning of the Transfiguration," in *Auferstehung—Resurrection*, ed. Friedrich Avemarie and Hermann Lichtenberger (Tübingen: Mohr Siebeck, 2001), 247–98, at 282. Fletcher-Louis makes several other suggestive connections between the Caesarean-Philippi episode and Azazel traditions in ibid., 280–81; see also G. W. E. Nickelsburg, "Enoch, Levi, and Peter: Recipients of Revelation in Upper Galilee," *JBL* 100 (1981): 575–600, at 590–91, 598.

62. On the Watchers tradition, see the essays in Angela Kim Harkins, Kelley Coblentz Bautch, and John C. Endres S. J., eds, *The Watchers in Jewish and Christian Traditions* (Minneapolis: Fortress, 2014).

63. According to Davies and Allison, ὕπαγε, σατανᾶ is probably redactional (*Matthew*, 1:372). They note a further connection between Matt. 4:10 and 16:23: "'Begone, Satan!' points to more than a verbal link with 16.21–3. In both places Jesus is choosing the path of duty: the end ordained by the Father is to be achieved by the manner ordained by the Father, namely, the cross" (ibid.). Luz adds that both scenes involve Jesus ascending a high mountain (Matt. 4:8; 17:1), "where the second divine proclamation of the Son of God takes place" (*Matthew*, 1:153).

64. Luz, *Matthew*, 1:151.

65. While he also describes a period of fasting, Luke does not employ the term νηστεία or νηστεύω in his version of the story. Luke 4:2: "And he did not eat anything in those days. And when they were completed, he was hungry." Mark 1:13: "And he was in the desert for forty days, being tempted by Satan. And he was with the beasts."

66. Allison, *New Moses*, 166–72. So also 1 Kgs 19:8 in reference to Elijah, whose fast appears to be an imitation of that of Moses.

67. Mark 1:13 has τεσσεράκοντα ἡμέρας, whereas Luke 4:2 contains ἡμέρας τεσσεράκοντα. It is likely, then, that Q originally recorded ἡμέρας τεσσεράκοντα. But why would Matthew deviate from the phrase utilized in the Septuagint and his Markan *Vorlage*?

68. Ziegler, *Isaias*, 125. See Stökl Ben Ezra, *Impact of Yom Kippur*, 15.

69. 1QpHab XI, 6–8 (Martínez and Tigchelaar, *Dead Sea Scrolls*, 1:20–1).

70. Pss. Sol. 3.7–8 (*OTP* 2:655; Alfred Rahlfs, *Septuaginta*, 2 vols. [Stuttgart: Deutsche Bibelgesellschaft, 1935, 1979], 2:474). According to R. B. Wright, the widest range for the dating of the Psalms of Solomon is 125 BCE to the early first century CE (*OTP* 2:640–41). See also Stökl Ben Ezra, *Impact of Yom Kippur*, 34 n. 92.

71. Philo, *Spec.* 1.168, 186; 2.41, 193, 194, 197, 200; *Legat.* 306; *Mos.* 2.23; *Decal.* 159.

72. Philo, *Spec.* 1.186 (Colson).

73. Philo, *Mos.* 2.23 (Colson).

74. Josephus, *J.W.* 5.236 (Thackeray).

75. Josephus, *Ant.* 3.240 (Thackeray). Apparently, Josephus uses νηστεία with regard to Yom Kippur in *Ant.* 17.165, 166; 18.94 as well.

76. Pseudo-Philo, LAB 13.6 (*OTP* 2:321).

77. Apoc. Ab. 12.1–2 (Kulik, *Slavonic Pseudepigrapha*, 19).

78. M. Yoma 8:1 (Danby, *Mishnah*, 171).

79. McNamara et al., *Targum Pseudo-Jonathan*, 169–70 (emphasis original). See ibid. (170 n. 63) for versions of the targum that translate the Hebrew root *'nh* (Pi.), "to afflict," as *ṣwm*, "to fast." According to Stökl Ben Ezra, "In the Palestinian rabbinic sources, Yom Kippur may be called *the* fast (צומא) or the great fast (צומא רבא)—*yBer* 4:1, 7b, 7c; *yPe'ah* 7:4, 20b, 8:9, 21b; *yTer* 8:5, 45c = *yAZ* 2:3, 41a. In the Babylonian Talmud I found only one passage (*bTem* 29a) using this form" (*Impact of Yom Kippur*, 16).

80. See Stökl Ben Ezra, *Impact of Yom Kippur*, 214.

81. Barn. 7.3 (Ehrman); also 7.4–5.

82. *Dial.* 40.4–5 (Thomas B. Falls, *St. Justin Martyr: Dialogue with Trypho*, rev. Thomas P. Halton, ed. Michael Slusser, SFC 3 [Washington, DC: Catholic University of America Press, 2003], 62; Miroslav Marcovich, ed., *Iustini Martyris: Dialogus cum Tryphone*, PTS 47 [Berlin: Walter de Gruyter, 1997], 147).

83. *Dial.* 40.4 (Falls, *Dialogue with Trypho*, 62; Marcovich, *Dialogus cum Tryphone*, 147) (emphasis original).

84. *Marc.* 3.7 (Evans, *Tertullian*, 191). So also Tertullian, *Adv. Jud.* 14.9.

85. Hom. Jer. 12.13.

86. *Dem. ev.* 1.3.2. On fasting on Yom Kippur, see further Stökl Ben Ezra, *Impact of Yom Kippur*, 15–16, 34 n. 92, 70–73, 100.

87. Cf. Matt. 6:16–18.

88. Davies and Allison, *Matthew*, 1:363.

89. Davies and Allison add that Israel is spoken of as God's son in Deut. 8:5 and that stones are mentioned in Deut. 8:9 (ibid.).

90. Philo, *Leg.* 3.174 (Colson).

91. Philo, *Spec.* 2.198–99 (Colson) (emphasis mine).

92. According to Daniel K. Falk, 1Q22 "demonstrate[s] concerns about the calendar, submission to the community's teachers, and atonement. These are common concerns of the Qumran sectarian literature, but distinctive features pointing to a Qumran origin are lacking. On the basis of paleography, one may conclude that this manuscript was probably copied no later than the early first century BCE" ("Moses, Texts of," in *Encyclopedia of the Dead Sea Scrolls*, ed. Lawrence H. Schiffman and James C. VanderKam, 2 vols. [Oxford: Oxford University Press, 2000], 1:577–81, at 578). As D. Barthélemy and J. T. Milik note, "elle commence avec l'année sabbatique (iii 1–7), après quoi suit probablement le rituel du *Yom hak-Kippurim*" (*Qumran Cave 1*, DJD 1 [Oxford: Clarendon, 1955], 91–97, at 91).

93. Barthélemy and Milik, *Qumran Cave 1*, 95. However, this contradicts Josh 4:19, which attributes this event to the tenth day of the first month.

94. 1Q22 III, 7–12 (Martínez and Tigchelaar, *Dead Sea Scrolls*, 1:63). See the critical edition of Barthélemy and Milik, who reconstruct 1Q22 III, 12 differently: [הכוהנים ו]י קחו [את שני השעירים ] ("and the priests shall take two goats") (*Qumran Cave 1*, 94–95).

95. There is some debate whether the occasion of this prayer is indeed Yom Kippur. Based upon the presence of the word כופרנו, Maurice Baillet places the prayer in the liturgy of the Day of Atonement (*Qumran Cave 4. Vol. 3: [4Q482–4Q520]*, DJD 7 [Oxford: Clarendon, 1982], 177–78). But according to Daniel K. Falk, "Passover is as plausible an identification for this prayer as the Day of Atonement" (*Daily, Sabbath, and Festival Prayers in the Dead Sea Scrolls*, STDJ 27 [Leiden: Brill, 1998], 178). Yet, Stökl Ben Ezra notes that manna is also linked to Yom Kippur in Philo and 1QWords of Moses, and that the motif of "the righteous and the wicked" appears in 11QMelchizedek in connection to the Day of Atonement (*Impact of Yom Kippur*, 41). Furthermore, the term "lot" (גורל) appears twice in an antithetical combination as it does in Lev. 16:8–10.

96. Lines 2–6 from 1Q34 3 I, 1–8 (//4Q508 1 1–3) (text and translation from Falk, *Festival Prayers*, 177–78).

97. Stökl Ben Ezra, *Impact of Yom Kippur*, 41.

98. B. Yoma 74b: "Our Rabbis taught: Ye shall afflict your souls . . . Who fed thee in the wilderness with manna . . . that He might afflict thee" (Epstein, *Babylonian Talmud*). Accordingly, the rabbis find Israel's desert afflictions a more fitting analogy to Yom Kippur than Pharaoh's oppression of the nation, since the afflictions of the Israel's wanderings and Yom Kippur were imposed by God and not by a human agent.

99. To be fair, the scapegoat typology is significantly stronger than the immolated goat typology.

100. Though (e), (g), and (h) have conceptual parallels in Luke 4:1–13, the Third Evangelist does not accentuate these parallels as Matthew does, and so they are not counted here.

101. Huizenga, *New Isaac*, 268.

# Chapter 3

# Jubilary Release of Sins and the Scapegoating of Jesus in Nazareth (Luke 4:16–30)

Luke's Nazareth discourse (Luke 4:16–30) has bothered interpreters for its rather perplexing conclusion, in which the townspeople, having marveled at Jesus's words in the synagogue (Luke 4:22), proceed to exile the prophet from his hometown, leading Jesus to a cliff's edge to cast him to his death (Luke 4:29). As Luke Timothy Johnson observes, "Many readers are puzzled by the apparent shift from 4:22, where the response of the listeners is if not admiring at least neutral, to 4:28, where wrath spills over into attempted manslaughter."[1]

Students of Luke's Gospel may lack a clear explanation for this shift, because they have largely neglected to consider the episode within a ritual framework. Noting Luke's omission of the ransom logion (cf. Mark 10:45; Matt. 20:28), failure to impute atoning significance to Jesus's blood (Luke 22:20; cf. Matt. 26:28), and the cursory role of the crucifixion in the apostolic preaching in Acts, Benjamin Wilson notes that "many interpreters have found that the Lukan cross is most distinctive for what it lacks . . . that Jesus's death actually stands at the margin of Lukan thought."[2] Since scholars generally agree that Luke's Gospel does not evince a robust theology of atonement, especially as it pertains to Jesus's death,[3] they have understandably neglected to consider the influence of Yom Kippur on the Nazareth narrative. Yet this lacuna is striking, given that the two Isaianic texts from which Jesus reads in the synagogue, Isa. 58:6 and 61:1–2, bear a close relationship to the Day of Atonement: the background of Isaiah 58 appears to be Yom Kippur, and the Jubilee year, to which Isa. 61:1–2 alludes, began on the Day of Atonement (Lev. 25:9).

Considering the question of the possible impact of the Day of Atonement on the Nazareth discourse, Christopher James Luthy has recently argued that "there is no mention or hint of Yom Kippur in Luke 4:16–30, which would be expected if Luke included Isa. 58:6 specifically because of this association [with Yom Kippur]."⁴ Yet, Luthy's claim, while seemingly correct on the surface, is questionable upon closer inspection, given the strong *prima facie* similarity between the attempted execution of Jesus and the manner of the scapegoat's death in Second Temple tradition. According to these traditions, the scapegoat was exiled from the city (Jerusalem), brought to a height, and cast down to its demise.⁵ The Day of Atonement, therefore, may have exercised a subtle yet significant influence upon the redaction of Luke 4:16–20, or, more likely, the special material utilized by the gospel author.⁶

To arrive at a conclusion on this topic, we will consider the Jubilary allusion in Luke 4:18–19//Isa. 61:1–2, the Yom Kippur background of Isaiah 58, Luke's use of the combined Isaianic citation in connection with the Day of Atonement, and the possibility that a scapegoat typology has informed the scene of the townspeople's attempt to execute Jesus by lethal plummet.

## JESUS'S CITATION OF ISAIAH 61 AND THE JUBILEE YEAR

Since the Jubilee year was commanded to begin on the Day of Atonement (Lev. 25:9), the question of whether Yom Kippur has influenced Luke's Nazareth narrative must take into account the possible Jubilary imagery underlying Luke 4:18–19, the scene in which Jesus reads aloud from the Isaianic scroll in the synagogue, conflating together Isa. 61:1–2 and 58:6.⁷

Many commentators affirm, in one form or another, the influence of the Jubilee tradition on Luke 4:18–19.⁸ Advancing this viewpoint, Robert Sloan has argued that the Third Evangelist not only purposefully alludes to the Jubilee year in the Nazareth story, but that the "image of Jubilee is very important for Luke in the construction of his Gospel."⁹ Indeed, the Jubilee may well be the basis of the imagery of "proclaiming liberty to the captives" and the "favorable year of the Lord" (Isa. 61:1–2).¹⁰ Sloan argues that Jesus's citation of Isaiah 61 is programmatic for Luke's "Jubilary theology," which is allegedly evinced in passages such as Luke 7:22; 6:20–38; 11:2–4; 14:13, 21; 24:47; Acts 1:6; 3:21.¹¹ He points to 11QMelchizedek, which links Isaiah 61 and Leviticus 25 to the concept of an eschatological Jubilee, as a contemporary Jewish parallel to Luke's interpretation of the Isaianic text.¹² Building on these insights, Richard Hays suggests that the double occurrence of the word "release" and the phrase, "the favorable year of the Lord" (Luke 4:18–19), creates an echo of Lev. 25:10 LXX, which refers to the Jubilee as the "year of release":

This extra line from Isaiah 58:6, inserted in this context, creates an emphatic repetition of the noun ἄφεσις ("release") in Jesus's reading of the scriptural text.

Jesus's mission includes both proclaiming *release* to the prisoners (Isa 61:1) and sending those who are broken into a condition of *release* (Isa 58:6). This double sounding of ἄφεσις turns up the volume of one more submerged echo in the last line of Jesus's lection: the concluding reference to "the year of the Lord's favor" (ἐνιαυτὸν κυρίου δεκτόν, following Isa 61:2) should be heard as an allusion to the year mandated by Leviticus 25, the "year of release" (25:10 LXX: ἐνιαυτὸς ἀφέσεως) in which all debts are to be cancelled and all slaves set free.[13]

This verbal argument appears to be the strongest evidence for the evocation of Jubilee in the Third Gospel. Hays contends that an allusion to the Jubilee year fits particularly well with Luke's emphasis on God's concern for the poor and vulnerable.[14]

Recently, however, Christopher James Luthy has cast doubt on the common view that Luke has the Jubilee year in mind, contending that the holy year was rarely linked to Isaiah 61 in Second Temple Judaism and that all alleged allusions to the Jubilee in Luke-Acts are better explained without reference to Jubilee.[15] Luthy echoes David Pao and Eckhard Schnabel's conclusion, that "distinct Jubilee themes and references are entirely absent in the Lukan writings, and there is no evidence that Luke was aware of the Jubilee interpretation in his use of Isa 61:1–2."[16] With regard to 11QMelchizedek (11Q13), Luthy claims that, "in the entire body of Second Temple and early church documents which address Isa 61, it is only 11Q13 which refers to the Jubilee . . . it is precisely because of this scroll that a reference to the Jubilee is seen in the Isaianic quotation in Luke 4:18–19 . . . however, it seems unlikely that the scroll had any bearing on Luke's work whatsoever."[17] Pao, Schnabel, and Luthy point to the non-sectarian "Messianic Apocalypse" (4Q521) as a closer parallel to Luke's use of Isaiah 61, which does not mention the Jubilee year but links an eschatological "anointed one" with the mission of Isa. 61:1–2, that is to say, releasing captives, preaching good news to the poor, and healing the wounded.[18] In short, Luthy's argument makes it more difficult to posit an allusion to the Jubilee in Luke 4:18–19, let alone suggest that the trope of Jubilee is programmatic for the remainder of the gospel, as Sloan contends.[19] Luthy instead proposes that the language of "release" (ἄφεσις) possesses the same meaning as observed throughout the entirety of Luke-Acts, that of "spiritual release" in the form of forgiveness of sins.[20]

That being said, Luthy takes the alleged Jubilee imagery of the Isaianic quotation too literalistically, proscribing the possibility of a mere Jubilary shading of the language employed in Luke 4:18–18. As John Nolland remarks, "The salvation in view is represented with Jubilee imagery, but is no call for an implementation of Jubilee legislation."[21] Darrell Bock adds that "the passage takes that picture of [Jubilary] freedom to show what God is doing spiritually and physically through his commissioned agent, Jesus. Jubilee, by analogy, becomes a picture of total forgiveness and salvation, just as it was in its pro-phetic usage in Isa 61."[22] Joel Green similarly concludes that it "seems more prudent, then, to speak of 4:18–19 as encouraging our reading of Jesus's mis-sion against the backdrop of the theme of the eschatological Jubilee, but not our concluding that Luke thus develops or is controlled by a theology of Jubilee."[23] Nolland, Bock, and Green's view is, on the whole, more balanced, since it acknowledges the relatively clear Jubilary imagery of Isa. 61:1–2, yet does not overinterpret this imagery as Sloan seems to do.

Luthy also overlooks one valuable piece of evidence that strengthens the case for a Jubilary shading of Luke 4:18–19: the evangelist's genealogy of Jesus (Luke 3:23–38). As Richard Bauckham observes, the genealogy con-sists of seventy-seven human generations from Adam to Jesus, which sug-gests some kind of numerical scheme.[24] Enoch occupies the seventh genealogical position, and Jesus the seventy-seventh, elevating Jesus as more ultimate than his Enochic counterpart.[25] Bauckham also notices that, "for a mind concerned with the symbolic significance of sevens, special significance also attaches to *seven times seven*—the Jubilee figure of forty-nine. It cannot be accidental that in the Lukan genealogy the name Jesus occurs not only in seventy-seventh place but also in forty-ninth place—where the only name-sake of Jesus among his ancestors appears (Luke 3:29)."[26] In other words, Luke's genealogy covertly underscores the number forty-nine—the Jubilee year—as an aspect of Jesus's identity.

Advancing Bauckham's thesis, George Brooke notes a similarity between the Lukan genealogy and two Second Temple texts.[27] In the Book of Watchers, the final judgment of the Watchers, following Asael's scapegoat-like banishment, is destined to occur at the end of ten periods of seven genera-tions (1 En. 10.12). In 11QMelchizedek, the eschatological Yom Kippur and final Jubilee is to begin at the end of the tenth Jubilee period.[28] According to Brooke, "The periodization of history in all three texts (1 Enoch, 11Q13, Luke) is similar, and for understanding the genealogy of Luke these Jewish parallels disclose that Luke's Jesus can be understood to belong at the end of the tenth Jubilee period from Enoch."[29] That is to say, Jesus is born after ten generations of seven, counting from Enoch, "the one person whose numerical place in a genealogy beginning from Adam was widely known and regarded as significant."[30] In light of Brooke's observations, the periodization of ten generations of seven between Enoch (Luke 3:37) and Jesus (Luke 3:23) may be explained by the Jubilee year. Thus, two peculiar phenomena in the Lukan genealogy seem to employ a Jubilary motif.

In conclusion, though there is slender evidence to maintain that the Jubilee constitutes a guiding motif of Luke 4:16–30, let alone of the entirety of the gospel, the verbal allusion to Lev. 25:10 LXX in Jesus's reading from the

Isaianic scroll (Luke 4:18–19), in light of the Jubilary evocations in the evangelist's genealogy (Luke 3:23–38), makes a Jubilee motif probable in the synagogue episode. Yet, the Jubilary motif only partially explains why the Third Evangelist has Jesus read not only from Isa. 61:1–2 but also Isa. 58:6. For this, we must turn to the other Isaianic passage cited by Jesus in the Lukan account.

## ISAIAH 58 AND THE DAY OF ATONEMENT

Many scholars have argued that the Day of Atonement supplies some of the imagery employed in Isaiah 58. Though frequently overlooked by Lukan commentators, the Yom Kippur background of Isaiah 58 bears significance for the larger question of the impact of Yom Kippur on Luke 4:18–19 and its surrounding narrative.

Michael Fishbane suggests three points of contact between Isaiah 58 and Yom Kippur. First off, the phrase, "to afflict yourselves" (piel of ענה with נפש as direct object), appears twice in Isaiah 58: "Why have we afflicted ourselves [ענינו נפשנו], and you take no knowledge of it . . . Is such the fast that I choose, a day for a person to afflict himself [ענות אדם נפשו]?" (Isa. 58:3, 5; cf. 58:10).[31] This phrase echoes the prolifically repeated biblical command to "afflict yourselves" on Yom Kippur: "And it shall be a statute to you forever that in the seventh month, on the tenth day of the month, you shall afflict yourselves [תענו את־נפשתיכם] and shall do no work" (Lev. 16:29; also Lev. 16:31; 23:27, 29, 32; Num. 29:7).[32] In the second place, just as the Jubilee year began on Yom Kippur with the sounding of the trumpet (שופר) (Lev. 25:9), so Isaiah 58 begins with the call to "lift up your voice like a trumpet [כשופר]" (Isa. 58:1).[33] Third, the vocabulary in Isa. 58:1, "Announce to my people their transgression [פשעם] and to the house of Jacob their sins [חטאתם]," matches that of Lev. 16:16, 21, in which the "transgressions" (פשע) and "sins" (חטאת) of Israel are the object of expiation.[34] According to Bohdan Hrobon, "As is often the case with a cumulative argument, its individual parts can be questioned . . . However, the fact that all three expressions are characteristic of the Day of Atonement, and that they occur together elsewhere only in Isa 58 makes Fishbane's case very strong."[35]

Hrobon contributes two additional links between the Isaianic text and Yom Kippur.[36] First, the language of "drawing near to God/Yahweh" (+ יהוה/אלהים קרב) occurs in Lev. 16:1 and Isa. 58:2: "[T]he role of the prophet is to change this approaching from being ineffective (v. 3a and 4b), even offensive to God (v. 5), into being efficacious (vv. 8–9a, 10b–12, 14) and pleasing to him (v. 6a)."[37] Second, Isa. 58:13 rebukes Israel for violating the Sabbath (שבת), and the Day of Atonement is one of only three occasions known as a "Sabbath of complete rest" (שבת שבתון) in the Hebrew Bible (Lev. 16:31; 23:32).[38]

A compelling clue that Yom Kippur lurks behind Isaiah 58 is the heavy emphasis on fasting in the first seven verses of the chapter, which becomes a guiding motif of the exhortation in the remainder of the passage. Julian Morgenstern had noted this years ago, arguing that the clause, "the fast that I [God] choose, a day to humble oneself" (Isa. 58:5), implies that God has chosen a day for fasting, namely, the Day of Atonement.[39] While God commanded Israel to abstain from food and drink on other occasions, fasting became so ubiquitous on Yom Kippur in the post-exilic era that the holy day came to be known as "the Fast."[40] Strikingly, Morgenstern was convinced that the Day of Atonement supplied the fasting motif in Isaiah 58 without apparent awareness of this rich early Jewish tradition.[41]

Finally, Stökl Ben Ezra suggests that the "frequent allusions to Isaiah 58 in Christian texts on Yom Kippur, beginning with Justin Martyr, may also point to an early association in Jewish ritual [with the Day of Atonement] . . . I suggest that some synagogues may have read the passages already in Tannaitic times, or even earlier even if they are attested to only in Amoraic traditions."[42] In relaying a Christological goat typology in his *Dialogue with Trypho*, which was written about a half-century later than the Gospel of Luke, Justin Martyr attests to a likely Second Temple tradition that reads Isaiah 58 in light of the Day of Atonement: "[In] that same place of Jerusalem you shall recognize him [Christ] whom you had subjected to shame, and who was a sacrificial offering for all sinners who are willing to repent and to comply with that fast [Yom Kippur] which Isaiah prescribed when he said, *loosing the strangle of violent contracts* [Isa 58:6], and to observe likewise all the other precepts laid down by him."[43] Thus, the ancient reception history of Isaiah 58 makes a perceived allusion to Yom Kippur in Isaiah 58 more probable.

In summary, in light of the points discussed above, the Day of Atonement likely supplies some of the imagery contained in Isaiah 58: (a) the emphasis on fasting in Isa. 58:1–7 and in post-exilic Yom Kippur traditions, (b) the phrase, "to afflict yourself" (נפש ענה), which occurs in Isa. 58:3, 5 and Lev. 16:29, 31; 23:27, 29, 32; Num. 29:7, (c) mention of the trumpet (שופר) in Isa. 58:1 and the sounding of the trumpet (שופר) on Yom Kippur of the Jubilee year (Lev. 25:9), (d) the announcing of Israel's "transgressions" (פשע) and "sins" (חטאת) in Isa. 58:1 and Lev. 16:16, 21, (e) the language of "drawing near to God/Yahweh" (קרב + אלהים/יהוה) in Isa. .58:2 and Lev. 16:1, (f) mention of the "Sabbath" (שבת) in Isa. 58:13 and Yom Kippur being designated a "Sabbath of complete rest" (שבת שבתון) (Lev. 16:31; 23:32), and (g) the early reception history of Isaiah 58 that reads the Isaianic passage in light of the Day of Atonement. We may now return to the question of Luke's use of Isa. 58:6 and 61:1–2 LXX.

## LUKE'S USE OF ISA. 58:6; 61:1–2 AND
## THE DAY OF ATONEMENT

Scholars have proffered multiple explanations for Luke's conflation of Isa. 58:6 and 61:1–2 LXX in his Nazareth scene, but none of them are entirely satisfactory. The reason for this lacuna may be that students of the Third Gospel have neglected to consider the Day of Atonement and the notion of forgiveness of sins as a possible link that connects the two Isaianic passages.

According to Green, the alleged Jubilary imagery in both Isaianic chapters explains the conflation of Isa. 58:6 and 61:1–2 LXX.[44] However, while Isa. 61:1–2 very likely evokes Jubilee imagery, Isaiah 58 does not appear to contain any Jubilary motifs, except perhaps for the call to "lift up your voice like a trumpet [כשופר]" (Isa. 58:1). This proposal therefore seems unlikely. Pao and Eckhard suggest that Isa. 58:6 and 61:1 were already linked in certain messianic textual traditions, such as 4Q521.[45] Yet they cite no evidence for this claim, and an allusion to Isa. 58:6 is by no means apparent in the extant fragments of 4Q521.[46] Following Charles Perrot, François Bovon suggests that passages such as Isa. 57:15–58:14 and 61:1–11 "became associated with each other on the occasion of the celebration of Yom Kippur, the first because of fasting and contrition, the second because of the beginning of the Year of Jubilee."[47] But neither Perrot nor Bovon supply evidence for the conjoining of Isa. 57:15–58:14 and 61:1–11 in the Second Temple period. Other scholars point to the presence of the catchword ἄφεσις in both passages as the reason for the conflation: "to preach release [ἄφεσιν] to the captives . . . to send those who have been oppressed in release [ἀφέσει]" (Luke 4:18//Isa. 58:6; 61:1–2 LXX).[48] This explanation is more compelling, especially since Isa. 58:6 and 61:1 are the only two verses in Isaiah LXX that contain the term. But why has Luke chosen to highlight the word ἄφεσις?

According to Hays, Luke's dual sounding of ἄφεσις, in combination with the phrase, "the year of the Lord's favor" (ἐνιαυτὸν κυρίου δεκτόν, Luke 4:19//Isa. 61:2), is intended to evoke the Jubilary "year of release" (ἐνιαυτὸς ἀφέσεως, Lev. 25:10 LXX).[49] But since Isaiah 58 is not a Jubilary text, this explanation is not wholly adequate. Joseph Fitzmyer notices that Luke employs ἄφεσις elsewhere to mean the forgiveness of sins.[50] In fact, of the ten total appearances of ἄφεσις in Luke-Acts, eight of these occur within the phrase "forgiveness of sins" (ἄφεσις [τῶν] ἁμαρτιῶν) (Luke 1:77; 3:3; 24:47; Acts 2:38; 5:31; 10:43; 13:38; 26:18), while the remaining two occur in the Isaianic citations in Luke 4:18. The dual use of ἄφεσις in the Nazareth narrative, therefore, suggests that Luke's readers would likely interpret this "release" as including a release from sins.[51] As Luthy concludes, Luke employs the term ἄφεσις "exclusively in connection to God's forgiveness of human sins."[52] In the context of Luke's Gospel as a whole, then, the term ἄφεσις not only betrays a Jubilary connection but also a link to the forgiveness of sins, in which case, an evocation of the Day of Atonement, on which the Jubilee year began, is also possibly in view.[53]

Not only are Isa. 58:6 and 61:1–2 LXX connected by the word ἄφεσις, which occurs in Leviticus 16 LXX with reference to the release of Israel's sins upon the scapegoat,[54] but both texts also contain the term ἀποστέλλω: "He has sent [ἀπέσταλκέν] me to preach release to the captives . . . to send [ἀποστεῖλαι] those who have been oppressed in release" (Luke 4:18//Isa. 58:6; 61:1–2 LXX). The term ἀποστέλλω also features prominently in Leviticus 16 LXX to describe the sending of the scapegoat into the wilderness:[55] "And he [Aaron] shall present it [the scapegoat] living before the Lord, to make expiation over it, so as to send it away [ἀποστεῖλαι] for banishment (of sins). He shall release [ἀφήσει] it into the wilderness" (Lev. 16:10 LXX).[56] Thus, two central terms pertaining to the scapegoat's sending (i.e., ἀποστέλλω) and the scapegoat's release of sins (i.e., ἄφεσις) occur in both Isaianic passages cited by Jesus in Luke 4:18–19.

Finally, Perrot had noticed that the adjective "favorable" (δεκτός) occurs in Isa. 58:5 and 61:2 LXX and further conjoins the two passages.[57] Although the word appears with regard to the "favorable year of the Lord" (ἐνιαυτὸν κυρίου δεκτόν) in Isa. 61:2 LXX, that is, the Jubilee year, the term pertains to the "favorable fast" (νηστείαν δεκτήν) performed on the Day of Atonement in Isa. 58:5 LXX.

In sum, the combination of Isa. 58:6 and 61:1–2 LXX is better explained not only with reference to the Jubilee year as a metaphor for the spiritual liberation inaugurated by Jesus but also in connection to the forgiveness of sins associated with the Day of Atonement, on which the Jubilee began (Lev. 25:9). That is to say, the repeated vocabulary generated by the use of Isa. 58:6 and 61:1–2 LXX, namely, ἄφεσις, ἀποστέλλω, and δεκτός (implicitly), suggests that the Day of Atonement was an impetus for the scriptural conflation. This conclusion is strengthened by the Yom Kippur background of Isaiah 58. The Qumran scroll 11QMelchizedek lends further support to this reading, which understands the proclaimed Jubilary "liberty" of Isa. 61:1 in terms of the release of God's chosen from "all their iniquities," culminating in an eschatological Day of Atonement (11Q13 II, 6–7). The next logical question is whether Yom Kippur has left an imprint on the remainder of the Nazareth narrative.

## JESUS'S EXPULSION FROM
## NAZARETH AS A SCAPEGOAT

Having proclaimed "the favorable year of the Lord" (Luke 4:19), the townspeople speak well of Jesus (Luke 4:22) until he offends them with a parable regarding Elijah and Elisha's dealings with Gentile people (Luke 4:25–27), provoking the Nazarenes to cast Jesus out of the city and lead him to the brow of a hill, where they intend to throw Jesus off a cliff (Luke 4:29). Scholars often claim that this procedure would be the first step in the process of death by stoning, citing m. Sanh. 6 in support.[58] Yet, this halakhic tradition requires the place of stoning to be only "twice the height" of the person being stoned, which is quite different from the height of Jesus's attempted murder.[59] Amy-Jill Levine and Ben Witherington III take issue with this theory as well:

> Problems here are manifold, from the factual observation that there is no cliff in Nazareth; the cliff, as such, is about 2.5 miles away from the location of the town, to the point that there is no indication of stoning in the scene, to the problem of building historical context from one verse from a second century text, such as *m. Sanh.* 6.4, which includes an entire legal procedure missing from Luke's story, for determining practices in the late Second Temple period. Nor, finally, does Jesus say anything that would prompt the death penalty.[60]

A better explanation, therefore, is forthcoming as to the townspeople's rather bizarre (see below) form of punishment chosen for Jesus.

In a recent article, Margaret Froelich and Thomas E. Phillips argue that the same cultural assumptions that undergird Aesop's death by fatal plunge in the *Life of Aesop* are operative in the Lukan account of Jesus's attempted expulsion in Nazareth.[61] Having surveyed a wide range of literature, using Suetonius's *Twelve Caesars* as a case study, Froelich and Phillips conclude that "death by lethal plummet was relatively uncommon in the ancient world."[62] Raising the question of why the inhabitants of Nazareth choose this peculiar form of execution for Jesus, they propose that "Aesop's accusers presume that death by lethal plunge is the appropriate punishment for Aesop's crimes [of blasphemy and temple theft]; the Nazarenes in Luke's Gospel share the cultural assumption of Aesop's *Vita* regarding the appropriate end for a blasphemer."[63] That is, Aesop had blasphemed the Delphians by regarding them as descendants of slaves, thereby questioning their privileged relationship to Apollos, and Jesus had blasphemed his Jewish townsfolk by including Gentiles—the widow of Zarephath and Naaman the Syrian (Luke 4:26–28)—in the eschatological blessings announced in Isaiah, thereby questioning their privileged relationship to Yahweh. The implied audiences of both stories presuppose, according to Froelich and Phillips, that expulsion off a cliff is a fitting form of capital punishment for such perceived blasphemy.

The parallels between the execution (attempts) in the *Life of Aesop* and Luke 4 are intriguing. However, since they only provide these two examples from antiquity, it is questionable whether Froelich and Phillips have provided enough evidence to establish a "common cultural trope" of death by lethal plummet for the offense of blasphemy. Alternatively, both accounts may reflect the exceedingly more common cultural phenomenon of ancient elimination rituals. Typically in such rituals, an offense to a deity occasions the need to eliminate a particular evil from a community by transferring that evil onto a "scapegoat" and then expunging that evil from the community by means of the scapegoat.[64] These rituals are well attested throughout a wide geographical, cultural, and temporal range. The most famous elimination ritual practiced in ancient Judaism was, of course, the rite of the scapegoat as described in Lev. 16:7–10, 20–22.

In fact, several classicists have suggested that the death of Aesop is modeled upon the *pharmakos* ritual, an ancient elimination rite practiced in Ionia and Athens during the Thargelia festival to Apollo, in which the people of a community feasted a victim (or victims) of lowly status, led him in procession, physically abused him, and expunged him from their city as a scapegoat. Francisco Adrados made the following observations years ago:

> It is certain that Aesop is the reviled *pharmakos* who is on the point of being killed time and again. He is an unfortunate, ugly, limping slave who is dumb and has a hunch-back . . . Even the figs Aesop is supposed to have eaten in the first anecdote of the work are symbolic: the *pharmakos* was adorned with necklaces of figs, he was given figs to eat . . . He is called *katharma*, "impure object," like the *pharmakos* . . . The stealing of a gold cup from Apollo is the *aition* of the death of the *pharmakos* in the Thargelia of Athens according to Ister, and all the facts which are given about the *pharmakos* coincide with those of Aesop and viceversa.[65]

Leslie Kurke has more recently affirmed this portrait of the Greek fabulist as a scapegoat: "Aesop already conforms to the type of the *pharmakos* in the he is grotesquely ugly and of low social status . . . When he is caught and convicted, Aesop is, like a scapegoat, led through the town for execution and ultimately condemned to a death enacted by the whole people, either by stoning or being thrown off a cliff."[66]

Given the broad knowledge and practice of elimination rituals in the ancient world, this cultural phenomenon may better explain the similarities between Aesop's expulsion from Delphi and the attempted elimination of Jesus from Nazareth.[67] According to Froelich and Phillip, the blasphemy of Aesop is only directed toward the townspeople and not the deity.[68] But this claim is contradicted by the story itself, since immediately after Aesop asserts that the Delphians are the descendants of "freed slaves," sent as spoils of war to Apollo (G, 126), the narrator announces that "Apollo was also angry" (G, 127).[69] Similarly, James Sanders ventures that the "real prophetic offense in Jesus's sermon was theological: it was serious and ultimate. Jesus told the congregation that God was not Jewish."[70] In other words, the greater slight against the Nazarenes was likely the perceived blasphemy against their God, whom they believed to be the God *of the Jews*. Such implied attacks against the peoples' deities would provoke divine wrath and require a scapegoat. A far greater percentage of the ancient world would readily comprehend this scenario than the peculiar scenario proposed by Froelich and Phillip, wherein a community determines that death by legal plummet is the appropriate punishment for a blasphemer.

One might object that this proposal falls into the same trap as Froelich and Phillip's thesis, in that two historical examples are not enough to posit a common cultural trope. However, the scapegoat's death by lethal plummet is known in other ancient literature as well. Regarding the *pharmakos* ritual, Strabo reports, "It was an ancestral custom among the Leucadians, every year at the sacrifice performed in honour of Apollo, for some criminal to be flung from this rocky look-out for the sake of averting evil."[71] The Suda records an annual custom in which a youth was cast, presumably from a height, into waters to divert an impending evil.[72] In the book of Jonah, the rebellious prophet is hurled off a ship as a scapegoat by its sailors to achieve safety, after Jonah had provoked the wrath of the deity by defying his commission to Nineveh.[73]

Most intriguingly is the case of the goat for Azazel in Second Temple tradition. Though Leviticus 16 does not prescribe this custom, the scapegoat was reportedly taken to a ravine outside of Jerusalem and cast downward to its demise. According to the Mishnah, the scapegoat's handler "pushed it from behind; and it went rolling down, and before it had reached half the way down the hill it was broken in pieces."[74] Targum Pseudo-Jonathan attests to this tradition as well: "The goat shall go up on the mountains of Beth Haduri, and a blast of wind from before the Lord will thrust him down and he will die."[75] Philo seems to be aware of this practice, writing that the scapegoat was "banished, driven from the most holy places, tumbling into desolate and vile gulfs."[76] The downward movement of the scapegoat is also attested in Jewish apocalyptic traditions. 1 Enoch 10 relates Asael's banishment into the cosmic wilderness of the underworld: "Bind Azazel [Asael] by his hands and his feet, and throw him into the darkness. And split open the desert which is in Dudael, and throw him there" (1 En. 10.4–5).[77] The Animal Apocalypse elaborates on Asael's punitive plunge into the netherworld: "And I saw one of those four who had come before; he seized that first star that had fallen from heaven [Asael/Azazel], and he bound it by its hands and feet and threw it into an abyss, and that abyss was narrow and deep and desolate and dark" (1 En. 88.1).[78] In the Apocalypse of Abraham, Azazel is exiled into a subterranean domain: "May you be the firebrand of the furnace of the earth! Go, Azazel, into the untrodden parts of the earth."[79] According to Andrei Orlov,

"The aforementioned mishnaic passage also hints to the fact that the final destination of the scapegoat's exile was not merely the desert but rather the underworld or abyss, a descent symbolically expressed by the pushing of the animal off the cliff."[80] Whether the reality reflects the myth or visa-versa, the scapegoat's descent was apparently a widely known trope in the Second Temple period.

The chances that Luke's readers heard an echo of this scapegoat tradition in the people's attempt to cast Jesus off a cliff increases in light of the allusion to Yom Kippur earlier in the story. The emphasis on the words "release" (ἄφεσις) and "send" (ἀποστέλλω) in Jesus's reading from Isaiah (Luke 4:18–19//Isa. 58:6; 61:1–2 LXX)—two words used for the scapegoat's sending and release of sins (Lev. 16:10, 26 LXX; cf. Lev. 16:21, 22, 26)—amplifies the volume of this echo. In the context of this scriptural evocation, the townspeople's expulsion of Jesus from the town and attempt to hurl him down a cliff (Luke 4:29) foreshadows that, in addition to Jesus being sent to proclaim release to the captives (Luke 4:18), he will be sent out of Jerusalem as a scapegoat for the release of sins.[81]

## CONCLUSION

Given the lack of an explicit theology of atonement vis-à-vis the Jewish temple cult in the Gospel of Luke, we may more safely conclude that the Day of Atonement has informed Luke's special material, from which he seems to have composed the Nazareth synagogue and expulsion episodes (Luke 4:18–19, 29).[82] This link to Yom Kippur could go a long way in explaining the conjoining of these two episodes despite their stark juxtaposition in the evangelist's final redaction. Whether Luke was aware of the evocation of the Jubilee and Yom Kippur in his source material is difficult to discern. Many think Luke's genealogy, which also employs Jubilary motifs, derives from a Jewish source.[83] If this is the case, then that source may be related to the material from which the Nazareth discourse derives. Otherwise, Luke may have been keener to these Jewish traditions than is widely thought. I will return to this question when discussing Luke's redaction of the Gerasene demoniac pericope in chapter 4.

To sum up, while the Gospel of Luke may not evidence a sustained Jubilee typology, the allusion to Lev. 25:10 LXX in Jesus's reading from the Isaianic scroll (Luke 4:18–19//Isa. 58:6; 61:1–2) remains quite clear, especially in light of the Jubilary evocations in Isa. 61:1–2 and the genealogy of Jesus (Luke 3:23–38). Yet the Jubilary motif does not adequately explain why Jesus also reads from Isa. 58:6. The Day of Atonement supplies some if not much of the imagery contained in Isaiah 58, especially the phrase, "to afflict yourself" (Isa. 58:3, 5; Lev. 16:29, 31; 23:27, 29, 32; Num. 29:7), and the motif of fasting (Isa. 58:1–7)—a major component of Yom Kippur as practiced in post-exilic Judaism. Jesus's combination of Isa. 58:6 and 61:1–2 LXX is better explained not only with reference to the Jubilee year but also in connection to the forgiveness of sins associated with the Day of Atonement, on which the Jubilee began (Lev. 25:9). The repetition of ἄφεσις and ἀποστέλλω in the combined Isaianic citation—two important terms in Leviticus 16 LXX—suggests that the Day of Atonement was an impetus for this scriptural conflation. This interpretation finds support in 11QMelchizedek, which reads the Jubilary "liberty" of Isa. 61:1 in terms of the elect's release from "all their iniquities," culminating in an eschatological Day of Atonement (11Q13 II, 6–7).

The parallel between the Delphian's execution of Aesop by lethal plummet in the *Life of Aesop* and the attempted execution of Jesus in Luke 4:29 is best explained by the common cultural practice of elimination rituals in the ancient world, not the direct influence of Aesop traditions on the Lukan material. In the light of the echo of Yom Kippur in Luke 4:18–19, the townspeople's expulsion of Jesus and attempt to hurl him down a cliff (Luke 4:29) evokes the scapegoat's exile from the city (Lev. 16:10, 21–22) and subsequent descent down an abyss (Philo, *Plant.* 61; m. Yoma 6:6; Tg. Ps.-J. Lev. 16:22; cf. 1 En. 10.4–5; 88.1; Apoc. Ab. 14.5). From a literary perspective, the attempted expulsion of Jesus from Nazareth foreshadows Jesus's ultimate banishment from Jerusalem, beginning a series of events that will culminate in the forgiveness of sins (Luke 1:77; 3:3; 24:47; Acts 2:38; 5:31; 10:43; 13:38; 26:18).

## NOTES

1. Luke Timothy Johnson, *The Gospel of Luke*, SP 3 (Collegeville, MN: Liturgical, 1991), 81.

2. Benjamin R. Wilson, *The Saving Cross of the Suffering Christ: The Death of Jesus in Lukan Soteriology*, BZNW 223 (Berlin: De Gruyter, 2016), 1.

3. For example, Scot McKnight claims that "the only place Luke has atonement theology explicitly is at Acts 20:28" (*Jesus and His Death: Historiography, the Historical Jesus, and Atonement Theory* [Waco, TX: Baylor University Press, 2005], 165; cf. 361–63).

4. Christopher James Luthy, *Rethinking the Acceptable Year: The Jubilee and the Basileia in Luke 4 and Beyond* (Eugene, OR: Wipf and Stock, 2019), 137.

5. Philo, *Plant.* 61; m. Yoma 6:6; Tg. Ps.-J. Lev. 16:22; cf. 1 En. 10.4–5; 88.1; Apoc. Ab. 14.5.

6. Scholars debate whether Luke 4:14–30 derives principally from Mark 6:1–6a, a pre-Lukan tradition, or Luke's own hand. Taking the view that the composition's

structure is owed to Mark, Joseph A. Fitzmyer is ambivalent as to the source of the remainder of the passage: "The Lucan form of the story of the Nazareth visit owes its inspiration to Mark 6:1–6a; in vv. 16, 22, 24 the wording probably comes from 'Mk.' As for the rest, vv. 17–21, 23, 25–30, one may debate whether they are derived from Luke's private source ('L') or are to be ascribed to Lucan composition" (*The Gospel According to Luke*, 2 vols., AB 28 [Garden City, NY: Doubleday, 1981–1985], 1:526). On the contrary, François Bovon concludes that the story's origin resides in a unique Lukan source: "The Markan passage is only distantly related to our pericope, and it appears in another context. Luke is familiar with it, but is probably not using it as his model here . . . In Q, or more likely in Luke's special source, Luke found the saying in an expanded version, in which the Scripture citation and its interpretation already had their place, and perhaps also the Hebrew Bible examples (vv. 25–27), and the inhabitants' attack on Jesus the prophet (v. 29), though indeed in another formulation" (*A Commentary on the Gospel of Luke*, 3 vols., trans. Christine Thomas, Donald Deer, and James Couch, Hermeneia [Minneapolis: Fortress, 2002–2013], 1:153). Darrell L. Bock takes a similar approach but attributes a slightly more influential role to Mark 6:1–6a: "This approach to the problem is the most satisfying, since it recognizes Luke's research and summarizing hand in the material, while explaining how the parallels between the accounts can exist" (*Luke*, 2 vols., BECNT [Grand Rapids: Baker Academic, 1994–1996], 1:397).

7. The scriptural citation is comprised of four lines from Isa 61:1–2 and one line from Isa. 58:6, both of which very closely follow the LXX, with the exception that Luke writes ἀποστεῖλαι instead of ἀπόστελλε (Isa. 58:6) and κηρύξαι instead of καλέσαι (Isa. 61:1). Notably, he omits from Isa. 61:1–2 the phrases ἰάσασθαι τοὺς συντετριμμένους τῇ καρδίᾳ, καὶ ἡμέραν ἀνταποδόσεως, and παρακαλέσαι πάντας τοὺς πενθοῦντας (Ziegler, *Isaias*, 337, 348).

8. See A. Strobel, "Die Ausrufung des Jobeljahrs in der Nazarethpredigt Jesu: Zur apokalyptischen Tradition Lc 4,16–30," in *Jesus in Nazareth*, ed. W. Eltester, BZNW 40 (Berlin: De Gruyter, 1972), 38–50; John Howard Yoder, *The Politics of Jesus*, 2nd ed. (Grand Rapids: Eerdmans, 1994 [1972]), 28–33; I. Howard Marshall, *The Gospel of Luke: A Commentary on the Greek Text*, NIGTC (Exeter, UK: Paternoster, 1978), 184; Donald W. Blosser, "Jesus and the Jubilee: The Year of Jubilee and Its Significance in the Gospel of Luke" (PhD diss., The University of St. Andrews, 1979); Sharon H. Ringe, "The Jubilee Proclamation in the Ministry and Teaching of Jesus: A Tradition-Critical Study in the Synoptic Gospels and Acts" (PhD diss., Union Theological Seminary, 1981); John Nolland, *Luke*, WBC 35A–C (Dallas: Word Books, 1989–1993), 1:197; Margaret Barker, "The Time is Fulfilled: Jesus and the Jubilee," *SJT* 53 (2000): 22–32; Christopher Bruno, "Jesus is our Jubilee . . . But How? The OT Background and Lukan Fulfillment of the Ethics of Jubilee," *JETS* 53 (2010): 81–101; Paul Hertig, "The Jubilee Mission of Jesus in the Gospel of Luke: Reversals of Fortunes," *Missiology* 26 (1998): 167–79; Nicholas Perrin, *Jesus the Temple* (Grand Rapids: Baker Academic, 2010), 134–44.

9. Robert B. Sloan, *The Favorable Year of the Lord: A Study of Jubilary Theology in the Gospel of Luke* (Austin, TX: Scholars, 1977), 174.

10. Brevard S. Childs, *Isaiah*, OTL (Louisville, KY: Westminster John Knox, 2001), 505; Nolland, *Luke*, 1:197; Robert T. Tannehill, *Luke*, ANTC (Nashville:

Abingdon, 1996), 92–93. The phrase "to proclaim liberty" (קרא דרור) in Isa. 61:1 occurs elsewhere in the Hebrew Bible only in Lev. 25:10, which provides legislation for the Jubilee year, and Jer. 34:8, 15, 17, which concerns the release of slaves on the closely related Sabbatical year (Exod. 21:2; Deut. 15:12). The reception of Isa. 61:1–2 in 11QMelchizedek affirms this interpretation as well.

11. Sloan, *Favorable Year*, 111–53. Among these gospel passages, Luke 6:24–26; 14:13, 21; 24:47 are unique to the Gospel of Luke. Sloan concludes that "the notion of Jubilee serves a very important function in the overall theology and literary presentation of the Gospel of Luke" (ibid., 175).

12. Ibid., 43–44. As Merrill P. Miller has pointed out, "the three major Scripture texts quoted from the Torah, the Prophets, and the Writings (Lev 25:13; Isa 52:7; Ps 82:1–2) unfold their inner relation and meaning for the community with reference to Isa 61:1–2" ("The Function of Isa 61:1–2 in 11QMelchizedek," *JBL* 88 [1969]: 467–69).

13. Hays, *Echoes of Scripture in the Gospels*, 228–29.

14. Ibid., 229, 278.

15. Luthy, *Acceptable Year*. Luthy examines the purported allusions to the Jubilee year in Luke 1:68; 2:3–4; 3:1; 5:17–26; 6:1–11, 27–38; 9:1–6, 14; 14:1–6; Acts 2:1–4; 6–9 and concludes that "none of the texts seem to meet Hays's criteria for determining the validity of Old Testament allusions" (*Acceptable Year*, 185). According to Luthy, "the absence of references to many of the distinct Jubilee year practices [in Luke's Gospel] is surely significant. There is no blowing of the trumpet, no exhortation for people to return to their ancestral land and no literal release of slaves, nor is there any mention of the word 'Jubilee,' and debt cancellation (which itself is not a clear Jubilee year provision) is only mentioned sparingly and never exhortatively. Given that Luke frequently provides explanatory notes for a Gentile readership about Jewish customs and traditions, it seems highly unlikely that he was seeking to communicate some type of Jubilee release, much less present it as a key theme . . . Finally, it is also of significance that the Early Church did not consider the Jubilee theme to be an explanation or explication of the message of Jesus . . . there were no distinctively Christian interpretations of the Jubilee until the writings of Hippolytus of Rome and Origen of Alexandria in the early third century" (ibid., 187–88).

16. David W. Pao and Eckhard J. Schnabel, "Luke," in *Commentary on the New Testament Use of the Old Testament*, ed. G. K. Beale and D. A. Carson (Grand Rapids: Baker, 2007), 251–414, at 290. So also Johnson, *Luke*, 81; Amy-Jill Levine and Ben Witherington III, *The Gospel of Luke*, NCBC (Cambridge: Cambridge University Press, 2018), 117.

17. Luthy, *Acceptable Year*, 189.

18. Pao and Eckhard, "Luke," 289–90; Luthy, *Acceptable Year*, 104–7. 4Q521 also mentions Malachi's (3:24) prediction of Elijah's return; cf. Luke 4:25–25.

19. Sloan, *Favorable Year*, 166.

20. Luthy, *Acceptable Year*, 189.

21. Nolland, *Luke*, 1:202. Nolland keenly observes that even Isa. 61:1–2 "are clearly no call to implement Jubilee legislation" (ibid, 197).

22. Bock, *Luke*, 1:410.

23. Joel B. Green, *The Gospel of Luke*, NICNT (Grand Rapids: Eerdmans, 1997), 212 n. 33.

24. Richard Bauckham, "The Lukan Genealogy of Jesus," in *Jude and the Relatives of Jesus in the Early Church* (London: T&T Clark, 1990), 315–73, at 315–18.

25. This point is underscored by the fact that the final judgment of the Watchers, according to 1 En. 10:12, is to occur after the Watchers endure seventy generations if being bound under the earth, that is to say, seventy-seven generations from the creation of Adam, given that the binding occurs in the generation immediately succeeding Enoch (Bauckham, "Lukan Genealogy," 320).

26. Ibid., 319 (emphasis original).

27. George J. Brooke, "Shared Intertextual Interpretations in the Dead Sea Scrolls and the New Testament," in *Biblical Perspectives: Early Use and Interpretation of the Bible in Light of the Dead Sea Scrolls*, ed. Michael E. Stone and Esther G. Chazon, STDJ 28 (Leiden: Brill, 1998), 35–57, at 46–50.

28. According to William K. Gilders, "This text divided the temporal period of its concern into ten jubilees. The eschatological enactment of the year of release will occur at the beginning of the tenth jubilee (ll. 6–7). The culmination of this period of release from the debt of sin will be the Day of Atonement at the end of the tenth jubilee" ("The Day of Atonement in the Dead Sea Scrolls," in Hieke and Nicklas, *Day of Atonement*, 63–74, at 71).

29. Brooke, "Shared Intertextual Interpretations," 49.

30. Bauckham, "Lukan Genealogy," 319.

31. Michael Fishbane, *Biblical Interpretation in Ancient Israel* (Oxford: Clarendon, 1985), 305.

32. The phrase occurs only two other times in the Hebrew Bible (Num. 30:14; Ps. 35:13).

33. Fishbane, *Biblical Interpretation*, 305.

34. Ibid.

35. Bohdan Hrobon, *Ethical Dimensions of Cult in the Book of Isaiah*, BZAW 418 (Berlin: De Gruyter, 2010), 203. Hbrobon adds the following caveat: "One can object that, besides proclaiming Yom Kippur, the sound of שופר was used to announce various other things, such as danger, war, etc. Also the expression 'to afflict oneself'. . . is not exclusive to the Day of Atonement, as documented by Num 30:14 and Ps 35:13. Finally, the occurrence of פשע and חטאת in both texts is not decisive, for this pair is fairly frequent in the OT" (ibid.).

36. In support, Hrobon cites Hans Kosmala, "Form and Structure of Isaiah 58," *ASTI* 5 (1967): 69–81, at 80; Arthur Sumner Herbert, *The Book of the Prophet Isaiah, Chapters 40–66*, CBC (Cambridge: Cambridge University Press, 1975), 144.

37. Hrobon, *Ethical Dimensions*, 204.

38. Ibid., 204–5. The other two occasions are the weekly Sabbath (Exod. 31:15; 35:2; Lev. 23:3) and the Sabbatical Year (Lev. 25:4).

39. Julian Morgenstern, "Two Prophecies from the Fourth Century B.C. and the Evolution of Yom Kippur," *HUCA* 24 (1952–1953): 1–71, at 38. Morgenstern also submits that Isaiah 58 presents the prophet as speaking to his contemporaries while

they are engaged in fasting, and that this fasting appears to be conventional; that is, there is no indication that this fasting is being performed in response to a national catastrophe (ibid.).

40. See Isa. 1:13–14 LXX; 1QpHab XI, 6–8; Pss. Sol. 3.7–8; Philo, *Spec.* 1.168, 186; 2.41, 193, 194, 197, 200; *Legat.* 306; *Mos.* 2.23; *Decal.* 159; Josephus, *J.W.* 5.236; *Ant.* 3.240; 17.165, 166; 18.94; Pseudo-Philo, LAB 13.6; Apoc. Ab. 12.1–2; m. Yoma 8:1; Tg. Ps.-J. Lev. 16:29; Barn. 7.3; Justin Martyr, *Dial.* 40.4–5; Tertullian, *Marc.* 3.7; *Adv. Jud.* 14.9; Origen, *Hom. Jer.* 12.13; Eusebius, *Dem. ev.* 1.3.2. See further in chapter 2.

41. The inference made by Levine helps explain Morgenstern's conclusion: "In biblical literature the idiom *'innah nefesh* always connotes fasting, as Ibn Ezra observed and as we may deduce from the contexts of Isaiah 58:3, 10 and Psalms 35:13" (*Leviticus*, 109).

42. Stökl Ben Ezra, *Impact of Yom Kippur*, 56. He also cites Origen, *Hom. Lev.* 10.2.4; Ephrem, *Hymn on Fasting* 2.1; Basil, *Homily on Fasting* 1–2; Leo, *Sermon* 92.2. Stökl Ben Ezra adds the caveat, "I cannot preclude that Christians alluded to this chapter for its contents without knowledge of Jewish liturgical traditions" (ibid., 56). According to b. Meg. 31a, the Haftara on Yom Kippur begins with Isa. 57:15 and would presumably continue to include Isaiah 58.

43. *Dial.* 40.4 (Falls, *Dialogue with Trypho*, 62) (emphasis original).

44. Green, *Luke*, 212.

45. Pao and Eckhard, "Luke," 288–89.

46. David L. Washburn finds no allusion to Isaiah 58 in 4Q521 (*A Catalogue of Biblical Passages in the Dead Sea Scrolls*, TCSt 2 [Leiden: Brill, 2003], 126).

47. Charles Perrot, *La Lecture de la Bible dans la Synagogue: Les anciennes lectures palestiniennes du Shabbat et des fêtes* (Hildesheim: Gerstenberg, 1973), 197–98; Bovon, Luke, 3 vols, 1:153.

48. Fitzmyer, *Luke*, 533; Bovon, *Luke*, 1:153; Pao and Eckhard, "Luke," 289.

49. Hays, *Echoes of Scripture in the Gospels*, 228–29.

50. Fitzmyer, *Luke*, 533.

51. It is difficult to know whether Luke is responsible for the conflation of Isa. 58:6 and 61:1–2 LXX. If he is, then the interpretation set forth in this chapter would challenge the census view that Luke is uninterested in a theology of atonement. However, given the paucity of an explicit theology of atonement in the Gospel of Luke, it seems safer to conclude that this conflation precedes the gospel author.

52. Luthy, *Acceptable Year,* 83.

53. Lev. 25:9: "Then you shall sound the loud trumpet on the tenth day of the seventh month. On the Day of Atonement you shall sound the trumpet throughout all your land." According to Stökl Ben Ezra, "In the Septuagint of Leviticus the word ἀφίημι usually implies the metaphysical release of *sins*. In Leviticus 16:10, ἀφίημι signifies the *physical* release of the goat . . . In Leviticus 16:26, the word ἄφεσις was probably chosen to combine the two meanings, i.e. the physical sending away of the goat and the metaphysical release of sins . . . In the context of Yom Kippur, ἄφεσις bears a second 'social' meaning, the release of slaves (דרור) in the Jubilee: Lev 25:10" (*Impact of Yom Kippur*, 104, 104 n. 115).

54. Lev. 16:26 speaks of "the man who sends out the goat designated for release/ forgiveness [εἰς ἄφεσιν]." The meaning of ἄφεσις here is quite literal: Israel's sins are physically "released" or "sent away on a trajectory," being conveyed onto the scapegoat and then sent into the wilderness (Lev. 16:21–22). The cognate ἀφίημι occurs in Lev. 16:10 LXX.

55. The close cognate, ἐξαποστέλλω, occurs in Lev. 16:21, 22, 26 LXX.

56. Luke's change of ἀπόστελλε (Isa. 58:6 LXX) to ἀποστεῖλαι is striking, given that ἀποστεῖλαι is the form of the word in Lev. 16:10 LXX. However, this change is motivated by the evangelist's desire to maintain the chain of infinitives begun with εὐαγγελίσασθαι and ending with κηρύξαι.

57. Perrot, *La Lecture de la Bible dans la Synagogue*, 198.

58. Josef Blinzler, "The Jewish Punishment of Stoning in the New Testament Period," in *The Trial of Jesus: Cambridge Studies in Honour of C.F.D. Moule*, ed. E. Bammel, SBT 2 (London: SCM, 1970), 147–61; Marshall, *Luke*, 190; Nolland, *Luke*, 1:201; James A. Sanders, "Isaiah in Luke," in *Luke and Scripture: The Function of Sacred Tradition in Luke-Acts*, ed. Craig A. Evans and James A. Sanders (Eugene, OR: Wipf and Stock, 1989), 14–25, at 24; Bock, *Luke*, 1:419; Green, *Luke*, 218–19. Often Deut 13:1–11; John 8:59; 10:31; Acts 7:54–8; 21:31–2 are cited as well.

59. M. Sanh. 6:4: "The place of stoning was twice the height of a man. One of the witnesses knocked him down on his loins; if he turned over on his heart the witness turned him over again on his loins. If he straightway died that sufficed; but if not, the second [witness] took the stone and dropped it on his heart" (Danby, *Mishnah*, 390).

60. Levine and Witherington III, *Luke*, 123.

61. Margaret Froelich and Thomas E. Phillips, "Throw the Blasphemer off a Cliff: Luke 4.16–30 in Light of the *Life of Aesop*," *NTS* 65 (2019): 21–32. The authors seem to be wary of positing any kind of literary dependence between the two texts.

62. Froelich and Phillips, "Throw the Blasphemer off a Cliff," 27.

63. Ibid., 31–2.

64. On which, see Hans Martin Kümmel, "Ersatzkönig und Sündenbock," *ZAW* 80 (1968): 289–318; Walter Burkert, "Transformations of the Scapegoat," in *Structure and History in Greek Mythology and Ritual* (Berkley: University of California Press, 1979), 59–77; Wright, *Disposal of Impurity*; Dennis D. Hughes, "The Pharmakos and Related Rites," in *Human Sacrifice in Ancient Greece*, repr. (London: Routledge, 2010), 139–65; Jean Bottéro, "The Substitute King and His Fate," in *Mesopotamia: Writing, Reasoning, and the Gods*, trans. Zainab Bahrani and Marc van de Mieroop (Chicago: University of Chicago Press, 1992), 138–55; Bradley H. McLean, "Apotropaeic Rituals," in *The Cursed Christ: Mediterranean Expulsion Rituals and Pauline Soteriology*, JSNTSup 126 (Sheffield: Sheffield Academic, 1996), 65–104; Stephen Finlan, "Curse Transmission Rituals and Paul's Imagery," in *The Background and Content of Paul's Cultic Atonement Metaphors* (Atlanta: SBL, 2004), 73–121; Richard E. DeMaris, "Jesus Jettisoned," in *The New Testament in its Ritual World* (London: Routledge, 2008), 91–111; Jan N. Bremmer, "The Scapegoat between Northern Syria, Hittites, Israelites, Greeks and Early Christians," in *Greek Religion and Culture, the Bible and the Ancient Near East*, JSRC 8 (Leiden: Brill, 2008), 169–214.

65. Francisco R. Adrados, "The 'Life of Aesop' and the Origins of Novel in Antiquity," *QUCC* 1 (1979): 93–112, at 105, 107–108. Adrados follows the seminal thesis of Anton Wiechers (*Aesop in Delphi*, Beiträge zur Klassischen Philologie 2 [Meisenheim: Anton Hain K. G., 1961], 31–49), that Aesop's *Life* is a mythological etiology for the *pharmakos* ritual at Delphi, a thesis that Gregory Nagy also accepted and adapted (*The Best of the Achaeans: Concepts of the Hero in Archaic Greek Poetry* [Baltimore: John Hopkins University Press, 1979], 279–97). More recently, see Leslie Kurke, *Aesopic Conversations: Popular Tradition, Cultural Dialogue, and the Invention of Greek Prose* (Princeton: Princeton University Press, 2011), 75–94.

66. Kurke, *Aesopic Conversations*, 85. Kurke adapts Wiechers's thesis by positing that both the Delphians and Aesop engage in "competitive scapegoating," so that not only do the Delphians cast Aesop in the role of the *pharmakos*, but Aesop also casts the Delphians in that same role.

67. Froelich and Phillips acknowledge the *pharmakos* reading of Aesop's death but cast doubt upon it, claiming that classists are "increasingly questioning the characterization of Aesop as a φαρμακός" ("Throw the Blasphemer off a Cliff," 29 n. 35). Yet, to substantiate this claim, they point only to "the devastating criticisms in Kurke, *Aesopic Conversations*, 29–31, 75–94" ("Throw the Blasphemer off a Cliff," 29 n. 35). But Froelich and Phillips are misled in this regard, as Kurke actually affirms a *pharmakos* interpretation of Aesop's death on these pages in his work, though he disagrees with other aspects of Wiechers and Nagy's proposals. In addition to the aforementioned quotation, take, for example, the following statement made by Kurke: "I suggested in chapter 1 that criticizing the idiosyncratic sacrificial practices and allotments of a particular community is precisely what Aesop does at Delphi—and the reason he is finally framed and killed as a scapegoat by the irate Delphians" (*Aesopic Conversations*, 211).

68. Froelich and Phillips, "Throw the Blasphemer off a Cliff," 31.

69. Translation from Lawrence M. Wills, *The Quest of the Historical Gospel: Mark, John, and the Origins of the Gospel Genre* (London: Routledge, 1997), 221. Wills's translation is based off the G text of Manolis Papathompoulos. Granted, the author states that Apollo was angry "because Aesop had slighted him in Samos by not including him with the statues of the nine Muses" (G, 127) (Wills, *Quest*, 221). However, the author's choice to include this detail *immediately* after Aesop disparages the Delphians, who straightaway decide to kill Aesop, cannot be accidental. Apollo was undoubtedly insulted by the degradation of his followers at Delphi as "freed slaves."

70. Sanders, "Isaiah in Luke," 24.

71. Strabo, *Geogr.* 10.2.9 (Jones).

72. Suda, s.v. περίψημα.

73. McLean, *Cursed Christ*, 101.

74. M. Yoma 6:6 (Danby, *Mishnah*, 170).

75. Tg. Ps.-J. Lev. 16:22 (McNamara et al., *Targum Pseudo-Jonathan*, 169).

76. *Plant.* 61 (Colson and Whitaker).

77. Knibb, *1 Enoch*, 87. On the subterranean locale of Asael's punishment in 1 Enoch 10, see Tawil, "Azazel," 53–54.

78. Nickelsburg and VanderKam, *1 Enoch*, 121.

79. Apoc. Ab. 14.5 (Kulik, *Slavonic Pseudepigrapha*, 21).

80. Orlov, *Divine Scapegoats*, 57–58.

81. Given that only Luke cites Ps. 16:10, in which David states, "You will not abandon my soul to Hades" (Ps. 15:10 LXX), it is possible that the Nazarene's attempted execution of Jesus by lethal plunge also foreshadows Jesus's descent to the underworld.

82. The evangelist's source material in this case was most likely Jewish, given the intimate knowledge of traditions pertaining to the Day of Atonement.

83. Raymond Brown, *The Birth of the Messiah* (New York: Doubleday, 1993 [1977]), 74–85, 90 n. 68; Fitzmyer, *Luke*, 491; Bauckham, "Lukan Genealogy," 326.

## Chapter 4

# The Gerasene/Gadarene Exorcism as Apocalyptic Mimesis of the Scapegoat Ritual

## *A Synoptic Analysis*

The Gerasene/Gadarene exorcism (Mark 5:1–20; Matt. 8:28–34; Luke 8:26–39) is one of the most memorable stories in the Synoptic Gospels, yet one commentator has also called it "one of the strangest stories."[1] Scholars especially struggle to make sense of the demons' transference into the swine and their plunge into the sea. At the same time, Markan scholars have appreciated the apocalyptic dimensions of this pericope in recent years.[2] According to Elizabeth Shively, in Mark 5:1–20, the evangelist employs "apocalyptic *topoi* to interpret Jesus's ministry as a skirmish in a dualistic cosmic contest in which the Spirit-empowered Jesus wages war against Satan to rescue people held captive by demonic powers."[3] Several scholars have even posited Mark's appropriation of traditions deriving from the Enochic corpus, particularly the Book of Watchers (see below). Yet these recent proposals have overlooked the possible influence of the apocalyptic scapegoat tradition, which seems to derive from 1 En. 10.4–8. In this enigmatic passage, Asael's punishment is depicted as an eschatological rendition of the scapegoat ritual (Lev. 16:8, 10, 20–22). This leader of the rebellious angels is bound and hurled into an abyss, resulting in the restoration of the earth. In the Gerasene/Gadarene exorcism story, the demons are effectively bound and hurled down a precipice, resulting in the restoration of the demoniac(s).

In his *Exorcism Stories in Luke-Acts*, Todd Klutz considers whether Leviticus 16 has influenced the Lukan account, noting that "Jesus's transferal of the impure spirits from the demoniac to the bodies of the swine is similar to the Levitical ritual's removal of iniquity from Israel to the wilderness."[4] However, Klutz concludes that too many incongruities between Leviticus 16 and the exorcism account make such influence unlikely.[5] Yet Klutz's careful analysis takes only the biblical text into account and not the early Jewish traditions surrounding the Yom Kippur ritual. When these traditions are considered, it becomes more apparent the scapegoat ritual has molded the exorcism story to a certain degree.[6]

In this chapter, I propose that ancient elimination rituals generally and Second Temple scapegoat traditions specifically have impacted the Gerasene/ Gadarene pericope in all three Synoptic accounts, though to varying degrees. Jesus transfers an evil onto a vehicle for disposal, which then eliminates that evil in an uninhabitable realm, leading to the restoration of the demoniac(s). In light of the echoes of the Watchers tradition, this expulsion mimics that of Asael/Azazel and anticipates God's eschatological judgment of the Devil/ Satan and his associates.

## MARK 5:1–20 AND THE WATCHERS TRADITION

Two independent investigations recently have concluded that the Watchers tradition exercised a notable influence on Mark's Gerasene account.[7] Prior to these studies, Graham Twelftree had suggested that Legion's pleas before Jesus (Mark 5:7, 10//Matt. 8:29//Luke 8:28, 31) resemble the Watcher's petition for mercy from God (1 En. 13.4–7).[8] Archie Wright has also noted that the brutality of the Gerasene demons (Mark 5:3–5) seems to recall the savagery of the Giants, whose disembodied spirits "do violence, make desolate, and attack and wrestle and hurl upon the earth" (1 En. 15.11).[9] The sexual innuendo implied in Legion's desire to "go into the pigs" (Mark 5:12) additionally evokes the sexual perversion of the Giants' fathers (1 En. 8.2; 9.8; 86.1–4). Given that the Enochic interpretation of Gen. 6:1–4 was commonplace in Second Temple Judaism,[10] it is not surprising to discover its imprint on the most elaborate exorcism story in the Synoptic tradition.

In an article subtitled, "Reading the Gerasene Demoniac (Mark 5:1–20) with the Book of Watchers (*1 Enoch* 1–36)," Nicholas Elder proposes about seven parallels between the two traditions, arguing that Mark 5:1–20 betrays a verbal and conceptual "interplay" with 1 Enoch 6–16.[11] These parallels include: (1) The immoral nature of the Watchers' sexual encounter with the daughters of men better explains Mark's choice of "unclean spirits" (ἀκάθαρτον πνεῦμα, Mark 5:2, 8, 13) instead of "demon" (δαιμόνιον; cf. Luke 8:27, 29–30).[12] (2) The appellation Legion gives to Jesus, "son of God Most High" (υἱὲ τοῦ θεοῦ τοῦ ὑψίστου, Mark 5:7), evokes 1 En. 9.3–4 and 10.1, where God is called "Most High" (ὕψιστος) just before the binding and expulsion of the fallen angels (1 En. 10.4–6, 11–14).[13] (3) Mark's *hapax legomenon*, "abode" (κατοίκησις, Mark 5:3), echoes the fourfold use of this term in 1 En. 15.7–10. Just as God circumscribes the "abode" of the Giants to the earth, where they wreak havoc (1 En. 15:8–10), so the "abode" of the impure spirits is in tombs, where they are a menace to others (Mark 5:3–5).[14] (4) Both texts mention "stones" (λίθοι). The demoniac injures himself with stones (Mark 5:15), which recalls how Asael is thrown upon jagged stones (1 En. 10:5).[15] (5) As the Watchers swear an oath (ὅρκος) on the mountain (ὅρος) known as "Hermon" (1 En. 6:4–6), so the demoniac requests an oath (ὁρκίζω) from Jesus while on a mountain (ὅρος, Mark 5:5, 7).[16] (6) Attempts had been made to "bind" (δέω) the demoniac with chains and fetters (Mark 5:3–4), which evokes the infamous "binding" (δέω) of the transgressive Watchers (1 En. 10:4, 12; 54:3–5). Also, both texts mention the "torturing" (βασανίζω/βάσανος) of their malevolent subjects (Mark 5:7; 1 En. 10.13).[17] (7) Just as God punishes the Giants by drowning them in the Flood (1 En. 15.8–10; 16.1), resulting in the earth's healing (10.16–22), so the impure spirits are drowned in the sea (Mark 5:13), resulting in the demoniac's healing (Mark 5:15).[18]

The most striking correspondences that Elder proposes are (4), (5), (6), and (7). Intriguingly, these particular correspondences, with the exception of (5), pertain to the punishment of Asael and the rebellious angels.[19] So, if the Watchers myth has indeed touched the construction of Mark's Gerasene account, the traditions contained in 1 Enoch 10 appear to have made the greatest impact. Yet Elder leaves one wondering why Mark evokes the Watchers tradition in the first place, and what function these allusions play in the Gerasene narrative, especially in the scene of the swine's fatal plummet (Mark 5:13).

In the same year, Thierry Murcia published an article in *Judaïsme Ancien*, arguing that Mark 5:1–20 evokes both the Day of Atonement and the Watchers tradition.[20] Murcia submits six parallels between the latter and the Markan narrative: (1) the attempted bindings of the demoniac (Mark 5:3–4; cf. Matt. 8:28–29; Luke 8:26–28) and Asael's binding (1 En. 10:4); (2) the demoniac's use of stones to afflict himself (Mark 5:5) and the jagged stones implemented in Asael's punishment (1 En. 10.5); (3) Asael banishment into an abyss (1 En. 10.4) and the swine's expulsion into the sea (Mark 5:13); (4) the name Λεγιών (Mark 5:9) and Asael's role as leader of a host of Watchers (1 En. 6.7; 8.1–2; 9.6; 13.1–2; cf. 54.5; 55.4; 69.2; 88.1); (5) the demoniac's abode in tombs (Mark 5:2–3, 5) and the darkness of Asael's place of torment (1 En. 10.4); (6) Legion's angst concerning his demise (Mark 5:7) and the judgment prepared for Asael and his host (1 En. 10.6; cf. 10.12–14).[21] Reflecting on these parallels, Murcia conclusively remarks, "The ensemble of these elements seems well to show, on the part of the evangelist, a precise knowledge of the Azazel cycle recorded in the Enochic literature, an ensemble of texts rather than a single book then quite in vogue."[22] The first three of Murcia's proposed correspondences are particularly impressive, though his other points may have some merit.[23]

In addition to positing influence from the Asael/Azazel tradition upon Mark 5:1–20, Murcia submits that the Jewish scapegoat ritual has also contributed toward shaping the Markan narrative.[24] He proposes three parallels: (1) As the high priest transfers sins onto the scapegoat (Lev. 16:21), so Jesus transfers the demons into the pigs (Mark 5:12–13).[25] (2) As the scapegoat was pushed down a ravine in Second Temple tradition (see below), so the swine plunge down a steep promontory (Mark 5:13).[26] (3) As the locale to which the scapegoat sending was desolate and rocky (Lev. 16:22),[27] so the Gerasene man lives alone in a cave and afflicts himself with stones (Mark 5:5).[28] The first two of these parallels are particularly compelling. Yet, Murcia fails to address the relationship between Mark's evocation of the Watchers myth and the scapegoat tradition. Furthermore, why are the demons transferred not into goats but into swine, and sent not into the wilderness but into the sea? And are other traditions concerning the scapegoat reflected in Mark's episode? Before engaging these issues, it will be expedient first to contextual the exorcism narrative within a broader ritual context.

## THE IMPACT OF ANCIENT ELIMINATION RITUALS ON LEGION'S EXPULSION (MARK 5:13)

The scene in which the herd of swine, having been possessed by the impure spirits, rush off the cliff into the sea (Mark 5:13), has puzzled Markan scholars for ages.[29] Yet this scene is hardly perplexing when read in light of the elimination rituals that were widely practiced in the ancient world. In his landmark work, *The Disposal of Impurity*, David P. Wright analyzes a multitude of Hittite and Mesopotamian rituals, wherein an impurity is transferred upon an animal that is then banished to a desolate area, to dispose of that impurity.[30] Wright observes that the "river is the most usual place for disposal" in Mesopotamian praxis.[31] As part of the famous New Year ritual, a ram's corpse is utilized to absorb the impurities of a sanctuary, and then a priest "throws the carcass of that ram into the river."[32] The wiping material of another expulsion rite is disposed "in either the unin[habited ] steppe or in the river."[33] In a different ritual, an imminent evil is transferred to a dog figurine, which is then cast into a river with the following words: "Car[ry] that dog to the depths. Do no[t re]lease it! Take it down to your depths. Remove[e] the evi[l] of the dog from my body!"[34] In another custom, according to Wright, "the evil of creaking beams is put upon a fish in the form of dust and then the fish is apparently put back into the river."[35] He notes that cathartic materials in Hittite rituals were typically discarded in rivers, whereby the pollutant was believed to vanish into the underworld.[36]

Usually a human became the vehicle for disposing of an impurity in Greek elimination rituals.[37] These "scapegoats" were sometimes hurled off cliffs into bodies of water, as Strabo reports concerning the *pharmakos* victim: "It was an ancestral custom among the Leucadians, every year at the sacrifice performed in honour of Apollo, for some criminal to be flung from this rocky look-out [into the sea] for the sake of averting evil."[38] The Suda records an annual custom in which a youth was cast, presumably from a height, into waters to divert an impending evil.[39] As discussed in the previous chapter, some classicists think a "similar line of reasoning occurs in the legend of Aesop who is pictured as a *pharmakos* and who is thrown over a cliff."[40] According to Tzetzes, the ashes of the *pharmakos* were scattered into the sea.[41] Herodotus records an Egyptian custom in which a steer's head, a curse having been transferred upon it, is cut off and "thrown into the river."[42] Familiar with this ritual, Plutarch states that "they invoke curses on the head of the victim and cut it off, and in earlier times they used to throw it into the river."[43]

The Old Testament is also acquainted with elimination rituals, even those that dispose of impurities in bodies of water. Deut. 21:1–9 contains instructions for a ritual in which a priest transfers the community's bloodguilt onto a heifer and washes it downstream by means of the heifer's blood: "The stream removes the cow's blood and thus represents the removal of the victim's blood and concomitant bloodguilt."[44] In the book of Jonah, after the prophet provokes divine wrath and a deadly storm at sea by defying his commission to Nineveh, Jonah is hurled off the ship as a scapegoat by its sailors to propitiate the deity and achieve safety (Jonah 1:11–15).[45] A brief line from the prophet Micah (7:18–19) employs a metaphor from expulsion ritual praxis: "Who is a God like you, pardoning iniquity . . . You will cast all our sins into the depths of the sea."[46] Israel's most famous elimination ritual occurred on the Day of Atonement, though the impurities were disposed in the desert, not water. On this solemn holy day, the high priest removed Israel's defiant sins from the inner sanctuary and transferred them onto the goat for Azazel, which was then banished into the wilderness (Lev. 16:8, 10, 21–22).[47] The scapegoat's expulsion into the wilderness is functionally equivalent to the disposal of impurities in water, namely, to eliminate the threating evil or impurity from the habitable world, subsequently sending it into the domain of demons or disorder.[48]

A distinctive characteristic of most ancient elimination rituals is the dual action of transferring an evil/impurity onto an object and then disposing of that object in an uninhabitable realm.[49] Strikingly, the exorcism described in Mark 5:7–13 involves both notions of transference and disposal.[50] These tropes uniquely appear together in the Gerasene account and no other Markan exorcism or healing episode (cf. Mark 1:6, 34, 42; 3:5, 10, 11, 15; 4:39; 5:28–29; 6:13, 56; 7:30, 33–35; 8:22–25; 9:26; 10:52).[51] Moreover, according to the Markan literary context, the "sea" (θάλασσα) into which the swine plummet (Mark 5.13) is associated with chaos and the demonic, which corresponds to the type of domain into which elimination ritual victims were typically sent.[52] Legion's exorcism, therefore, appears to be informed by ancient elimination rituals: an evil (the impure spirits) is transferred from a subject (the demoniac) into an object (the swine) and disposed in an uninhabitable realm (the sea), resulting in a positive outcome (the man is healed). Pointing to parallel Mesopotamian exorcisms that involve a rite of transference, Graham Twelftree had already anticipated this conclusion, suggesting that "it is probably more appropriate to view the destruction of the pigs as part of the cure rather than . . . deliberate proof of the exorcism's success."[53] Bradley McLean had similarly posited that the exorcism story "was probably based upon the author's personal knowledge of apotropaeic rituals."[54] While it would be mistaken to reckon the Gerasene episode in Mark 5:13 as an elimination ritual per se, this exorcism in particular, without a doubt, possesses an "elimination ritual" flavor and appropriate tropes from such rites.

## THE INFLUENCE OF SCAPEGOAT
## TRADITIONS ON MARK 5:1–20

Thus far I have argued two central points: first, that Mark 5:1–20 betrays significant influence from the Asael tradition, and second, that Mark 5:1–20 employs tropes from ancient elimination ritual praxis. My contention here is that these two phenomena are conceptually connected in Mark's Gerasene narrative. In early Judaism, some Jews had identified Azazel of Leviticus 16 with the Asael of the Watchers tradition. The former figure, Azazel, was the recipient of sins in Israel's most well-known elimination rite, the scapegoat ritual, and the latter figure, Asael, became a cosmic scapegoat in the apocalyptic imagination of certain early Jewish communities. It is therefore quite possible that Mark, or his tradition, has been influenced by Second Temple scapegoat traditions, not least those that conflated Azazel of Leviticus 16 with the Asael of the Watchers myth.

As I have discussed elsewhere, the Jerusalem scapegoat ritual helped shape the composition of 1 Enoch 10, especially in the account of Asael's eschatological banishment to the netherworld (10:4–8) and the restoration of the cosmos (10:20–22).[55] As Stökl Ben Ezra summarizes, both Asael and the scapegoat become vehicles for the disposal of sin, both are abused, brought to a desert, and cast into an abyss, resulting in purification: "The goat originally sent *to* As'azel was seen as the personification *of* As'azel, the demonic source of sin *himself*."[56] Similar to Hellenistic elimination rituals, which acquired self-referential, mythical renditions,[57] so the apocalyptic scapegoat motif came to reflect the Jewish temple ritual and visa-versa: "the relationship between myth and ritual, word and deed, is reciprocal . . . The annual Yom Kippur was perceived—at least by some—as a ritual anticipation of the eschatological purification of God's creation from sin."[58] In light of these traditions, I propose that early Jewish Yom Kippur traditions have shaped the Markan Gerasene account in several significant ways.

First, the transference of the impure spirits into the pigs (Mark 5:13) evokes the transference of sins onto the scapegoat. In the temple ritual, the high priest conveyed Israel's moral evils—their sins and iniquity—onto the head of the scapegoat (Lev. 16:21–22). In 1 En. 10.8, the angel Raphael is commanded to "write all the sins" upon Asael. Similarly, in the Apocalypse of Abraham, the angel Yahoel transfers Abraham's filthy garments onto Azazel, so that he becomes an inheritor of iniquity (Apoc. Ab. 13.14). Asael/Azazel's role as a sin-bearing figure seems to be reflected in 4Q180 1 7–9 and 4Q203 7 I, 5–7 as well.[59] Murcia keenly identifies this parallel between Mark 5:13 and the scapegoat tradition: "In the two cases, it is the same theme: a transfer of evil from man to animal—on the one hand, sins to the goat, on the other hand, demons to the pigs."[60] We are simply adding that this trope is present in the apocalyptic renditions as well.

Second, the swine's plunge off the cliff (Mark 5:13) evokes the scape-goat's precipitous demise as attested in Second Temple tradition. The term "cliff" (κρημνός) does not describe a hillock or mild bank leading gradually to the sea, rather, it denotes a steep promontory with sharp exposure, a fall from which is typically injurious or fatal.[61] That is to say, one does not "rush down" (ὁρμάω) a κρημνός unless, of course, one is precipitously plummeting down it. This must be the meaning of the phrase, "The herd rushed down the cliff into the sea" (ὥρμησεν ἡ ἀγέλη κατὰ τοῦ κρημνοῦ εἰς τὴν θάλασσαν, Mark 5:13). The image is not one of swine running down a gentle bank across a sandy beach into the sea, but of swine tumbling headlong down a steep, rugged precipice overhanging the water.

According to early Jewish tradition, the scapegoat's final destination was not merely the wilderness but a rocky height in the wilderness, down which it was pushed by its handler unto its demise. Though I covered this tradition in the previous chapter, it will be helpful to relay it again here. The Mishnah reports that the scapegoat's handler "pushed it from behind; and it went roll-ing down, and before it had reached half the way down the hill it was broken in pieces."[62] Targum Pseudo-Jonathan records this tradition as well: "The goat shall go up on the mountains of Beth Haduri, and a blast of wind from before the Lord will thrust him down and he will die."[63] Philo appears to know this custom, writing that the scapegoat was "banished, driven from the most holy places, tumbling into desolate and vile gulfs."[64] The Book of Watchers describes Asael's descent into the underworld: "Bind Azazel [Asael] by his hands and his feet, and throw him into the darkness. And split open the desert which is in Dudael, and throw him there" (1 En. 10.4–5).[65] The Animal Apocalypse elaborates on this tradition: "And I saw one of those four who had come before; he seized that first star that had fallen from heaven [Asael/Azazel], and he bound it by its hands and feet and threw it into an abyss, and that abyss was narrow and deep and desolate and dark" (1 En. 88.1).[66] Azazel is exiled into a subterranean domain in the Apocalypse of Abraham. Abraham is instructed to say to the celestial entity, "May you be the firebrand of the furnace of the earth! Go, Azazel, into the untrodden parts of the earth."[67]

Returning to Mark 5:13, the swine's plummet down the steep promontory recalls the scapegoat's precipitous demise, especially given the elimination-ritual flavor of this particular exorcism. The rugged terrain of the Gerasene "cliff" (κρημνός) is also consistent with the rocky terrain of the scapegoat's wilderness destination.[68] In light of the apocalyptic atmosphere of the Markan account and its echoes of the Watchers tradition,[69] the choice of "the sea" as the swine's destination, as opposed to the desert (Lev. 16:21–22), may be linked to the waters used to judge Asael/Azazel and the Giants in certain early Jewish traditions.[70] According to Yarbro Collins, the sea is "symbolically equivalent to the abyss,"[71] and thus the swine's final destination is similarly subterranean, as it is for Asael/Azazel.

Third, the demoniac's self-debasing behavior (Mark 5:5) echoes the biblical command to "afflict yourselves" on the Day of Atonement: "This shall be a statute to you forever: In the seventh month, on the tenth day of the month, you shall afflict yourselves, and shall do no work . . . It is a sabbath of complete rest to you, and you shall afflict yourselves; it is a statute forever" (Lev. 16:29, 31; cf. 23:27, 29, 32; Num 29:7). The performance of self-abasing activities became a key feature of the Day of Atonement in the Second Temple period. According to Philo, there was no food, drink, entertainment, alcohol, festive decorations, merriment, dancing nor music played on Yom Kippur.[72] The Mishnah forbids eating, drinking, anointing, washing, marital intercourse, and putting on sandals.[73] In the Book of Jubilees, Jacob's tumultuous mourning for Joseph becomes an etiological framework for the Day of Atonement.[74] Observant Jews practiced other penitential deeds as well: "Some may wear sackcloth and place ashes on the head; they abstain from sleep, induce tears and cry, stand for long hours during the prayer, or suffer more extreme afflictions."[75]

Looking to Mark 5:5, the Second Evangelist uniquely emphasizes the self-deprecating behavior of the demoniac: "And day and night among the tombs and mountains he was incessantly crying out and cutting himself with stones."[76] This description, perhaps in a heightened form, evokes the elaborate forms of self-affliction practiced by the people in anticipation of their "cleansing" (Lev. 16:30).[77] From the perspective of the implied author, the "man" (ἄνθρωπος, Mark 5:2, 8) seems to be preparing himself for the cleansing of impure spirits from his own body. There is a parallel in the Apocalypse of Abraham, where the patriarch is commanded to "abstain from every kind of food cooked by fire, and from drinking of wine and from anointing with oil" for forty days (Apoc. Ab. 9.7; cf. 12.2) before his own impurity is expunged and placed upon Azazel by the angel Yahoel (Apoc. Ab. 13.14). As with Abraham and the Jewish community generally on Yom Kippur, the demoniac's self-affliction precedes the elimination of his (demonic) impurities.

Fourth, the Gerasene exorcism uniquely involves the cruel treatment of the demon(s) being expelled, which recalls the maltreatment of the scapegoat as attested in early Jewish tradition.[78] The halakhic source of Barn. 7.8 stipulates that "all of you shall spit on it and pierce it." The Mishnah reports that the goat's hair was tugged by the people as they cried, "Bear [our sins] and be gone! Bear [our sins] and be gone!" (m. Yoma 6:4).[79] According to Tertullian, the goat for Azazel was "cursed and spit upon and pulled about and pierced."[80] In the apocalyptic milieu, Asael is to be bound "hand and foot," "thrown" into an abyss, lain upon "sharp and jagged stones" and "covered with darkness," so that his face does "not see the light," and he is to "dwell there for an exceedingly long time" (1 En. 10.4–5).[81] Verbal abuse is heaped upon Azazel in the Apocalypse of Abraham: "This is disgrace, this is Azazel! . . . Shame on you, Azazel! For Abraham's portion is in heaven, and yours is on earth . . . Hear, counselor, be shamed by me!" (Apoc. Ab. 13.6–7, 11–12).[82]

The physical and verbal abuse of the scapegoat corresponds to the harsh treatment of Legion in the Markan account. The pluperfect of Mark's ἔλεγεν ("For Jesus had been saying to him" Mark 5:8) implies that the exorcism involved a protracted struggle before the expulsion was accomplished.[83] According to Yarbro Collins, Legion's request that Jesus not torture him (Mark 5:7) "signifies that [the] exorcism is painful or at least distressing for the spirit."[84] Legion's prostration before and imploring of Jesus (Mark 5:6, 10, 12) are also humiliating to the otherwise powerful demons.[85] Finally, Mark chooses an imperfect verb with a violent connotation—πνίγω, meaning to "choke," "drown," or "strangle"[86]—vividly to describe the demon's fate: "And they were being drown in the sea" (Mark 5:13).[87]

Fifth, Mark's arresting account of the demoniac's miraculous healing (Mark 5:15) evokes the theme of restoration known in apocalyptic Yom Kippur traditions. In Zechariah's fourth night vision in Zechariah 3, Joshua the high priest's dirty garments are exchanged for "festal apparel" (Zech 3:4–5), signaling an act of atonement to be executed "in a single day" (3:9), that is, on the Day of Atonement most likely.[88] 11QMelchizedek links Isaiah 61 and Leviticus 25 to the concept of an eschatological Jubilee and final restoration, culminating in an eschatological Day of Atonement. Following

Asael's prescribed banishment in 1 Enoch 10.4–6, Raphael is commanded to "heal the earth, which the Watchers have desolated; and announce the healing of the earth, that the plague may be healed" (1 En. 10.7).[89] In the Apocalypse of Abraham, the patriarch's transgressions are removed, and he is endowed with new heavenly garments, signifying "an eschatological return to the protoplast's original condition" (Apoc. Ab. 13.14).[90]

Mark recounts that, following the exorcism, the townspeople "came to Jesus and saw the man who had a demon, sitting, clothed, and in his right mind, the very man who had possessed the legion. And they were afraid" (Mark 5:15). The evangelist's use of the historical present (ἔρχονται . . . θεωροῦσιν) makes this scene particularly vivid.[91] In a manner similar to Abraham and Joshua, the man's (ἄνθρωπος, Mark 5:2, 8) new clothing symbolizes that he has been "restored to normality."[92] The fear of the townspeople indicates that a mighty act of God has occurred,[93] their awestruck attitude recalling the atmosphere of Yom Kippur: "For all stand in awe, overcome by the sanctity of the day . . . as a time of purification and escape from sins."[94]

In conclusion, five parallels between early Jewish Day of Atonement traditions and the Markan Gerasene narrative suggest that the Second Evangelist has molded this pericope with Yom Kippur motifs in view: (1) the transference of evil/impurity onto the scapegoat, (2) the descent of the scapegoat unto its demise, (3) the command to "afflict yourselves" on Yom Kippur, (4) the physical and verbal abuse of the scapegoat, and (5) the eschatological restoration associated with the scapegoat's demise. These correspondences are especially compelling in light of the elimination-ritual flavor of this particular exorcism.[95] In the context of the Gospel of Mark, this exorcism signals the eschatological expulsion of the cosmic powers of Satan's kingdom (Mark 3:22–24) from their privileged positions of authority over the nations, and augurs God's kingdom reign, in which Gentiles are released from bondage to cosmic forces, and their oppressive earthly counterparts (the Roman military), and welcomed into the family of God.[96] Mark employs the potent imagery of Yom Kippur and its apocalyptic variations to communicate this message.

## LUKE'S REDACTION OF THE GERASENE
## EXORCISM (LUKE 8:26–40)

Luke retains elements of this pericope from the Gospel of Mark that broadly evoke the Watchers tradition.[97] With regard to the five parallels to the Day of Atonement identified above, Luke repeats four of them: (A) the transference of evil/impurity onto a vehicle of disposal (i.e., a scapegoat) (Luke 8:33), (B) the descent of the scapegoat unto its demise (Luke 8:33), (C) the physical and verbal abuse of the scapegoat (Luke 8:28, 31, 33), and (D) the eschatological restoration associated with the scapegoat's demise (Luke 8:35–36).[98] The Lukan rendition introduces two additional features that further suggest the influence of Yom Kippur on this pericope.[99]

First of all, the Third Evangelist augments the description of the demoniac's behavior by adding, "And he would break through the bonds and be driven by the demon into the deserts [εἰς τὰς ἐρήμους]" (Luke 8:29). As one recalls, the phrase "into the desert" occurs three times in Leviticus 16 with regard to the scapegoat (Lev. 16:10, 21–22). Now, the phrase, "he would be driven by the demon into the deserts," is not likely a verbal allusion to the biblical text, since "desert" (ἔρημος) is singular in Leviticus 16 LXX and plural in Luke 8:29. However, the scapegoat's journey to the wilderness was well known in early Judaism. According to Philo, the scapegoat "was to be sent out into a trackless and desolate wilderness."[100] Josephus reports that the scapegoat "is sent alive into the wilderness beyond the frontiers."[101] In 1 Enoch 10, Raphael is told to "bind Asael hand and foot, and cast him into the darkness; and make an opening in the wilderness that is in Doudael. Throw him there."[102] Azazel becomes "the firebrand of the furnace of the earth" and is banished "into the untrodden parts of the earth."[103] Of course, the "goat for Azazel" was also sent *to* Azazel (Lev. 16:10), a figure that was once regarded as a deity or demon of the desert.[104]

While there is no *terminus technicus* for the scapegoat's "sending" in extant Greek literature (the LXX itself uses three different terms), Luke's choice of ἐλαύνω ("he would be *driven* into deserts") finds a parallel in Philo's employment of that same verb to depict the scapegoat's banishment: "An illustration of what has been said is afforded by that which is done year by year on the day called the 'Day of Atonement' . . . that which exalts creation [the 'scapegoat'] shall be banished [ἐλαυνόμενος], driven from the most holy places, to find itself amid rocky chasms in trackless and unhallowed regions."[105] Luke's terminology is thus not at variance with contemporary verbiage vis-à-vis the scapegoat. The driving of the Gerasene man "into deserts" by the malevolent power (Luke 8:29) may therefore recall the driving of the scapegoat into the desert to Azazel.[106]

Second, Luke interprets the sending-place of the pigs and demons as "the abyss." Whereas Mark writes, "And he urged him greatly that he might not send them out of the country" (Mark 5:10), Luke reports, "And they urged him that he might command them to depart into the abyss [εἰς τὴν ἄβυσσον]" (Luke 8:31). In the Septuagint, the term "abyss" (ἄβυσσος) usually translates the Hebrew word תהום, which denotes the waters of the subterranean realm (Gen. 1:2; 7:11; 8:2; Isa. 51:10; Ezek. 31:15; Jonah 2:6; Job 38:16; cf. Sir. 1:3; 16:18; 24:5). The abyss also became the place of imprisonment for the disobedient fallen angels and powers in Enochic Judaism (1 En. 10.4–5, 13;

18:10–19:2;  21:7–10;  54:5;  88:1–3;  90:24–27;  Jub.  5:6),  the  Book  of
Revelation  (Rev.  9:1, 2, 11;  11:7;  17:8;  20:1, 3),  and  apparently  Jude 6 and 2
Pet.  2:4  (though  here  ἄβυσσος  is  not  employed).[107]  Lukan  commentators  generally  agree  that  "the  abyss,"  into  which  Jesus  effectively  sends  the  demons
(Luke 8:31),  has  as  its  background  this  tradition  regarding  the  punishment  of
fallen  angels  or  spirits.[108]  According  to  Bovon,  "it  is  assumed  that  the  demons
remain  imprisoned  in  the  ἄβυσσος."[109]

Regarding  this  Jewish  tradition,  the  infamous  angel  Asael/Azazel  occupies
a  prominent  place.  In  the  Book  of  Watchers,  this  chief  offender  is  to  be  bound
hand  and  foot,  cast  into  the  darkness,  thrown  into  an  opening  in  the  wilderness,  and  covered  with  darkness  for  a  long  time  (1 En. 10.4–5)  until  the  day
of  judgment  (1 En. 10.6).[110]  Represented  as  the  first  "fallen  star,"  Asael  is
singled  out  in  the  Animal  Apocalypse:  "[The archangel]  bound  it  by  its  hand
and  feet  and  threw  it  into  an  abyss,  and  that  abyss  was  narrow  and  deep  and
desolate  and  dark"  (1 En. 88.1).[111]  In  the  Parables  of  Enoch,  the  host  of  Asael/
Azazel  encounters  a  similar  fate:  "These  [chains]  are  being  prepared  for  the
host  of  Azazel,  that  they  might  take  them  and  throw  them  into  the  abyss  of
complete  judgment,  and  with  jagged  rocks  they  will  cover  their  jaws"  (1 En.
54.5;  cf.  55.4–56.4).[112]  Elsewhere  in  the  Enochic  corpus,  where  similar  pun-
ishments  are  described  (1 En. 18:10–19:2;  21:7–10;  90:24–27),  Asael/Azazel
is  most  certainly  in  view  as  one  of  the  chief  powers  placed  in  an  abyss  of
judgment.[113]  Additionally,  several  scholars  have  noted  the  influence  of  Asael/
Azazel  traditions  on  the  depiction  of  the  dragon's  punishment  in  Rev. 20:1–3,
7–10.[114]  The  demons'  fear  of  being  sent  into  the  "abyss"  (Luke 8:31),  therefore,  conforms  to  the  Enochic  template  of  the  fallen  angels'  punishment,
which  has  itself  been  influenced  by  the  scapegoat  tradition.

Intriguingly,  the  demons'  driving  the  Gerasene  man  "into  the  deserts"  (εἰς
τὰς ἐρήμους,  Luke 8:29)  structurally  corresponds  to  the  sending  of  demons
"into  the  abyss"  (εἰς τὴν ἄβυσσον,  Luke 8:31),  as  Joel  Green  observes:  "Jesus
allows  the  transfer  of  the  demons  into  the  swine  with  the  result  that  they,  like
the  demoniac  before  him,  are  'driven'  (v. 29)  into  self-destruction."[115]  This
association  between  the  wilderness  and  the  abyss  further  suggests  the  influence  of  the  scapegoat  tradition  upon  Luke's  version  of  the  pericope.

Thus,  while  Luke's  account  of  the  Gerasene  exorcism  does  not  embellish
most  of  the  Yom  Kippur  motifs  present  in  his  Markan  *Vorlage*,  it  retains  most
of  them  and  betrays  the  influence  of  scapegoat  traditions  concerning  the  goat
for  Azazel's  demonic  desert  destination  and  the  eschatological  fate  of  Asael/
Azazel  and  his  associates  in  an  abyss.  One  may  raise  the  question  of  whether
these  evocations  of  the  Day  of  Atonement  and  the  Watchers  myth  derive  from
Luke's  direct  knowledge  of  these  traditions  or  indirectly  through  one  of  his
Jewish  sources.  Given  that  "abyss"  (ἄβυσσος,  Luke 8:31)  is  a  *hapax legomenon*  in  Luke-Acts,  "desert"  in  the  plural  (ἔρημοι,  Luke 8:29)  is  not

characteristically Lukan,[116] and that neither Yom Kippur nor Enochic Judaism appear to have made a great impact on the Luke-Acts corpus,[117] I am inclined to think that these allusions are more subconscious for the Third Evangelist and to be credited to a Jewish source that influenced his composition of the scene.

## MATTHEW'S REDACTION OF THE
## GERASENE EXORCISM (MATT. 8:28–34)

Matthew has radically abbreviated this exorcism story, effectively omitting eleven of Mark's twenty verses (i.e., Mark 5:3–6, 8–10, 15, 18–20).[118] Though his account is so brief, he preserves several details that recall the Watchers traditions.[119] Of the five parallels between the Markan account and Yom Kippur, Matthew retains three of them: (A) the transference of evil onto a vehicle of disposal (i.e., a scapegoat) (Matt. 8:32a), (B) the descent of the scapegoat unto its demise (Matt. 8:32b), and (C) the abuse of the scapegoat (Matt. 8:29). The Matthean rendition introduces three additional features that also suggest the influence of Yom Kippur.

First, Matthew includes *two* demoniacs, a fact that has puzzled commentators for decades. Having relayed nine scholarly explanations for this phenomenon, Davies and Allison conclude, "In our judgment, while none of the nine proposals listed can be declared impossible, none of them is obviously probable. And as we cannot add to the catalog, we remain unenlightened. All we can do is call attention to the other places where our author multiples by two."[120] France similarly pleads ignorance of the reason for the two demoniacs, admitting that "I do not know of any really satisfactory explanation of Matthew's tendency to see double."[121] I propose a novel explanation, namely, that Matthew perceives the Yom Kippur evocations in his Markan *Vorlage* and is thinking of the Yom Kippur halakhic edict, that the two goats must be identical in appearance.

Although this requirement is not in Leviticus 16, m. Yoma 6:1 reports that "the two he-goats of the Day of Atonement should be alike in appearance, in size, and in value, and have been bought at the same time."[122] The halakhic material utilized in the Epistle of Barnabas instructs, "Take two fine and similar goats and offer them" (Barn 7.6 [Ehrman]). The author adds, "For this reason the goats are similar, fine, and equal" (Barn 7.10 [Ehrman]). Justin Martyr similarly records that the two goats "were commanded to be similar, one of which was to be the scapegoat and the other the sacrificial goat" (*Dial.* 40.4).[123] As I and others have argued, Matthew alludes to this tradition in his Barabbas episode, causing "Jesus Barabbas" and "Jesus the Messiah" (Matt. 27:16–17) to become virtually identical in appearance.[124]

One glaring problem with this reading, however, is that the two goats of Yom Kippur eventually obtained opposing designations, one becoming the "goat for Yahweh" and the other the "goat for Azazel" (Lev. 16:7–10), and only the latter inherited iniquity and was banished into the wilderness (Lev. 16:20–22). In response, one could conjecture that Matthew was content with just a passing evocation of the image of the two goats without further reflection. A more satisfying explanation, however, is that the evangelist intends the two demoniacs to foreshadow the two scapegoats that appear later in his gospel, namely, Jesus Barabbas/the crowd (Matt. 27:24–26) and Jesus the Messiah (Matt. 27:27–31).[125] The sins of others are transferred onto both of these figures (Matt. 23:35–36; 26:28), similar to the transfer of the two demons into pigs (Matt. 8:32). Both of these figures, like the two Gadarene demons, are finally expunged in an act of purgation.

Second, Matthew underscores the eschatological dimension of the exorcism by having the demons ask Jesus, "Have you come here to torment us *before the time?*" (ἦλθες ὧδε πρὸ καιροῦ βασανίσαι ἡμᾶς, Matt. 8:29). Matthew employs the cognate, "tormentor" (βασανιστής), in the conclusion to the Parable of the Debtor to describe the eschatological fate of the wicked (Matt. 18:34). Matthew also uses καιρός in descriptions of the eschaton (Matt. 13:30; 16:3; 21:41; 24:45).[126] These factors strongly suggest that the torment which the demons fear is the eschatological torment of the disobedient powers known well in Jewish apocalyptic.[127] For the most part, this eschatological tradition is the same as that evoked by the demons' fear of the "abyss" in Luke 8:31 (see above), that is, the tradition widely attested in 1 En. 10.4–5, 13; 18:10–19:2; 21:7–10; 54:5; 88:1–3; 90:24–27; Jub. 5.6, 10–11; 10.5–7, 11; 4Q180 1 7–10; 4Q203 7 I, 5–7; Rev. 20:1–3, 10; Jude 6; 2 Pet 2:4; Apoc. Ab. 14.5, 7; and elsewhere. In this tradition, Asael/Azazel, leader of the troop of fallen angels, features prominently.

Matthew knows this tradition and references it in his Final Judgment scene, in which the Son of Man judges the unrighteous lot of "goats" on his left side (cf. Matt. 25:33): "Then he will say to those at his left hand, 'Depart from me, cursed ones, into the eternal fire prepared for the Devil and his angels'" (Matt. 25:41). As argued in chapter 1, Matthew assimilates the Devil's profile to that of Asael/Azazel in this verse (cf. 1 En. 54.4; 55.4), which is evinced in the parallel between "the eternal fire prepared for the Devil and his angels" (Matt. 25:41) and the "prepared" judgment of "Azazel, and all his associates and all his host" (1 En. 54.4; 55.4) at the behest of the Son of Man/Elect One seated on a "throne of glory" (Matt. 25:31; 1 En. 55.4).[128] Thus, the Gadarene demons' fear of being "tormented before the time" (Matt. 8:29) anticipates the final judgment of the Devil and his associates, which, in Matthew's thought, follows a scapegoat-like archetype.

Third, Matthew changes Mark's verb πέμψον (Mark 5:12), used in the demons' request to be "sent" into the pigs, to one of the terms for the scapegoat's "sending" in Leviticus 16 LXX, ἀποστέλλω (Lev. 16:10): "If you cast us out, send us into the herd of swine" (Matt. 8:31).[129] In stark contrast to his Markan *Vorlage*, Matthew has Jesus utter a single word in response to this request (Matt. 8:32). Here, "Jesus speaks for the first time. He utters one little word: 'Go!' The result is dramatic. The herd thunders over a cliff and perishes in the water. The sovereign power of Jesus could not be more effectively presented. His word is compulsion."[130] Jesus's stark command to "go" better fits the image of expulsion or banishment than "and he permitted them" (Mark 5:13; Luke 8:32). The evangelist's choice of the verb ὑπάγω is noteworthy, since he employs the same term when Jesus rebukes Satan in Matt. 4:10 and 16:23. As noted in chapter 2, both of these passages appear to assimilate the Satan's profile to that of Asael/Azazel, who, like the scapegoat, is verbally commanded to "go" or "depart" in extra-biblical tradition (m. Yoma 6:4; Apoc. Ab. 13:12; 14:7).

In sum, Matthew's radically abridged account—his omission of the demoniac(s)' description (Mark 5:3–6), Jesus's dialogue with the demons (Mark 5:8–10), and the man's request to become a disciple (Mark 5:18–20)—has the effect of highlighting Jesus's powerful expulsion of the demons. Hence, it more elegantly (though less vividly) evokes the scapegoat ritual, though admittedly in a less obvious manner. In Matthew's narrative universe, the demons' demise adumbrates the Son of Man's eschatological victory over the Devil (Matt. 25:41; cf. 22:13), and it may foreshadow the two sin-bearing "scapegoats"—Jesus Barabbas/the crowd and Jesus the Messiah—who later appear in his passion narrative (Matt. 27:15–26; 27–31).

## CONCLUSION

Elimination ritual traditions have molded the Markan Gerasene exorcism story, as the gospel account manifests the predominant features of such rituals that were widely known throughout the Mediterranean world: an evil (the impure spirits) is transferred from a subject (the demoniac) onto an object (the swine) and disposed in an uninhabitable realm (the sea), resulting in a positive outcome (the man is healed). Often in such rituals, the impure object of elimination is disposed in a body of water, as is the case in the exorcism story. Matthew and Luke retain the basic elements of this template, though Matthew does not narrate the healing of the demoniacs. Graham Twelftree's suggestion therefore seems to be correct, that "it is probably more appropriate to view the destruction of the pigs as part of the cure rather than . . . deliberate proof of the exorcism's success."[131]

The most famous elimination ritual in the Jewish world was the scapegoat ritual, which received an apocalyptic reworking in the mythology of Asael/ Azazel and the fallen angels' punishment. As scholars have recently argued, and as was affirmed in this chapter, the Watchers tradition appears to have made a noticeable impact upon Mark's Gerasene narrative. But Mark's evocation of the Enochic myth is not unrelated to the elimination-ritual atmosphere of the exorcism. Rather, in light of the former, the Gerasene exorcism mimics the cosmic, scapegoat-like expulsion of Asael/Azazel, anticipating God's eschatological judgment of Satan and his associates. The demons' fear of being cast into the "abyss" (Luke 8:31) or of being tormented "before the time" (Matt. 8:29) confirms this apocalyptic and ritual component of the exorcism tradition.

Todd Klutz had rejected the idea that Luke alludes to Leviticus 16 in his exorcism story for five reasons, all of which apply equally to the three Synoptic accounts: (1) the scapegoat ritual serves a collective interest, while only the demoniac(s) is healed; (2) Azazel dwells outside the community, whereas the demons dwell within the demoniac(s); (3) the scapegoat ritual is performed annually, but Jesus's exorcism is eschatological; (4) the scapegoat ritual utilizes a goat, while Jesus utilizes pigs; and (5) the officiate of Yom Kippur changes clothes (Lev. 16:4, 24), whereas the recipient of the exorcism receives new clothes.[132] These incongruities, reasonable as they are on the sole grounds of Leviticus 16, can be reconciled on the basis of Second Temple *traditions* regarding the Day of Atonement, most of which have been covered in this investigation: (1) the Apocalypse of Abraham, in which the patriarch is the direct beneficiary of Azazel's banishment (Apoc. Ab. 13.14), shows that the scapegoat does not always serve a collective interest; (2) in Second Temple Judaism, the threat "outside" the community (Azazel) became a threat "inside" the community (1 En. 15.11; Jub. 10.8–9, 11); (3) in the apocalyptic *imaginaire*, the scapegoat ritual signals the eschatological expulsion of evil; (4) the choice of swine can be explained by Mark's intended mockery of the *Legio X Fretensis*, the earthly counterparts of the cosmic powers being vanquished;[133] and (5) Apoc. Ab. 13.14 and Zech 3:4–5 both use clothing imagery to symbolize the atonement made for the beneficiaries of the ritual. Thus, this study demonstrates the importance of considering not only the biblical text but also subsequent Jewish traditions when weighing scriptural echoes or allusions.

For Mark, Jesus's scapegoat-like expulsion of Legion signals God's banishment of hostile cosmic powers from their positions of authority over the nations (i.e., binding the "Strong Man," Mark 3:27) and augurs God's kingdom reign, in which Gentiles are released from bondage to these powers (and their earthly counterparts) and welcomed into the family of God (Mark 3:13–19, 31–35). Luke's version tells a similar tale, correlating the "deserts" into which the demons would drive the demoniac (Luke 8:29) with the "abyss" into which they are finally sent (Luke 8:31), arguably making the scapegoat-Asael/Azazel typology even stronger. While Matthew greatly abridges the exorcism account, the expulsion scene now becomes explicitly eschatological (as in Luke) and is the focal point of the story, adumbrating the Son of Man's victory over "the Devil and all his angels" (Matt. 25:41). The presence of two demoniacs, while evoking the two goats of Yom Kippur, may foreshadow the two scapegoats that later appear in Matthew's passion narrative.

## NOTES

1. Eduard Schweizer, *The Good News According to Mark*, trans. Donald H. Madvig (Richmond: John Knox, 1970), 111.

2. Joel Marcus, *Mark: A New Translation with Introduction and Commentary*, AB 27–27A (New York: Doubleday, 2002–2008), 1:352; Adela Yarbro Collins, *Mark: A Commentary*, Hermeneia (Minneapolis: Fortress, 2007), 269–70; Elizabeth E. Shively, *Apocalyptic Imagination in the Gospel of Mark: The Literary and Theological Role of Mark 3:22–30* (Berlin: Walter de Gruyter, 2012), 177.

3. Shively, *Apocalyptic Imagination*, 39.

4. Todd Klutz, *The Exorcism Stories in Luke-Acts: A Sociostylistic Reading* (Cambridge: Cambridge University Press, 2004), 144–48, quote at 145.

5. Klutz, *Exorcism Stories in Luke-Acts*, 146. Klutz's analysis is directed toward Mark but equally applies to all three gospels.

6. See below for my response to Klutz's objections.

7. I conducted the bulk of this study without prior knowledge of either of these articles.

8. Graham H. Twelftree, *Jesus the Exorcist: A Contribution to the Study of the Historical Jesus*, WUNT 2:54 (Tübingen: Mohr Siebeck, 1993), 154–55.

9. Archie Wright, "The Demonology of 1 Enoch and the New Testament Gospels," in *Enoch and the Synoptic Gospels: Reminiscences, Allusions, Intertextuality*, ed. Loren T. Stuckenbruck and Gabriele Boccaccini, EJL 44 (Atlanta: Scholars, 2016), 215–44, at 239, 242.

10. Nickelsburg, *1 Enoch 1*, 71–88; Annette Yoshiko Reed, *Fallen Angels and the History of Judaism and Christianity: The Reception of Enochic Literature* (Cambridge: Cambridge University Press, 2005), 116–21; Loren T. Stuckenbruck, "The Book of Enoch: Its Reception in Second Temple Jewish and in Christian Tradition," *EC* (2013): 7–40.

11. Nicholas A. Elder, "Of Porcine and Polluted Spirits: Reading the Gerasene Demoniac (Mark 5:1–20) with the Book of Watchers (*1 Enoch* 1–36)," *CBQ* 78 (2016): 430–46. According to Elder, "We are not, then, dealing with *direct, literary* dependence . . . Mark does, however, demonstrate strong conceptual parallels with the Enochic template" (Elder, "Gerasene Demoniac," 433 n. 9). Nevertheless, Elder contends for certain verbal parallels between the two texts (ibid., 431, 446).

12. Ibid., 434–36.

13. Ibid., 436–39.

14. Ibid., 439–41.

15. Ibid., 441–42.

16. Ibid., 442.

17. Ibid., 442–45.

18. Ibid., 445.

19. Parallels (1), (2), and (3) are not very convincing. The phrase "unclean spirit" (ἀκάθαρτον πνεῦμα, Mark 5:2, 8, 13) may broadly recall the Watchers tradition, but it never occurs in 1 Enoch 6–16 (although Jub. 10.1 employs the phrase "impure demon" within a discourse pertaining to the Watchers and their progeny). Moreover, the title "God Most High" (ὁ θεὸς ὁ ὕψιστος, Mark 5:7) is quite common in the Septuagint, so a specific allusion to 1 En. 9.3–4; 10.1 seems doubtful. Similarly, the term "abode" (κατοίκησις, Mark 5:3) is very broad in meaning, so an allusion to 1 En. 15.7–10 is also uncertain (κατοίκησις appears eight times in the LXX, ten times in Josephus, zero times in Philo, and very rarely in the Greek pseudepigrapha).

20. Thierry Murcia, "La question du fond historique des récits évangéliques. Deux guérisons un jour de Kippour: l'hémorroïsse et la résurrection de la fille de Jaïre et le possédé de Gérasa/Gadara," *Judaïsme Ancien* 4 (2016): 123–64.

21. Murcia, "Deux guérisons un jour de Kippour," 153–56.

22. "L'ensemble de ces éléments paraît bien montrer, de la part des évangélistes, une connaissance précise du cycle d'Azazel consigné dans la littérature hénochienne, un ensemble de textes plutôt qu'un livre unique, alors très vogue" (ibid., 157–58).

23. The link between the tombs and the darkness of Asael's punishment is weak. As the fallen Watchers were the most infamous conglomerate of angels in Second Temple Judaism, that the Watchers tradition lurks behind the name Λεγιών is not an improbable postulate (cf. Matt. 26:53), though it is by no means self-evident. We could revise Murcia's sixth parallel by comparing Legion's petition to Jesus (Mark 5:10, 12) to the Watchers' petition to God (1 En. 13:1–7; cf. Jub. 10.8) (see below).

24. Notably, the present author also observed several connections between Mark 5:1–20 and the scapegoat tradition before consulting Murcia's article. Murcia additionally contends that the Day of Atonement has molded the Markan narrative about the hemorrhaging woman and Jairus's daughter (Mark 5:21–43), suggesting that the historical events reflected in the stories may have occurred on Yom Kippur ("Deux guérisons un jour de Kippour," 138–47). I have found this particular thesis less convincing, however.

25. Ibid., 152–53.

26. Ibid., 151–52.

27. Stökl Ben Ezra, *Impact of Yom Kippur*, 88.

28. Murcia, "Deux guérisons un jour de Kippour," 155.

29. Scholars typically understand this episode as signaling the effectiveness of Jesus's exorcism (e.g., Campbell Bonner, "Technique of Exorcism," *HTR* 36 [1943]: 39–49, at 47–49; idem, "Additions and Corrections," *HTR* 37 [1944]: 333–39, at 334–36; Robert H. Gundry, *Mark: A Commentary on His Apology for the Cross* [Grand Rapids: Eerdmans, 1993], 252; Yarbro Collins, *Mark*, 271). Twelftree,

however, has cast serious doubt on this interpretation (*Jesus the Exorcist*, 74–75). The effectiveness of the exorcism, as Martin Dibelius and Twelftree suggest, is exhibited when the townspeople discover the former demoniac "sitting there, clothed, and in his right mind" (Mark 5:15) (*From Tradition to Gospel*, trans. Bertram Lee Woolf [New York: Charles Scribner's Sons, 1971 (1919)], 87; Twelftree, *Jesus the Exorcist*, 74).

30. For example, see Wright, *Disposal of Impurity*, 47, 50–51, 56–59, 64–67, 70–71.

31. Ibid., 252.

32. Ibid., 64; Milgrom, *Leviticus*, 1:1068.

33. Wright, *Disposal of Impurity*, 293.

34. Ibid., 71–72; Milgrom, *Leviticus*, 1:1079.

35. Wright, *Disposal of Impurity*, 252.

36. Ibid., 266.

37. Bremmer, "The Scapegoat," 169–214.

38. Starbo, *Geogr.* 10.2.9 (Jones).

39. Suda, s.v. περίψημα. See Hughes, "The Pharmakos," 111–13.

40. Jan N. Bremmer, "Scapegoat Rituals in Ancient Greece," in *Oxford Readings in Greek Religion*, ed. Richard Buxton (Oxford: Oxford University Press, 2000), 280. See *Life of Aesop* 124–42; Plut. *Mor.* 557a; Wiechers, *Aesop in Delphi*, 31–49; Nagy, *Best of the Achaeans*, 279–97; Adrados, "Life of Aesop," 105, 107–108; Kurke, *Aesop Conversations*, 75–94.

41. Tzetzes, *Child.* 5.728–45.

42. Herodotus, *Hist.* 2.39 (Godley).

43. Plutarch, *Mor.* 363b (Babbitt 1936: 75, 77); cf. Aelian, *Nat. an.* 10.21. Diodorus Siculus describes a fictitious Ethiopian ritual of purification, in which two strangers are sent to traverse a stormy sea (*Lib. Hist.* 2.55).

44. David P. Wright, "Deuteronomy 21:1–9 as a Rite of Elimination," *CBQ* 49 (1987): 387–403.

45. McLean, *Cursed Christ*, 101.

46. Wright, *Disposal of Impurity*, 272 n. 149.

47. See Wright, *Disposal of Impurity*, 16–30; Milgrom, *Leviticus*, 1:1071–79; Schwartz, "Bearing of Sin," 17–21.

48. Tawil, "Azazel," 47–52; Wright, *Disposal of Impurity*, 252; Milgrom, *Leviticus*, 1:1042, 1046, 1072. As a point of technicality, the scapegoat did not bear impurities but Israel's deliberate sins (Lev. 16:21) (Milgrom, *Leviticus*, 1: 1033–34; Schwartz, "Bearing of Sin," 17–19). According to Tawil and Milgrom, the scapegoat ultimately deposited the sins in the netherworld, since in Mesopotamian cosmology the wilderness was believed to be a portal to the underworld ("Azazel," 48–59"; Milgrom, *Leviticus*, 1:1072). Yet, Wright contends that the Hebrew Bible, though it associates the wilderness with demons (Lev. 17:7; Isa. 13:21; 34:14; 2 Chron. 11:15), does not link the desert, impurities, nor demons with the netherworld (*Disposal of Impurities*, 25–30). The community that composed 1 En. 10.4–5, however, links the underworld, the desert, and a fallen angel by making the nether-regions of the cosmos, accessed by means of the desert, the locale of Asael's punishment. See also Apoc. Ab. 14.5.

49. Bottéro, "Substitute King," 142; McLean, "Apotropaeic Rituals," 74; Wright, *Disposal of Impurity*, 32; Burkert, "Scapegoat," 61; DeMaris, "Jesus Jettisoned," 106. The act of transference is implicit in some of the discussed elimination rituals.

50. Mark notably uses πνεῦμα ἀκάθαρτον three times (5:2, 8, and 5:13), whereas Matthew omits the phrase (cf. Matt. 8:28, 31, 33) and Luke reproduces it once (Luke 8:29). Regarding the term πνεῦμα ἀκάθαρτον, Loren T. Stuckenbruck notes that "the Gospels offer very little information about what it is that made the exorcized spirits unclean," though he states that the expression, "a spirit of uncleanness," in the Dead Sea Scrolls "suggests that the effect of the bad spirit is to make its victim ritually unclean and therefore unable to participate in the religious life of Israel" (*The Book of Giants from Qumran: Texts, Translation, and Commentary* [Tübingen: Mohr Siebeck, 1997], 174). Wright cautiously suggests that "the [gospel] authors were aware of the Watchers traditions of 1 En. 7.5 in which the Giants are rendered 'unclean' by the drinking of blood, which, upon their physical deaths, would render the Giants' spirits unclean" ("The Demonology of 1 Enoch and the New Testament Gospels," 235 n. 74). Jub. 10.1 refers to the Giants' spirits as "impure demons."

51. The notion of transference may be implied in Mark 5:28–29; 6:56; 7:33–35; 8:22–25.

52. Jesus rebukes the "sea" θάλασσα on his way to the land of the Gerasenes (Mark 4:39), evoking the Old Testament image of God vanquishing the primordial chaotic waters (Isa 51:9–10; Job 26:11–12; Ps 18:15) (Marcus, *Mark*, 1:338–39).

53. Twelftree, *Jesus the Exorcist*, 75; cf. 155.

54. McLean, "Apotropaeic Rituals," 102.

55. See Moscicke, "Jesus, Barabbas, and the Crowd," 129–30 n. 19. See further in idem, *New Day of Atonement*, 66–71.

56. Stökl Ben Ezra, "Yom Kippur in the Apocalyptic Imaginaire," 354, quote at 356.

57. Bremmer, "The Scapegoat," 191.

58. Stökl Ben Ezra, "Yom Kippur in the Apocalyptic Imaginaire," 354, quote at 356.

59. 4Q180 1 8–9: "And concerning 'Azaz'el [is written . . .] [to love] injustice and to let him inherit evil for all [his] ag[e . . .]" (Martínez and Tigchelaar, *Dead Sea Scrolls*, 1:370–73; cf. John M. Allegro, *Qumran Cave 4. Vol. 1: [4Q158–4Q186]*, DJD 5 [Oxford: Clarendon, 1968], 78). As Reed notes, "it is intriguing that the author distinguishes this Watcher from the rest, singling him out as the one who 'inherits evil'" (*Fallen Angels*, 98). 4Q203 7 I, 5–6: "Then he punished, and not us [bu]t Aza[ze]l" (Martínez and Tigchelaar, *Dead Sea Scrolls*, 1:410–11; cf. Stuckenbruck, *Book of Giants*, 78). According to Milik, "Azazel appears here in his expiatory role (Lev. 16:8, 10, 26), for he seems to be punished for the sins of the giants" (*Enoch*, 313).

60. "Dans les deux cas, c'est bien la même thématique: un transfert du mal de l'homme vers l'animal—d'un côté, des péchés vers le bouc, de l'autre, des démons vers les porcs" (Murcia, "Deux guérisons un jour de Kippour," 152–53).

61. LSJ, 994; BDAG, 566. For example, the army of Judah conquers its enemies by hurling them down a κρημνός (2 Chron 25:12); the Romans casts Jews down κρημνοί to kill them (Josephus, *Ant.* 14.70); Potiphar's wife speaks of committing

suicide by throwing herself down a κρημνός (T. Jos. 7.3); a deer is crippled by a fall from a κρημνός (Dio. Chrys. 7.3); and humans are tossed from a κρημνός in an Hellenistic elimination ritual (Herodotus, *Hist.* 4.103). Josephus describes one particular κρημνός as follows: "[One] must firmly plant each foot alternately. Destruction faces him; for on either side yawn chasms [κρημνῶν] so terrific as to daunt the hardiest" (*J.W.* 7.283 [Thackeray]).

62. M. Yoma 6:6 (Danby, *Mishnah*, 170).

63. Tg. Ps.-J. Lev. 16:22 (McNamara et al., *Targum Pseudo-Jonathan*, 169).

64. *Plant.* 61 (Colson and Whitaker).

65. Knibb, *1 Enoch*, 87. On the subterranean locale of Asael's punishment in 1 Enoch 10, see Tawil, "Azazel," 53–54.

66. Nickelsburg and VanderKam, *1 Enoch*, 121.

67. Apoc. Ab. 14.5 (Kulik, *Slavonic Pseudepigrapha*, 21).

68. According to m. Yoma 6:8, the place of the scapegoat's sending was called "Beith Hadudo," which means "a place jagged and pointed" (Devorah Dimant, "1 Enoch 6–11: A Methodological Perspective," *SBLSP* [1978]: 323–39, at 336 n. 40) (see also Tg. Ps.-J. Lev. 16:10). This rockiness is reflected in Philo ("desolate and vile gulfs," *Plant.* 61) and in 1 En. 10.5 ("lay beneath him [Asael] sharp and jagged stones").

69. On Mark's use of apocalyptic in the Gerasene narrative, see Shively, *Apocalyptic Imagination*, 172–83.

70. Scholars commonly interpret the swine's drowning in the sea as echoing the Exodus narratives (J. Duncan M. Derrett, "Contributions to the Study of the Gerasene Demoniac," *JSNT* 3 [1979]: 2–17, at 6–8). Yet, in the Animal Apocalypse, the Giants meet their fate in the Flood: "And water began to boil up and rise above the ground . . . all the cattle, elephants, camels, and donkeys [the Giants] sank to the bottom along with all the animals . . . and they perished, sinking into the depths" (1 En. 89.3, 6) (Daniel C. Olson, *Enoch, A New Translation. The Ethiopic Book of Enoch, or 1 Enoch* [North Richland Hills: Bibal, 2007], 159–60; see also Wis. 14.6). The place of Azazel's punishment in the Book of Parables (see 1 En. 54.5–6) is elsewhere described as a valley filled with subterranean sulfuric water that becomes so hot that it is transformed into a tormenting fire (1 En. 67.4–13) (see Walck, *Son of Man*, 21–22). The rulers of the earth under Azazel's charge (1 En. 54.1–5; 55.4) are judged in these waters, suffering the same torment as their celestial representatives (67.8–13).

71. Yarbro Collins, *Mark*, 271.

72. Philo, *Spec.* 2.193; cf. 2.196.

73. M. Yoma 8:1.

74. Jub. 34.12, 17–19.

75. Stökl Ben Ezra, *Impact of Yom Kippur*, 34.

76. Scholars have traditionally interpreted the demoniac's violent behavior as reflecting his insanity (Robert A. Guelich, *Mark 1–8:26*, WBC 34A [Dallas: Word Books, 1989], 278) or the demon's destructive force (Marcus, *Mark*, 1:350).

77. See Milgrom, *Leviticus*, 1:1056.

78. Admittedly, there is an element of violence in the demonic possessions or expulsions of Mark 1:26; 9:18, 20, 22, 26.

79. Danby, *Mishnah*, 169.

80. *Marc.* 3.7.7–8 (Evans, *Tertullian*, 191).

81. Nickelsburg and VanderKam, *1 Enoch*, 28.

82. *OTP* 1:695.

83. Guelich, *Mark 1–8*, 280; Gundry, *Mark*, 250; R. T. France, *The Gospel of Mark. A Commentary on the Greek Text*, NIGTC (Grand Rapids: Eerdmans, 2002), 229.

84. Yarbro Collins, *Mark*, 268. So also Gerd Theissen, *The Miracle Stories of the Early Christian Tradition*, trans. Fancis McDonagh (Philadelphia: Fortress, 1983), 89.

85. Theissen, *Miracles Stories*, 57; John R. Donahue and Daniel J. Harrington, *The Gospel of Mark*, SP 2 (Collegeville, MN: Liturgical, 2002), 166. A verbal echo of Leviticus 16 is possibly present in the demon's plea that Jesus "not send them out of the country" (μὴ αὐτὰ ἀποστείλη ἔξω τῆς χώρας, Mark 5:10). The verb ἐξαποστέλλω is used with regard to the "sending out" of the scapegoat into the desert (Lev. 16:21–22, 26). While Mark does not write ἐξαποστέλλω but ἀποστέλλω, a search for ἀποστέλλω used with ἔξω in the New Testament, LXX, Philo, Josephus, the Greek Pseudepigrapha, and the Apostolic Fathers yields only Mark 5:10, making it a rather exceptional combination of words.

86. LSJ, 1425; BDAG, 838.

87. Gundry, *Mark*, 252.

88. On the influence of Yom Kippur on Zechariah 3, see Henri Blocher, "Zacharie 3: Josué et le Grand Jour des Expiations," *ETR* 54 (1979): 264–70; Stökl Ben Ezra, "Yom Kippur in the Apocalyptic Imaginaire," 360–61; M. A. Sweeney, *The Twelve Prophets: Vol. 2* (Collegeville, MN: Liturgical, 2000), 599; Lena-Sofia Tiemeyer, "The Guilty Priesthood (Zech 3)," in *The Book of Zechariah and its Influence*, ed. Christopher Tuckett (Burlington, VT: Ashgate, 2003), 1–19, at 8–11; Stökl Ben Ezra, *Impact of Yom Kippur*, 80–82; Thomas Pola, *Das Priestertum bei Sacharja: Historische und traditionsgeschichtliche Untersuchung zur frühnachexilischen Herrschererwartung* (Tübingen: Mohr Siebeck, 2003), 222; Mark J. Boda, *Haggai, Zechariah* (Grand Rapids: Zondervan, 2004), 258; Byron G. Curtis, *Up the Steep and Stony Road: The Book of Zechariah in Social Location Trajectory Analysis*, AcBib 25 (Atlanta: SBL, 2006), 136; Lena-Sofia Tiemeyer, *Priestly Rites and Prophetic Rage: Post-Exilic Prophetic Critique of the Priesthood* (Tübingen: Mohr Siebeck, 2006), 249–51; Michael R. Stead, *The Intertextuality of Zechariah 1–8*, LHBOTS 506 (London: T&T Clark, 2009), 159–60, 170–72; Orlov, *Atoning Dyad*, 43–48.

89. Nickelsburg and VanderKam, *1 Enoch*, 28.

90. Andrei A. Orlov, *Dark Mirrors: Azazel and Satanael in Early Jewish Demonology* (Albany, NY: State University of New York, 2011), 50.

91. Gundry, *Mark*, 253.

92. France, *Mark*, 232.

93. Collins, *Mark*, 272–73.

94. Philo, *Spec.* 1.186–87 (Colson).

95. In this light, the Gerasene exorcism acquires a distinct sacerdotal quality. See Acts 19:13–14. On priestly characteristics of Jesus in the gospels, see Oscar Cullman,

*The Christology of the New Testament*, trans. S. C. Guthrie and C. A. M. Hall (London: SCM, 1959), 83–89, 130–33; Crispin H. T. Fletcher-Louis, "Jesus as the High Priestly Messiah: Part 1," *JSHJ* 4 (2006): 155–75; idem "Jesus as the High Priestly Messiah: Part 2," *JSHJ* 5 (2007): 57–79; Perrin, *Jesus the Temple*; idem, *Jesus the Priest* (Grand Rapids: Baker, 2018); Joseph L. Angel, "Enoch, Jesus, and Priestly Tradition," in *Enoch and the Synoptic Gospels: Reminiscences, Allusions, Intertextuality*, ed. Loren T. Stuckenbruck and Gabriele Boccaccini, EJL 44 (Atlanta: Scholars, 2016): 285–316.

96. The Gentile man now begs Jesus to be "with him" (Mark 5:18), indicating his new status as a disciple (2:9, 25; 3:14; 5:4; 14:33) and acceptance into the family of God (3:31–35).

97. Luke retains the following parallels: (a) the brutality of the Gerasene demons (Luke 8:29) and the savagery of the Giants (1 En. 15.11), (b) Legion's pleas before Jesus (Luke 8:28, 31) and the Watcher's petition for divine mercy (1 En. 13.4–7), (c) the binding of the demoniac (Luke 8:29) and the binding of Asael (1 En. 10.4), (d) the "torturing" (βασανίζω) of the demoniacs (Luke 8:28) and the "torture" (βάσανος) of the fallen Watchers (1 En. 10.13), (e) the drowning of the pigs in water (Luke 8:33) and the Giants' drowning in the Flood (1 En. 15.8–10; 16.1), and now, (f) the sending of the demons into an abyss (Luke 8:31) and the fallen angels' punishment in an abyss (see above). Luke omits mention of "stones" (λίθοι) (Mark 5:15; cf. 1 En. 10:5), mitigates the sexual innuendo present in Mark 5:12 (cf. 1 En. 8.2; 9.8; 86.1–4), eliminates the "oath" (Mark 5:7; cf. 1 En. 6:4–6), and uses a different verb for "binding" in Luke 8:29 (cf. Mark 5:3–4; 1 En. 10:4, 12).

98. With regard to (C), Luke's narrative portrays the demon's humiliation and maltreatment only slightly less vividly, as he changes Mark's pluperfect verb (ἔλεγεν, 5:8) to a verb in the perfect tense (παρήγγειλεν, Luke 8:29). Regarding (D), Luke highlights the restoration of the demoniac by writing that "for a long time he had worn no clothes" (8:27).

99. Luke follows Mark more closely than Matthew in his redaction of the Gerasene exorcism account, the length and order of his narrative being roughly equivalent to the Markan version.

100. Philo, *Spec.* 1.188 (Colson). See also Philo, *Her.* 179.

101. *Ant.* 3.241 (Thackeray).

102. 1 En. 10.4–5 (Nickelsburg and VanderKam, *1 Enoch*, 28).

103. Apoc. Ab. 14.5–6 (Kulik, *Slavonic Pseudepigrapha*, 21).

104. See Tawil, "Azazel," 44–47; Milgrom, *Leviticus*, 1:1021; Wright, *Disposal of Impurity*, 21–25, 30; Janowski, "Der Bock," 130; Pinker, "Goat to Go to Azazel," 19–25.

105. Philo, *Plant.* 61 (Colson and Whitaker). Philo elsewhere uses the cognate ἀπελαύνω to describe the scapegoat's expulsion: "For the lot which fell to creation is called by the oracles the lot of dismissal, because creation is a homeless wanderer, banished [ἀπελήλαται] far away from wisdom" (*Her.* 179 [Colson and Whitaker]). Other verbs used to depict the scapegoat's "sending" include ἀποστέλλω (Lev. 16:10 LXX), ἀφίημι (Lev. 16:10 LXX), ἐξαποστέλλω (Lev. 16:21–22, 26 LXX; Philo, *Post.* 70), βάλλω (1 En. 10.4; Barn. 7.8), πέμπω (Josephus, *Ant.* 3.240), ἐκπέμπω (Philo, *Spec.* 1.188), παραπέμπω (Justin, *Dial.* 40.4), and ἄγω (Barn. 7.8).

106. Admittedly, the role of the malevolent power differs in both instances. One does the driving into the desert, while the other receives the scapegoat in the desert.

107. The term ἄβυσσος can also refer to the realm of the dead (Psa. 107:26; Rom. 10:7).

108. Jeremias, "ἄβυσσος," *TDNT* 1:9–10; Marshall, *Luke*, 339; Fitzmyer, *Luke*, 739; Nolland, *Luke*, 1:414; Bock, *Luke*, 1:775; Green, *Luke*, 340; Bovon, *Luke*, 1:329; Murcia, "Deux guérisons un jour de Kippour," 2016. On the contrary, Kim Papaioannou remarks, "It is unlikely that the sea is the Abyss to which the demons dread going since this is the one place they rush to as soon as they enter the pigs (*The Geography of Hell in the Teaching of Jesus: Gehenna, Hades, the Abyss, the Outer Darkness Where There is Weeping and Gnashing of Teeth* [Eugene, OR: Wipf and Stock, 2013], 168). Instead, he argues that "the abyss" indicates a place where the demons' powers "have been rendered ineffective" (ibid., 172). This interpretation is improbable, since it is solely premised upon Luke's use of singular verbs with regard to the demoniac's actions in 8:28, as opposed to plural verbs in 8:30. Yet, surely it is the demon, not the man, who recognizes Jesus as "Son of the Most High," as other malevolent powers have so articulated Jesus's heavenly identify prior in the gospel (Luke 4:3, 9, 34). It is therefore most natural to take, "I beg you, do not torment me," which immediately follows, "What have you to do with me, Jesus, Son of the Most High" (8:28), as the demon's speech. Furthermore, the explanatory γάρ clause in 8:29 ("for Jesus had commanded the unclean spirit to come out of the man") makes more sense this way. The demon has far greater reason to expect the exorcism to be tormenting than the man, as the conclusion of the exorcism clearly demonstrates. As Nolland observes, the request not to be tormented in 8:28 parallels the demons' demise in 8:31 (*Luke*, 1:408). And the switch between singular and plural verbs in the demon's speech may simply be a clever way of showcasing the man's possession by a "legion" of demons (8:30). Most Lukan commentators understand the request not to be tormented to be that of the demon(s), not the man (Marshall, *Luke*, 338; Fitzmyer, *Luke*, 738 Nolland, *Luke*, 1:408; Johnson, *Luke*, 137; Bock, *Luke*, 1:772; Green, *Luke*, 338–39; Bovon, *Luke*, 1:327).

109. Bovon, *Luke*, 1:329.

110. 1 En. 9.4 of Syncellus[1] reads: "Then the Most High commanded the holy archangels, and they bound their leaders and cast them into the abyss [εἰς τὴν ἄβυσσον], until the judgment" (Black and Denis, *Apocalypsis Henochi Graece*, 23). According to Archie Wright, "Asa'el is first to face his punishment for his role in the Instruction motif of *BW* (10.4–6, 8). He will be bound and cast into the darkness where he will be entombed until the Day of Judgment at which time he will be destroyed in the fire. The angels from the Shemihazah tradition face a similar punishment in 10.11–14. They will first view the death of their offspring (10.12) and secondly, they shall be bound under the earth until their judgment (10.12). The judgment occurs after seventy generations of entombment at which time they shall be cast into the fire where they will be destroyed (10.13–14)" (*The Origin of Evil Spirits: The Reception of Genesis 6:1–4 in Early Jewish Literature* [Tübingen: Mohr Siebeck, 2005], 145–46).

111. Nickelsburg and VanderKam, *1 Enoch*, 121.

112. Ibid., 68. Kelley Coblentz Bautch remarks that "the pattern recurs in the Animal Apocalypse as the Watchers are first consigned to an abyss (1 Enoch 88.1, 3) described as deep, dark and of the earth. At the time of the eschaton, the angels are brought forward for judgment (1 Enoch 90.21) and then thrown into a fiery abyss along with other sinners (1 Enoch 90.24–26). The Book of Parables describes a similar fate: chains are prepared for the host of Azazel (a later rendering of Asael and a reference to one of the Watchers) so that they might be thrown into an abyss of complete judgment and covered with jagged stones (cf. 1 Enoch 10.5). On the day of judgment, we are told, the archangels will throw the rebels into a burning furnace because they became servants of Satan and led astray humankind (54.3–6)" ("The Fall and Fate of Renegade Angels: The Intersection of Watchers Traditions and the Book of Revelation," in *The Fallen Angels Traditions: Second Temple Developments and Reception History*, ed. Angela Kim Harkins, Kelley Coblentz Bautch, and John C. Endres S.J., CBQMS 53 [Washington, DC: Catholic Biblical Association of America, 2014], 69–93, at 84).

113. Reflecting on the complexity of traditions regarding the punishment of the renegade angels, Patrick A. Tiller writes that "in both the Book of the Watchers and the Animal Apocalypse, there are two prisons into which the Watchers will be cast. The first, a temporary prison, is described as two separate places in 10.4–5 (=88.1) and 10.12 (=88.3). In 18.12–16 and 21.1–6 these two places are combined into a single prison for both the wandering and the fallen angles. In the later part of the Book of the Watchers (18.12–16; 21.1–6), the prison is not an abyss at all but a dark, desert wasteland. In chapters 6–12, it is not clear whether the temporary prisons are abysses or not. The permanent prison, the abyss of fire, is described in 10.6, 13; 18.9–11; and 21.7–10 in the Book of the Watchers and in 90.24–25 in the Animal Apocalypse. The abyss described by Jude seems to be a composite of all these prisons: it is dark (10.4–5; 88.1); it is reserved for the wandering stars (18.12–16; 21.1–6); and it is eternal (10.6, 13; 21.7–10)" (*A Commentary on the Animal Apocalypse of 1 Enoch*, EJL 4 [Atlanta: Scholars, 1993], 252–54).

114. Grabbe summarily remarks, "Although there is no explicit reference to the scapegoat ceremony, Rev. 20, 1–3, 10 has clear connections with 1 Enoch 10.4–5. Note the common features: Asael is bound prior to the judgment just as is Satan. (This binding seems to include chains, according to 1 Enoch 54.3–5. . .). Just as Satan is cast into the abyss, so are Asael and others according to Syncellus' version of 1 Enoch 9.4 . . . In the final judgment, just as Satan is cast into a 'lake of fire' . . . so Asael and his companions are cast into an 'abyss of fire' . . . Thus, the punishment of Satan has been assimilated to the Asael tradition of 1 Enoch" ("The Scapegoat Tradition," 160–61). According to David Aune, "Since the narrative pattern found twice in Rev. 20:1–10 (i.e., in vv. 1–3 and 7–10) also occurs twice in 1 Enoch [i.e., 10.4–6; 10.11–12], it seems likely that both authors are dependent on a traditional eschatological scenario. The enumeration of motifs found in these three passages exhibits a striking similarity, though John has introduced the innovation of the temporary release of Satan" (*Revelation 17–22*, WBC 52 [Nashville: Thomas Nelson, 1998], 1078–79). Andrei A. Orlov enumerates the impact of the scapegoat tradition on Revelation 20 even further (*Demons of Change: Antagonism and Apotheosis in Jewish and*

*Christian Apocalypticism* [Albany, NY: State University of New York, 2020], 109–118).

115. Green, *Luke*, 340 (cf. Nolland, *Luke*, 1:409).

116. "Desert" (ἔρημος) occurs 24 times in Luke-Acts, always in the singular except in Luke 1:80; 5:16; 8:29. The plural in Luke 5:16 is not redactional but taken from Mark 1:45, and the phrase ἐν ταῖς ἐρήμοις in Luke 1:80 differs from that in 8:29 (εἰς τὰς ἐρήμους).

117. On the influence of the Day of Atonement on Luke's Nazareth narrative (4:16–30), see chapter 3, in which I suggest that the allusions to Yom Kippur in that narrative derive principally from Luke's special material. Sverre Aalen ("St. Luke's Gospel and the Last Chapters of 1 Enoch," *NTS* 13 [1966]: 1–13) and George W. E. Nickelsburg ("Revisiting the Rich and the Poor in 1 Enoch 92–105 and the Gospel according to Luke," in *George W. E. Nickelsburg in Perspective: An Ongoing Dialogue of Learning*, ed. Jacob Neusner and Alan J. Avery-Peck, 2 vols., JSJSup 80 [Leiden: Brill, 2003], 2:547–71) have argued for the influence of the Epistle of Enoch on the Parable of the Rich Man and Lazarus (Luke 16:19–31). Leslie Baynes further argues for the impact of the Parables of Enoch on that same Lukan parable and in several other instances in the gospel ("The Parables of Enoch and Luke's Parable of the Rich Man and Lazarus," in *Enoch and the Synoptic Gospels: Reminiscences, Allusions, Intertextuality*, ed. Loren T. Stuckenbruck and Gabriele Boccaccini, EJL 44 [Atlanta: SBL, 2016], 129–52). As compelling as some of the proposed allusions may be, scholars are still generally doubtful that Luke was acquainted with the Enochic corpus.

118. Scholars struggle to explain the reason for Matthew's abbreviation of the Markan story. Luz remarks, "Thus the primary question for the interpretation is what Matthew was trying to do with his abridgment, or, perhaps, what is was about the Marcan narrative that bothered him" (*Matthew*, 2:23).

119. Matthew retains the following parallels: (a) the fierceness of the demoniac (Matt. 8:28) and the savagery of the Giants (1 En. 15.11), (b) the demons' plea before Jesus (Matt. 8:31) and the Watcher's petition for divine mercy (1 En. 13.4–7), (c) the "torturing" (βασανίζω) of the demons (Matt. 8:29) and the "torture" (βάσανος) of the fallen Watchers (1 En. 10.13), and (d) the drowning of the pigs in water (Matt. 8:32, here specifically called τοῖς ὕδασιν) and the Giants' drowning in the Flood (1 En. 15.8–10; 16.1). Matthew omits mention of "stones" (λίθοι) (Mark 5:15; cf. 1 En. 10:5), mitigates the sexual innuendo present in Mark 5:12 (cf. 1 En. 8.2; 9.8; 86.1–4), eliminates the "oath" (Mark 5:7; cf. 1 En. 6:4–6), and omits the "binding" of the demoniac (Mark 5:3–4; Luke 8:29; cf. 1 En. 10:4, 12).

120. Davies and Allison, *Matthew*, 2:80. The most popular of these seem to be (a) Matthew's desire to conform to the need for more than one witness (Deut. 17:6; cf. Matt. 18:15–16; 26:60), (b) Matthew is compensating for omitting the story of the demoniac in Mark 1:21–29, and, (c) since the demon's name is "Legion," Matthew feels at liberty to multiply the number of demoniacs for narrative effect.

121. France, *Matthew*, 339. As is often noted, Matthew doubles the number of blind individuals healed by Jesus (Matt. 9:27–28; 20:30; cf. Mark 10:46), doubles the number of animals that Jesus rides into Jerusalem (Matt. 21:2, 7; cf. Mark 11:2, 7),

and includes two witnesses at Jesus's trial before the Sanhedrin (Matt. 26:60; cf. Mark 14:57). As France notes, however, the instance of the donkey and the colt (Matt. 21:2, 7) has more to do with the scriptural fulfillment of Zech 9:9 (ibid.).

122. Danby, *Mishnah*, 169.

123. I have modified the translation of Falls, *Dialogue with Trypho*, 62.

124. See Wratislaw, *Notes and Dissertation*, 18; Stökl Ben Ezra, *Impact of Yom Kippur*, 165–74; idem, "Fasting with Jews," 179–84; Berenson Maclean, "Barabbas," 324–30; Moscicke, *New Day of Atonement*, 105–111.

125. See Moscicke, *New Day of Atonement*, 99–180.

126. On καιρός as a descriptor for the "end time" in other biblical and related literature, see Davies and Allison, *Matthew*, 2:582 n. 14.

127. So Meier, *Matthew*, 90; Gundry, *Matthew*, 182; Davies and Allison, *Matthew*, 2:81–82; Nolland, *Matthew*, 375–76; France, *Matthew*, 341. Cf. Luz, *Matthew*, 2:24.

128. This proposal was confirmed by the parallel scene of eschatological expulsion described in Matt. 22:13, the language of which almost certainly appropriates Asael/Azazel traditions (again, see Chapter One; 1 En. 10.4).

129. See note above on the various terms used for the scapegoat's "sending" in Leviticus 16 LXX and other early Jewish and Christian literature.

130. Davies and Allison, *Matthew*, 2:84

131. Twelftree, *Jesus the Exorcist*, 75.

132. Klutz, Exorcism Stories in Luke-Acts, 146.

133. The name Λεγιών brings to mind Roman military force, which explains the choice of swine—a comical jab at the *Legio X Fretensis*, who carried the standard of a boar (see Marcus, *Mark*, 1:351; Stephen D. Moore, *Empire and Apocalypse: Postcolonialism and the New Testament*, BMW 12 [Sheffield: Sheffield Phoenix, 2006], 24–44; Markus Lau, "Die *Legio X Fretensis* und der Besessene von Gerasa: Anmerkungen zur Zahlenangabe 'ungefähr Zweitausend' [Mk 5,13]," *Bib* 88 [2007]: 351–64; Yarbro Collins, *Mark*, 270; Ched Myers, *Binding the Strong Man: A Political Reading of Mark's Story of Jesus* [Maryknoll, NY: Orbis, 2008 (1988)], 190–92). The message seems to be that, as in 1 En. 54.1–5 and 67.4–13, the fate of Legion's earthly counterparts (the Roman army) are equally destined for eschatological judgment.

# Chapter 5

# Jesus's Atonement and Heavenly Ascent in John's Resurrection Narrative (John 20:11–23)

A number of scholars have suggested that John's empty tomb narrative evokes the imagery of the cherubim stationed at either side of the "mercy seat" or "atonement slate" slate in the Holy of Holies, when he writes that Mary Magdalene entered the tomb and "saw two angels in white, sitting where the body of Jesus had been lying, one at the head and the other at the feet" (John 20:12).[1] As such, the two angels arguably recall the cherubim situated at either end of the of atonement slate, "one cherub at one end, and one cherub at the other" (Ezek. 25:19).

Recently, two students of John's Gospel have attempted to bolster the case for this reading, but they have done so unconvincingly in my opinion.[2] Yet the case for an allusion to the image of the cherubim and the atonement slate in John 20:12 remains quite strong, and there is more evidence that has yet to be presented for it. Admittedly, this evidence is of an indirect nature and consists of neither scriptural allusions nor typological patterns. Nevertheless, it seems that the cultic imagery associated with Yom Kippur that has contributed to John's evocation of the Holy of Holies has indirectly impacted other aspects of his resurrection narrative as well. Not only does the conceptual clustering of themes pertaining to the Day of Atonement in John 20 strengthens the case for an allusion to the cherubim and atonement slate in 20:12 but it also enhances our understanding of John's notion of Jesus as the eschatological temple and sheds potential light on the evangelist's theology of atonement.

## JESUS AS ESCHATOLOGICAL TEMPLE
## IN THE GOSPEL OF JOHN

John's temple theology has received much scholarly attention in recent years, and it alerts us to his interest in sacerdotal traditions.[3] The evangelist's notion that Jesus is the fulfillment or replacement of the Jerusalem temple is perhaps clearest in John 2:18–22.[4] Here, while standing in the temple in dialogue with "the Jews," Jesus says, "Destroy this temple, and in three days I will raise it up" (2:19). Though he is taken to be threatening the existence of the Jerusalem temple, John clarifies Jesus's statement with a note that "he was speaking about the temple [ναός] of his body" (John 2:21). According to Mary Coloe, "The placement of this scene, at the beginning of Jesus's public activity rather than at its conclusion as depicted in the Synoptics (Mark 11:15–19 and par.), establishes the image of the temple as a major interpretive clue for understanding the gospel's portrait of Jesus and his mission."[5]

This Christological temple theme, however, first appears in John's prologue, in which the evangelist writes that "the Word became flesh and dwelt [ἐσκήνωσεν] among us, and we have seen his glory" (John 1:14). As Paul Hoskins notes, the LXX frequently uses the term σκηνή in reference to the tabernacle, and the tabernacle was designated a special dwelling place for God's "glory" in the Old Testament (Exod. 40:34–35; Lev. 9:23; Num. 14:10; 16:19, 42; 20:6).[6] The point of the evangelist is that the "Jesus is now the dwelling place of God. The glory once visible in Israel's tabernacle and temple can now be seen in Jesus."[7]

Then, in his conversation with Nathanael, Jesus says, "You will see heaven opened and the angels of God ascending and descending on the Son of Man" (John 1:51). This is an allusion to Gen. 28:12, where Jacob sees a vision of angels ascending and descending a ladder that reaches to heaven. As Greg Beale notices, Jacob, using a stone, establishes a miniature sanctuary in response to his theophanic vision: "And this stone, which I have set up for a pillar, shall be God's house" (Gen. 28:22). Expositing the scriptural allusion, Beale remarks that "Jesus's identification of himself with the temple stairway of Genesis 28 is thus another way of claiming that he, not the Jerusalem temple, is the primary link between heaven and earth."[8]

Following the explicit identification of Jesus as a temple in John 2:21, Jesus tells the Samaritan woman that "those who drink of the water that I will give them will never be thirsty. The water that I will give will become in them a spring of water gushing up to eternal life" (John 4:14). According to Hoskins, this story develops John's temple theology and insists that Jesus is the replacement of the Jerusalem temple, wherein God is to be worshiped "in spirit and truth" (John 4:23–24).[9] Beale notices that the image of "living water" (John 4:11) and a "spring of water" (John 4:14) recalls the rivers that flow forth from temples in the Old Testament.[10] This temple symbolism likely also undergirds Jesus's statement in John 7:37–38: "Let anyone who is thirsty come to me, and let the one who believes in me drink. As the Scripture has said, 'Out of the believer's heart shall flow rivers of living water'."[11] Finally, as Bruce Grigsby has suggested, the water that flows from Jesus's side when he is pierced in John 19:34 "appears to thematically culminate the Evangelist's development of the 'living water' theme," pointing to Jesus's fulfillment of the temple's cultic functions by establishing God's presence among his people by giving them the Holy Spirit (cf. John 20:22), which operates in conjunction with the symbolism of blood flowing from Jesus's side, signaling the expiation accomplished by Jesus's sacrifice (cf. John 1:29).[12]

While other verses in the Gospel of John may evoke the temple theme,[13] the foregoing is sufficient to establish the Fourth Evangelist's notion that Jesus is the fulfillment or replacement of the Jerusalem temple. Given the centrality of this theme in the gospel, one would expect to find further allusions to the temple in John's resurrection narrative. In fact, John likely alludes to the holiest domain within the temple precincts—the Holy of Holies—not long in his story of the risen Jesus.

## CHERUBIM AND ATONEMENT SLATE

In recent years, scholars have suggested that John's description of the "two angels in white, sitting where the body of Jesus had been lying, one at the head and the other at the feet" (John 20:12), is intended to evoke the cherubim stationed at either side of the atonement slate in the Holy of Holies.[14] The principal scriptural basis for this proposed allusion is Exod. 25:17–22 (cf. 37:7–9):

> Then you shall make a mercy seat of pure gold; two cubits and a half shall be its length, and a cubit and a half its width. *You shall make two cherubim of gold*; you shall make them of hammered work, *at the two ends of the mercy seat. Make one cherub at the one end, and one cherub at the other; of one piece with the mercy seat you shall make the cherubim at its two ends.* The cherubim shall spread out their wings above, overshadowing the mercy seat with their wings. *They shall face one to another; the faces of the cherubim shall be turned toward the mercy seat.* You shall put the mercy seat on the top of the ark; and in the ark you shall put the covenant that I shall give you. There I will meet with you, and from above the mercy seat, *from between the two cherubim that are on the ark of the covenant*, I will deliver to you all my commands for the Israelites.

According to Philippe Simenel, this biblical passage evinces "a very strong
spatial analogy with the text of John."[15] Rewriting the Exodus text with the
parallels in brackets, Simenel remarks, "And you will make two golden
cherubim [two angels], make a cherub at one end [one at the head], and the
other cherub at the other end [the other at the feet], you will place the mercy
seat above the ark, and in the ark, you will place the charter of the covenant
that I will give you [at the place where Jesus was deposited]."[16] As Izaak
Hulster notices, though not a direct verbal parallel, the phrase, "one cherub at
one end, and one cherub at the other" (Ezek. 25:19), closely resembles John
20:12, "one at the head, and one at the feet."[17]

    In biblical literature, the cherubim appear in two basic roles, "as guard-
ians of a sacred tree or as guardians and carriers of a throne."[18] The image
of two cherubim hovering over the atonement slate, on which God was
conceived as sitting enthroned (1 Sam. 4:4; 2 Sam. 6:2; 2 Kgs. 19:15; 1
Chron. 13:6; Psa. 80:1; 99:1; Isa. 37:16; Sib. Or. 3.1), whether in the tabernacle (Exod. 25:17–22; 37:7–9; 1 Chron. 28:18) or in the temple (1 Kgs.
6:23–28), was well known in the Second Temple period (11Q19 VII, 10;
Philo, *Cher.* 25; *Her.* 166; *Fug.* 100–101; *Mos.* 2.97; Josephus, *Ant.* 3.137;
7.378; 8.72–73; 8.103; LAB 26.12; Lad. Jac. 2.7). In apocalyptic circles
associated with *merkabah* mysticism, rooted in Ezekiel's vision of the
*kavod* (Ezek. 1:4–28; 10:1–22),[19] the cherubim are reimagined as celestial
beings ministering before the heavenly throne of God (1 En. 14.11, 18;
4Q286; 1 II, 1; 4Q403 1 II, 15; 4Q405 20–22; 1 En. 61.10; 71.7; 2 En. 21.1;
22.2). Cherubim also appear in a number of arboreal settings often associated with the garden of Eden (Gen. 3:24; 1 Kgs 6:29–35; Ezek. 28:14, 16;
41:18–20, 25; 1 En. 20.7; Philo, *Cher.* 11, 20–25, 28; Apoc. Mos. 19.2;
22.3; 28.3; 32.2; 38.3). Though their number in these contexts is not always
clear, these cherubim appear in pairs in Ezekiel's temple vision, in which
they are depicted as guardians of a sacred tree (Ezek. 41:18–20, 25). Philo
also understands the number of cherubim stationed in the garden of Eden to
be two (*Cher.* 20–25). Conflating both traditions, the Life of Adam and Eve
(Greek) describes God as traveling through the primordial garden while
seated upon a chariot of cherubim (Apoc. Mos. 22.3; 38.3).

    Hulster points out that cherubim could be regarded as "angels" (ἄγγελοι)
in the Second Temple period, in which ἄγγελοι could refer generically to
"heavenly beings."[20] As to why John places "angels" instead of "cherubim"
in the tomb, Hulster remarks that "ἄγγελοι was probably the best word which
fit the resurrection account (in line with the gospel's presumed sources) and
meanwhile could evoke the association with the beings on the cover of the
Ark of the Covenant."[21] He further notices that empty space occupies the ter-
ritory in between both the cherubim of the ark (Exod. 25:20; 1 Kgs. 6:27) and
the angels in Jesus's tomb (John 20:13).[22]

Not only is there a numeric and spatial correspondence between the two angels at either side of where Jesus lay and the two cherubim at either side of the atonement slate, but the garden context of the angelic figures in the Gospel of John recalls the arboreal setting often associated with the cherubim in Jewish thought.[23] The arboreal setting of Jesus's tomb strengthens the evocation of the cherubim in John 20:12, as only John reports that Jesus's tomb resided in a "garden" (κῆπος, John 19:41).[24]

Given the numeric, spatial, and arboreal connections between the angels at Jesus's tomb and the cherubim in the Holy of Holies, Hulster's conclusion is justified, that "while not every reader would have picked up this allusion, those rooted in the tradition of the Old Testament and aware of John's Gospel's dependence on the Jewish traditions probably would have noticed this allusion to the Ark."[25] This cultic and perhaps scriptural allusion to the ark of the covenant augments John's temple Christology, enjoining it to the conceptual matrix associated with the mercy seat in the Holy of Holies, which featured prominently on the Day of Atonement.

## GARDEN SETTING

Only the Fourth Evangelist reports that Jesus's tomb was located in a "garden" (John 19:41) and that Mary identified Jesus as "the gardener" upon first seeing him (John 20:15). This garden setting seems to be at the forefront of the evangelist's thought during the scene at the tomb, since he narrates that Mary, upon seeing the risen Jesus, thought that he was "the gardener" (ὁ κηπουρός, John 20:15). Some commentators doubt that John intends this arboreal context to evoke the garden of Eden, since the evangelist writes κῆπος instead of παράδεισος—the term that occurs throughout Genesis 2–3 LXX.[26] However, both Aquila and Theodotion employ κῆπος to refer to the garden of Eden (Gen. 3:1 LXX), and Jewish authors sometimes used this word when speaking of the primordial garden of God (Ezek. 36:35 LXX; Sib. Or. *Frag.* 3.47; Josephus, *Ant.* 1.38, 45, 51). That being said, a direct link to the garden of Eden seems unlikely. Yet, that John calls the reader's attention to the arboreal setting of the tomb twice throughout the short narrative is peculiar and may suggest the arboreal imagery associated with temple cults in the ancient world.

The prolific link between gardens and temples is well known and does not need to be established here.[27] Summarizing some of the symbolism associated with the Jewish temple, Alex Douglas remarks:

> The temple was viewed as a model of the cosmos, and we can clearly see both Eden's paradisiacal state and the creation of the world reflected in its

construction. In fact, much in the temple was designed to emulate and recreate the Garden of Eden for Israelite worshippers. For example, the interior of the temple was made entirely of cedar, and as Solomon decorated the walls, the Bible tells us that "he carved all the walls of the house round about with carved figures of cherubim and palm trees and open flowers, within and without" (1 Kings 6:29). The palm trees and flowers alone would conjure images of Eden, but the cherubim make the reference certain . . . In Eden, cherubim were placed to guard the way to the tree of life, and in the temple, two giant cherubim—each fifteen feet tall—guarded the entrance to the Holy of Holies (see 1 Kings 6:23–28) . . . According to Ezekiel 28:13–14, "Eden the garden of God" is located "upon the holy mountain of God." Eden was a temple where the presence of God dwelled . . . Consistent with the mountain imagery associated with Eden and the temple, both are also the source of rivers that flow out and provide life to the surrounding area . . . the restored millennial temple is also pictured with a river flowing out from its base to water the earth. (see Ezekiel 47:1–12; Zechariah 14:3–8; Joel 3:16–18)[28]

According to Jon Levenson, "in the ancient Near East, gardens, especially royal gardens, are not simply decorate. They are symbolic, and their religious message is very much involved with that of the Temple in or near which they are not infrequently found."[29]

Not only were some Jewish authors in the first century acquainted with such arboreal symbolism associated with the temple,[30] John himself seems to betray an awareness of it, when Jesus tells the Samaritan woman that "those who drink of the water that I will give them will never be thirsty. The water that I will give will become in them a spring of water gushing up to eternal life" (John 4:14). This temple symbolism likely also undergirds Jesus's statement in John 7:37–38: "Let anyone who is thirsty come to me, and let the one who believes in me drink. As the Scripture has said, 'Out of the believer's heart shall flow rivers of living water'."[31] While John does not explicitly employ garden imagery to speak of the eschatological temple, the link he creates between water and temple operates within the same symbolic domain. In fact, immediately after the empty-tomb narrative, the evangelist recalls this water-temple motif, when Jesus appears to his disciples and breathes the Holy Spirit upon them (John 20:22). This scene fulfills the water-Spirit saying of John 7:37–39, in which the phrase "rivers of living water" is interpreted as the Spirit, "which believers in him were to receive" (John 7:39).[32] As Hoskins notes, "Clearly, the Spirit is the key gift that flows out from Jesus, the true Temple."[33]

The garden setting of the empty tomb narrative enhances the cultic elements of the resurrection story. This cultic shading becomes more apparent in the following scene, in which Jesus fulfills the role of the eschatological temple by imparting the Holy Spirit to his disciples (John 20:22; cf. 7:37–39) and by endowing them with the priestly ability to forgive or retain sins (John 20:23).

## MOURNING AND WEEPING

While it is fitting for a disciple of Jesus to mourn at his burial site, the Fourth Evangelist writes the verb "to weep" (κλαίω) a total of four times in his story of Mary Magdalen's interaction with Jesus at the tomb, suggesting that the theme holds some significance for the gospel writer. First, John narrates that "Mary stood weeping [κλαίουσα] outside the tomb. As she wept [ἔκλαιεν], she stooped down into the tomb" (John 20:11). The angels then ask her, "Woman, why are you weaping [κλαίεις]?" (John 20:13). Finally, Jesus asks her, "Woman, why are you weeping [κλαίεις]? Whom do you seek?" (John 20:15).

While mention of Mary's weeping prepares the reader for her mistaking Jesus for "the gardener" (John 20:15), John's repeated emphasis on weeping reminds one of the traditions regarding mourning on the Day of Atonement. As noted earlier, the patriarch Jacob's intense mourning for his son Joseph becomes an etiological for the Day of Atonement in the Book of Jubilees:

> Jacob's sons slaughtered a he-goat, stained Joseph's clothing by dipping it in its blood, and sent (it) to their father Jacob on the tenth of the seventh month . . . [Jacob] continued mourning Joseph for one year and was not comforted but said: "May I go down to the grave mourning for my son." For this reason, it has been ordained regarding the Israelites that they should be distressed on the tenth of the seventh month—on the day when (the news) which made (him) lament Joseph reached his father Jacob—in order to make atonement for themselves on it with a kid—on the tenth of the seventh month, once a year—for their sins.[34]

Anke Dorman suggests that this phenomenon of mourning, a later interpretation of the command to "afflict yourselves" (Lev. 16:29, 31; 23:27–32; Num. 29:7), "seems to be the most important aspect of the festival in Jubilees."[35]

The Epistle of Barnabas, which makes use of early Jewish Yom Kippur traditions, also mentions mourning as part of the customs of the Day of Atonement: "What then does he say in the prophet? 'Let them eat some of the goat offered for all sins on the day of fasting' [Yom Kippur] . . . you alone are to eat, while the people fast and mourn in sackcloth and ashes."[36]

John's repeated emphasis on Mary's weeping, though not a direct allusion to the Day of Atonement, fits well within a cultic reading of the empty tomb narrative. If the empty slab where Jesus's body had lain evokes the atonement slate utilized on Yom Kippur, then Mary's mourning adumbrates the solemnity of the atonement achieved by Jesus's sacrifice for the people.

## HEAVENLY ASCENSION

After Mary Magdalene recognizes the risen Lord, Jesus makes the following enigmatic statement, "Do not hold on to me, for I have not yet ascended to the Father. But go to my brothers and say to them, 'I am ascending to my Father and your Father, to my God and your God" (John 20:17). This verse has proven difficult to interpret because the same risen Jesus invites Thomas to touch his body later in the narrative (John 20:27), which seems to contradict his statement to Mary. In his brilliant discussion of this passage, Raymond Brown shows that the scholarly confusion revolves around a misunderstanding of the ascension in Johannine theology. Just as John reinterprets the crucifixion to be part of Jesus's glorification, so he interprets the resurrection to be part of Jesus's ascension.[37] Thus, Mary "mistakes an appearance of the risen Jesus for his permanent presence with his disciples."[38] The statement, "I am ascending to my Father" (John 20:17), "is a theological statement contrasting the passing nature of Jesus' presence in his post-resurrectional appearances and the permanent nature of his presence in the Spirit."[39]

John's conflation of Jesus's resurrection with Jesus's ascension casts his allusion to the cherubim and atonement slate in a new light. One is reminded of the high priest's unique privilege of entering the Holy of Holies to purges sins from the atonement slate once a year (Lev. 16:11–17), a tradition which later Jewish writers utilized in their accounts of the patriarchs' ascensions into the cosmic sanctuary.[40] The explicit mention of Jesus's ascension in John 20:17 foregrounds the entire scene at the tomb (20:11–18) against the theme of Jesus's exaltation to the heavenly Father (cf. John 14:12, 28; 16:5, 10, 28).[41] It makes one wonder whether John's allusion to the sanctuary's adytum in 20:12 indicates that Jesus's atoning work was ultimately accomplished only after his ascension to the Father. If so, John's theology of atonement would seem to diverge from the Synoptic tradition and align more closely with the author of the Epistle to the Hebrews, who conceives the (resurrected and) ascended Jesus as a high priest who makes atonement before God in the heavenly sanctuary:[42]

> But when Christ came as a high priest of the good things that have come, then through the greater and perfect tent (not made with hands, that is, not of this creation), he entered once for all into the Holy Place, not with the blood of goats and calves, but with his own blood . . . But when Christs had offered for all time a single sacrifice for sins, he sat down at the right hand of God. (Heb. 9:24, 26; 10:12)

On this note, Raymond Brown had interestingly remarked, "Perhaps it would have been more logical if John had joined the author of the Epistle to the Hebrews in having Jesus go directly to the Father from the cross, for the resurrection does not fit easily into John's theology of crucifixion."[43] That is to say, Jesus's ascension/exaltation may factor into John's understanding of Jesus's atonement more than scholarship has previously considered.

## Theophanic Vision

Commentators often pass over Mary Magdalene's declaration to the disciples, "I have seen the Lord" (John 20:18), with little exposition.[44] Yet the notion of theophany or the vision of God is an important term in the conceptual lexicon of Yom Kippur. The Hebrew Bible stresses that the Holy of Holies, and more specifically the ark of the covenant, is the place of God's unique presence. At the beginning of the instructions for the Day of Atonement, Aaron is warned against entering the adytum at any time, "for I will appear in the cloud upon the mercy seat" (Lev. 16:2). God tells Moses, "There I will meet you, and from above the mercy seat, from between the two cherubim that are on the ark of the covenant" (Exod. 25:22). When the tabernacle and temple are respectively completed, the Hebrew Bible vividly narrates the coming and dwelling of God in the most holy place (Exod. 40:34–35; 1 Kgs. 8:10–12).

Stökl Ben Ezra notes that, in the post-exilic period, certain apocalyptic texts "depict the vision of God as an ascent of the visionary to the heavenly holy of holies, using allusions to the entrance of the high priest on Yom Kippur."[45] The clearest example is 1 Enoch 14, where the antediluvian patriarch ascends into the celestial sanctuary and sees the following:

> And I was looking and I saw a lofty throne; and its appearance was like ice, and its wheels like the shining sun, and the voice (*or* sound) of the cherubim, and from beneath the throne issued rivers of flaming fire. And I was unable to see. The Great Glory sat upon it; his apparel was like the appearance of the sun and whiter than much snow. No angel could enter this house and look at his face because of the splendor and glory, and no human could look at him.[46]

The Apocalypse of Abraham describes a similar scene upon the patriarch's ascent into the heavenly realm:

> And as the fire rose up, soaring hiring, I saw under the fire a throne [made] of fire and the many-eyed Wheels, and they are reciting the song. And under the throne [I saw] four singing fiery Living Creatures . . . And above the Wheels there was the throne which I had seen. And I was covered with fire and the fire encircled round about, and an indescribable light surrounded the fiery people.[47]

In a non-apocalyptic context, Philo of Alexandria conceptualizes the high priest's entrance into the Holy of Holies as the soul's journey toward virtue or the vision of God. In one of his works, he writes:

> To him [the high priest] it is permitted to enter once a year and behold the sights which are forbidden to others, because in him alone of all resides the winged and heavenly yearning for those forms of good which are incorporeal and imperishable. And so, when smitten by its ideal beauty he follows that archetype which creates by impress the particular virtues, beholding with ecstasy its most divine loveliness.[48]

Stökl Ben Ezra observes that "Philo is the first to refer explicitly to Yom Kippur and quote Leviticus 16 in order to depict the mystical ascent of the soul to God in his heavenly abode . . . this may have the character of a vision or even of a meeting with the divine."[49]

Again, while Mary Magdalene's revelatory statement, "I have seen the Lord," does not directly recall the Day of Atonement, it fits nicely within the larger conceptual matrix of the theophanic visions of God often associated with Yom Kippur and the high priest's entrance into the Holy of Holies. The language of theophany continues into the next narrative segment, when the disciples "see" the Lord (John 20:20, 25) and Thomas utters his famous declaration, "My Lord and my God!" (John 20:28).

## FORGIVENESS OF SINS

As noted previously, Jesus's gift of the Holy Spirit to his disciples (John 20:22) fulfills his promise to give "rivers of living water" to the one who believes in him (John 7:37–39), and that this imagery is rooted in the notion of Jesus as an eschatological temple. Thus, John's temple theology seems to lurk behind the episode of John 20:19–23. This is affirmed by the evangelist's choice to have Jesus show "his hands and his side [πλευρά]" to his disciples (John 20:20), recalling Jesus's pierced "side" (πλευρά), from which blood and water flowed on the cross (John 19:34) (recall that water symbolizes the Spirit in John).

The granting of authority to the disciples to forgive sins also appears to be a part of John's temple theology. As Herman Ridderbos remarks, "By the Spirit, whom Jesus bestows on the apostles for the fulfillment of their task, he shows himself to be present in them as the living Lord who forgives sins on earth."[50] In other words, Jesus extends the function of the eschatological temple, in its capacity to grant atonement, to his disciples by means of the Holy Spirit. Thus, three elements of John 20:19–23 should be understood within the evangelist's larger temple theology: (a) the revealing of Jesus's "side" to the disciples (20:20), which recalls the water and blood that flowed from Jesus's "side" on the cross (19:34), (b) the gift of the Holy Spirit (20:22), which recalls the promise of "living water" to believers (7:37–39), and the authority to forgive sins (20:23).

This final element directly relates to the principal theme of Yom Kippur, namely, atonement. As Lev. 16:30 states, "For on this day atonement shall be made for you, to cleanse you; from all your sins you shall be clean before the Lord." Philo provides a sense of how important this holy day was for Jews in the Second Temple period to procure personal forgiveness of sins:

> [T]he holy-day is entirely devoted to prayers and supplications, and men from morn to eve employ their leisure in nothing else but offering petitions of humble entreaty in which they seek earnestly to propitiate God and ask for remission of their sins, voluntary and involuntary, and entertain bright hopes looking not to their own merits but to the gracious nature of Him Who sets pardon before chastisement.[51]

Similarly, the Psalms of Solomon relay that, on the Day of Atonement, "[t]he righteous constantly searches his house, to remove his unintentional sins. He atones for (sins of) ignorance by fasting and humbling his soul, and the Lord will cleanse every devout person and his house."[52] The Qumran scroll 11QMelchizedek, the apocalyptic-minded community associated an eschatological Yom Kippur with the liberation of God's chosen from "the debt of all their iniquities" (11Q13 II, 6).

Jesus's discourse with his disciples on the forgiveness of sins (John 20:23), then, not only bears a direct relationship to John's larger Christological temple theology but is, once again, congruous with key themes associated with the Day of Atonement in the first century.

## CONCLUSION

It seems that the cultic imagery associated with Yom Kippur that has contributed to the evocation of the cherubim and atonement slate in the Holy of Holies in John 20:12 has subtly impacted other aspects of John's resurrection narrative, particularly in John 20:11–18, though it extends into 20:19–23 as well. These cultic motifs include the presence of arboreal imagery, the performance of weeping or mourning, ascension into the heavenly realm, beholding a vision of God, and the pardoning of sins. The clustering of these concepts suggests that, though it may not have had a direct influence on the evangelist's resurrection narrative, Yom Kippur was an available conceptual matrix that the gospel writer drew upon in composing his resurrection account.

The significance of these Day of Atonement motifs, especially that of the cherubim and the mercy seat, for John's theology of atonement remains to be fully explored. Indeed, the Fourth Evangelist portrays Jesus's death as a sacrifice that removes people's sins (John 1:29; cf. 11:50; 18:14; 19:34),[53] yet little consideration has been given to the role of Jesus's resurrection and exaltation in John's theology of atonement. John 20:12 may suggest that Jesus's atoning work is only complete upon his ascension to the Father in heaven (20:17). Given that John's resurrection narrative is also effectively an ascension narrative, this premise would seem to be confirmed in John 20:22, where Jesus grants authority to pardon sins and gives the Holy Spirit to his disciples, which he can only do because he has gone to be with the Father (John 14:26, 28; 15:26) and has been glorified (John 7:39). Jesus's granting of authority to the disciples to forgive sins (John 20:23) must therefore be understood as premised upon his resurrection and ascension to the Father as well. In short, the Gospel of John seems to blend together a cross-centric (i.e., Pauline-Markan) and an ascension-centric (i.e., Epistle to the Hebrews) vision of Jesus's atoning work. Yet this novel thesis remains to be scrutinized in more detail.

## NOTES

1. Philippe Simenel, "Les 2 anges de Jean 20:11–12," *ETR* 67 (1992): 71–76; Xavier Léon-Dufour, *Lecture de l'Évangile selon Jean: Tome IV: L'heure de la glorification (chapitres 18–21)* (Paris: Seuil, 1996), 218; Nicholas P. Lunn, "Jesus, the Ark, and the Day of Atonement: Intertextual Echoes in John 19:38–20:18," *JETS* 52 (2009): 731–46; Christian Grappe, "Les deux anges de Jean 20:12: Signes de la présence mystérieuse du Logos (à la lumière du targum d'Ex 25:22)?" *RHPR* 89 (2009): 169–77. According to Lunn ("Jesus, the Ark, and the Day of Atonement," 731 n. 2) and Grappe ("Les deux anges de Jean 20:12," 170), this interpretation was proposed by Matthew Henry in 1715, Jakobus Wettstein in 1751, John Lightfoot in 1859, Brooke Foss Westcott in 1882, and G. H. C. MacGregor in 1928. For a more recent history of scholarly opinion on this topic, see Izaak J. de Hulster, "The Two Angels of John 20:12: The Old Testament Background," *BN* 162 (2014): 97–120, at 98–100.

2. Christian Grappe appeals to Tg. Neof. Exod. 25:22 and Tg. Ps.-J. Exod. 25:22, which both state that God's Memra dwells upon the atonement slate between the cherubim ("Les deux anges de Jean 20:12," 172–73). Accordingly, Grappe posits John's knowledge of such a tradition that associated the mercy seat with the Word of God, suggesting that the evangelist has crafted an *inclusio* between his prologue and resurrection account concerning the motif of the λόγος (ibid.). But to find God's Memra in a text such as Exod. 25:22 is hardly surprising, given that the Memra

features ubiquitously in the Targumim, and, more crucially, Grappe cites no early sources that would date this tradition to the Second Temple period or earlier (though see Philo, *Fug.* 100–01; cf. *Cher.* 28). Nicholas Lunn draws a number of parallels between John's resurrection narrative and ark of the covenants traditions ("Jesus, the Ark, and the Day of Atonement," 732–34), yet most of these parallels are unconvincing. For instance, he posits a number of verbal correspondences, such as "to take up" (αἴρω) (Exod. 25:14; Num 4:15; John 19:38; 20:1–2), "to place" (τίθημι) (Exod. 40:2–3, 5–6, 22, 24, 26, 29; John 19:41–42; 20:3, 13, 15), "to touch" (ἅπτω) (Num 4:15; John 20:17), and "to go in" (εἰσέρχομαι) + "to see" (ὁράω) (Num 4:20; John 20:6–8) (ibid.). But these are among some of the most common words in Greek biblical literature, and they do not exhibit the kind of unique word combinations or syntactical patterns typical of genuine verbal echoes. Lunn also suggests several conceptual parallels, such as the use of a barrier (curtain [Exod. 40:3, 21], rock [John 20:1]) to separate the inner chamber (Holy of Holies, tomb) from the outside, the use of cloth to cover the ark (Num. 4:5) and Jesus's body (John 19:40), and the use of spices to anoint the ark (Exod. 30:26) and Jesus's body (John 12:3; 19:39) (ibid.). But these phenomena—the rock, cloth, and spices—are all easily explained as typical features of Palestinian burial customs.

3. J. T. Williams, "Cultic Elements in the Fourth Gospel," *Stud Bib* (1978): 339–50; Bruce H. Grigsby, "The Cross as an Expiatory Sacrifice in the Fourth Gospel," *JSNT* 15 (1982): 51–80; James McCaffrey, *The House with Many Rooms: The Temple Theme of Jn 14.2–3*, AnBib 114 (Rome: Pontifical Biblical Institute, 1988); Jonathan A. Draper, "Temple, Tabernacle, and Mystical Experience in John," *Neot* 31 (1997): 263–88; Mark Kinzer, "Temple Christology in the Gospel of John," SBLSP (Atlanta: Scholars, 1998), 447–64; Mary L. Coloe, *God Dwells with Us: Temple Symbolism in the Fourth Gospel* (Collegeville, MN: Liturgical, 2001); Alan Kerr, *The Temple of Jesus's Body: The Temple Theme in the Gospel of John*, LNTS 220 (London: T&T Clark, 2006); G. K. Beale, *The Temple and the Church's Mission: A Biblical Theology of the Dwelling Place of God*, NSBT (Downers Grove, IL: InterVarsity, 2004), 192–200; Steven M. Bryan, "The Eschatological Temple in John 14," *BBR* 15 (2005): 187–98; Stephen T. Um, *The Theme of Temple Christology in John's Gospel*, LNTS 312 (London: T&T Clark, 2006); Paul M. Hoskins, *Jesus as the Fulfillment of the Temple in the Gospel of John* (Eugene, OR: Wipf and Stock, 2007); Mary L. Coloe, "Temple Imagery in John," *Int* 63 (2009): 368–81; Margaret Barker, *King of the Jews: Temple Theology in John's Gospel* (London: SPCK, 2014).

4. Scholars debate the exact nuance of Jesus's relationship to the Jerusalem temple in the evangelist's thought, whether it be a relation of analogy, metaphor, typology, replacement, fulfillment, etc. This study cannot afford to engage that question. John employs the language of scriptural "fulfillment" numerous times in the Gospel (John 12:38; 13:18; 15:25; 17:12; 19:24, 28, 36).

5. Coloe, "Temple Imagery in John," 372.

6. Hoskins, *Jesus as the Fulfillment of the Temple*, 117.

7. Coloe, "Temple Imagery in John," 372.

8. Beale, *The Temple and the Church's Mission*, 195.

9. Hoskins, *Jesus as the Fulfillment of the Temple*, 135–45.

10. Beale, *The Temple and the Church's Mission*, 196. Alluding to the river flowing from the garden of Eden (Gen 2:10–14), Ezekiel's eschatological temple contains water flowing from within it (Ezek 47:1), so that "everything will live where the river goes" (Ezek 47:9). Joel 3:18 foretells that "a fountain shall come forth from the house [=temple] of the Lord," and Zech 14:8 prophesies that "living waters shall flow out from Jerusalem" on the Day of the Lord.

11. Hoskins, *Jesus as the Fulfillment of the Temple*, 160–70. Hoskins concludes that both water-from-the-rock and water-from-the-eschatological-temple traditions stand behind Jesus's reference to "Scripture" in John 7:38.

12. Grigsby, "Cross as an Expiatory Sacrifice," 61.

13. For example, some have argued that the "the Father's house" in John 14:2 should be identified with a (heavenly) temple (most recently, see Bryan, "The Eschatological Temple in John 14," 187–98).

14. See note above.

15. "[U]ne très forte analogie spatiale avec le texte de Jean" (Simenel, "Les 2 anges de Jean 20:11–12," 75).

16. "Et tu feras deux chérubins en or [deux anges], fais un chérubin à une extrémité [l'un à la tête], et l'autre chérubin à l'autre extrémité [l'autre aux pieds], tu placeras le propitiatoire au-dessus de l'arche, et dans l'arche, tu placeras la charte de l'alliance que je te donnerai [à l'endroit où avait été déposé Jésus]" (ibid.," 75–6). For Simenel, the tomb effectively becomes a new ark of the covenant, in which atonement is made and God is revealed.

17. Exod. 25:19: כרוב אחד מקצה מזה וכרוב־אחד מקצה מקצה מזה. Exod 25:19 LXX: χερουβ εἷς ἐκ τοῦ κλίτους τούτου καὶ χερουβ εἷς ἐκ τοῦ κλίτους τοῦ δευτέρου. John 20:12: ἕνα πρὸς τῇ κεφαλῇ καὶ ἕνα πρὸς τοῖς ποσίν.

18. See T. N. D. Mettinger, "Cherubim," in *Dictionary of Deities and Demons in the Bible*, 189–92, at 190.

19. On the identity of the *ḥayyot* and cherubim in Ezekiel 1 and 10 respectively, see David J. Halperin, *The Faces of the Chariot: Early Jewish Responses to Ezekiel's Vision*, TSAJ 6 (Tübingen: Mohr Siebeck, 1988), 39–44.

20. Hulster, "The Two Angels in John 20:12," 102–3.

21. Ibid., 103.

22. Ibid., 104. Hulster notes that the "Hebrew Bible's accounts of the cherubs on the Ark (Exod 25:17–22; 37:6–9; 1 Kgs 6:23–28; Heb 9:5) are unclear concerning their position—e.g., whether they stand or sit—hence, this element cannot be compared with John's description of sitting angels" (ibid.).

23. Cf. Hulster, "The Two Angels in John 20:12," 111.

24. On the relationship between the garden in John 19:41 and the garden of Eden, see below.

25. Ibid., 110.

26. Raymond E. Brown, *The Gospel according to John*, 2 vols., AB (Garden City, NY: Doubleday, 1966–1970), 2:990; Barnabas Lindars, *The Gospel of John*, NCBC (Grand Rapids: Eerdmans, 1972), 594; C. K. Barrett, *The Gospel According to St. John*, 2nd ed. (Philadelphia: Westminster, 1978), 560; Craig S. Keener, *The Gospel of John: A Commentary*, 2 vols. (Grand Rapids: Baker Academic, 2003) 1:1164.

27. Gordon J. Wenham, "Sanctuary Symbolism in the Garden of Eden Story," in *I Studied Inscriptions before the Flood* (Winona Lake, IN: Eisenbrauns, 1994), 399–404; Beale, *The Temple and the Church's Mission*, 66–80; Joshua Berman, *The Temple: Its Symbolism and Meaning Then and Now* (Northvale, NJ.: J. Aronson, 1995), 21–34; Jon D. Levenson, *Resurrection and the Restoration of Israel: The Ultimate Victory of the God of Life* (New Haven: Yale University Press, 2008), 82–90; Leigh M. Trevaskis, *Holiness, Ethics and Ritual in Leviticus* (Sheffield: Sheffield Phoenix, 2011), 93–95; L. Michael Morales, *Who Shall Ascend the Mountain of the Lord? A Biblical Theology of the Book of Leviticus* (Downers Grove, IL: IVP Academic, 2015), 39–74.

28. Alex Douglas, "The Garden of Eden, the Ancient Temple, and Receiving a New Name," in *Ascending the Mountain of the Lord: Temple, Praise, and Worship in the Old Testament*, ed. Jeffrey R. Chadwick, Matthew J. Grey, and David Rolph Seely (Provo, UT: Brigham Young University, 2013), 36–48 (accessed at https://rsc.byu.edu/ascending-mountain-lord/garden-eden-ancient-temple-receiving-new-name).

29. Levenson, *Resurrection and the Restoration of Israel*, 86.

30. E.g., Sir 50:8–12; Jub 3.12, 26–27; 4.25–26; 8.19; Philo, *Somn.* 1.215.

31. Hoskins, *Jesus as the Fulfillment of the Temple*, 160–70. Hoskins concludes that both water-from-the-rock and water-from-the-eschatological-temple traditions stand behind Jesus's reference to "Scripture" in John 7:38.

32. Barrett, *John*, 570.

33. Ibid., 167.

34. VanderKam, *Book of Jubilees*, 228–29.

35. Anke Dorman, "'Commit Injustice and Shed Innocent Blood': Motives Behind the Institution of the Day of Atonement in the Book of Jubilees," in *The Day of Atonement: Its Interpretation in Early Jewish and Christian Traditions*, 49–62, at 57.

36. Barn 7.4–5 (Ehrman).

37. Brown, *John*, 2:1011–17.

38. Ibid., 2:1012.

39. Ibid., 2:1015.

40. See below.

41. Lunn's suggestion that John's use of "ascend" in John 20:17 is a "veiled allusion" to the burnt offering made on the Day of Atonement seems far-fetched and unlikely ("Jesus, the Ark, and the Day of Atonement," 742–44).

42. David M. Moffitt, *Atonement and the Logic of Resurrection in the Epistle to the Hebrews*, NovTSup (Leiden: Brill, 2011). Moffitt's dissertation challenged the prevailing view that the author of the Epistle to the Hebrews held little or no room for Jesus's resurrection in his theology of atonement. His thesis has won favor with many scholars.

43. Brown, *John*, 2:1013.

44. E.g., Brown, *John*, 2:1017; Barrett, *John*, 566; George R. Beasley-Murray, *John*, WBC 36 (Waco, TX: Word, 1987), 378; Lindars, *John*, 608. The phrase ἑώρακα τὸν κύριον never occurs in the LXX. Brown notes the possibility that a verse from the "passion Psalms" is in mind here: "I will proclaim your name to my brothers; in front of the congregation I will praise you" (Psa 22:23) (*John*, 2:1017).

45. Stökl Ben Ezra, *Impact of Yom Kippur*, 100.

46. 1 En. 14.18–21 (Nickelsburg and VanderKam, 35).

47. Apoc. Ab. 18.3, 13 (Kulik, *Slavonic Pseudepigrapha*, 24).

48. Philo, *Ebr.* 136–37. Cf. Philo, *Spec.* 1.72.

49. Stökl Ben Ezra, *Impact of Yom Kippur*, 110.

50. Herman N. Ridderbos, *The Gospel according to John: A Theological Commentary*, trans. John Vriend (Grand Rapids: Eerdmans, 1997), 644.

51. Philo, *Spec.* 2.196 (Colson).

52. Pss. Sol. 3.7–8 (*OTP* 2:654–55).

53. On the background and meaning of the phrase, "Behold, the Lamb of God that takes away the sin of the world" (John 1:29), see George L. Carey, "The Lamb of God and Atonement Theories," *TynBul* 32 (1981): 97–122; Jesper Tang Nielson, "The Lamb of God: The Cognitive Structure of a Johannine Metaphor," in *Imagery in the Gospel of John: Terms, Forms, Themes, and Theology of Johannine Figurative Language*, ed. Jörg Frey, Jan G. van der Watt, and Ruben Zimmermann (Tübingen: Mohr Siebeck, 2006), 217–56. The dominant position seems to be that the phrase combines imagery from the Paschal lamb and the Suffering Servant (cf. Isa 53:7), though the Paschal lamb did not function in an expiatory manner.

# Conclusion

This investigation into the impact of the Day of Atonement on the New Testament Gospels has covered a lot of ground. A recapitulation of its principal arguments and findings is therefore warranted. A brief summary of each gospel author's use of Yom Kippur traditions follows, along with inquiries for future studies.

## SUMMARY

In chapter 1, I argued that Leviticus 16 and Second Temple Yom Kippur traditions have influenced the imagery of the Final Judgment scene in Matt. 25:31–46, so that the eschatological expulsion of all the unrighteous "into the eternal fire prepared for the Devil and his angels" becomes a purgative event resembling the yearly expulsion of iniquity from the earthly temple by means of the goat for Azazel (Lev. 16:21–22).

Not only the conception of the Son of Man as attested in the Parables of Enoch but also the Azazel traditions attested within that same Enochic booklet have shaped Matthew's redaction of the account. Most importantly, Matt. 25:31, 41—"Then he (the Son of Man) will sit on the throne of glory . . . he will say to those at his left hand, 'Depart from me, cursed ones, into the eternal fire prepared for the Devil and his angels'"—bears a striking resemblance to 1 En. 55.4—"My Chosen One (=Son of Man) . . . will sit on the throne of glory and judge Azazel, and all his associates and all his host." Given the evangelist's application of the Asael/Azazel tradition of 1 En. 10.4 in Matt. 22:13—another unique passage in which a divine king banishes the unrighteous in a manner reminiscent of Asael/Azazel—the influence of Azazel traditions on Matt. 25:41 becomes highly probable. However, Matthew appears to assimilate aspects of Asael/Azazel's profile to that of the Devil in Matt. 25:41.

The Matthean judgment scene betrays at least five points of correspondence with Second Temple Yom Kippur traditions. First, the imagery of goats is quite peculiar, given that very little in Matthew's cultural milieu suggests such a negative valuation of goats as Matt. 25:41–46 contains, and that the Hebrew Bible possesses a generally positive attitude toward goats, the scapegoat being the exception. An association between the goats of the Final Judgment and the scapegoat ritual provides a rationale for the negative appraisal of that lot of goats on the Son of Man's left side. Second, given that the reason why a shepherd would separate sheep from goats remains a puzzle, this separation is plausibly motivated by a Yom Kippur typology. The imagery of two opposing lots (Matt. 25:32–34, 41) is consistent with the way other Jewish authors interpreted the "lot for Yahweh" and the "lot for Azazel" (Lev. 16:8–10), mapping each lot onto antagonistic social groups (1QS II, 17; Philo, *Her.* 179; Apoc. Ab. 10.15; 13:7; 14.6; 20:5; Origen, *Hom. Lev.* 9.3.2; 9.4.2; 9.5.2). The later rabbis associated the right side with the lot for Yahweh and the left side with the lot for Azazel (m. Yoma 4:1; b. Yoma 39a–b; Tg. Ps.-J. Lev. 16:18–19, 21). Third, while Matthew's community may have been aware of certain blemishes on the reputation of goats, these qualities were not extreme enough to merit the harsh expulsion described in Matt. 25:41, 46. Yet, if the gospel writer intends the lot of goats on the Son of Man's left side to evoke the sin-bearing scapegoat that was expunged from Jerusalem and handed over to Azazel, then their jarring expulsion in Matt. 25:41, 46 is exceptionally fitting. Fourth, the Matthean *hapax legomenon*, "cursed" (καταράομαι, Matt. 25:51), has perplexed scholars, since the verse in which this word occurs otherwise bears the imprint of the evangelist's redactional hand. However, that the king identifies "those at his left hand" (i.e., the lot of goats) as "cursed" is quite expected in light of the fact that the scapegoat also became the inheritor of curses in Second Temple Jewish tradition (Philo, *Spec.* 1.188; Barn. 7.9; Tertuallian, *Marc.* 3.7; m. Yoma 6:4; Apoc. Ab. 13.7). Fifth, Matthew employs the motif of the antithetical destinations of the two animals—one goat *to* Yahweh and one goat *to* Azazel (Lev. 16:8, 10)—as other Jewish writers of his time had done (1 En. 10.4; 14:8–24; 87.3; 88.1; Barn. 7.9; Apoc. Ab. 14.5–6; 15–32). One lot is destined to the kingdom of the Father (Matt. 25:34), and one lot is destined to the fire prepared for the Devil (Matt. 25:41). As with the apocalyptic Day of Atonement traditions, the movements of both entities acquire a cosmic and eschatological significance.

The ritual shading that Matt. 25:31–46 acquires in light of its use of Yom Kippur imagery fits exceptionally well into Matthew's overarching interest in moral purity. The logical conclusion to the drama of moral impurity in

Matthew's theological imagination involves the Son of Man's eschatological purgation of iniquity from the cosmos in a manner reminiscent of the yearly expulsion of moral impurity from Israel's temple by means of the scapegoat ritual.

Chapter 2 contended that Matthew has constructed a Day of Atonement typology in his baptism-temptation narrative (Matt. 3:16–4:11), whereby Jesus is portrayed as both the goat for Yahweh and the goat for Azazel. By means of the criterion of recurrence, this typology lends additional support for the Christological goat typology in Matthew's passion narrative. While the presentation of Jesus as both goats is not the evangelist's primary motive in narrating the baptism and temptation stories, it is an overlooked aspect of the author's redactional agenda. The clustering of the following conceptual parallels suggests that this is the case.

First, as opposed to Luke, Matthew preserves the structural parallel between the rite of the two goats (Lev. 16:7–10, 15–22) and the baptism-temptation narrative (Matt. 3:16–17; 4:1–11). Second, Matthew, again in contrast to Luke, follows Mark by situating the baptism in a context where all of Israel's sins are being confessed (Matt. 3:5–6), which parallels the confession of all the sins of Israel on Yom Kippur (Lev. 16:21). Third, the scriptural echoes of Isaiah 42 and possibly Genesis 22 in the heavenly voice (Matt. 3:17) evoke Jesus's sacrificial vocation. The sequence of a bodily cleansing (Matt. 3:16), followed by an encounter with the deity (3:17), brings to mind the distinctive rites of the high priest's bathing (Lev. 16:4) and entrance into the Holy of Holies with the blood of the goat for Yahweh (Lev. 16:15–17). Fourth, the priestly baptizer's elimination ritual uniquely associates Jesus with the sinful people in the First Gospel (Matt. 3:14–15), which recalls how the high priest caused the goat for Azazel to inherit Israel's sins in the elimination rite known as the scapegoat ritual (Lev. 16:21). Fifth, Jesus is sent "into the wilderness" (Matt. 4:1), similar to how the scapegoat was sent "into the wilderness" on the Day of Atonement (Lev. 16:10, 21–22). Contrary to Luke, Matthew's decision to retain the form εἰς τὴν ἔρημον recalls Leviticus 16 LXX, where that phrase occurs three times. Sixth, Like the goat for Azazel on Yom Kippur (Lev. 16:8, 10, 26), Jesus encounters a nefarious deity in the desert (Matt. 4:1–11). Moreover, the First Evangelist seems to uniquely conflate the Devil and possibly Satan with the figure of Azazel elsewhere in the gospel (Matt. 16:23; 25:41). Seventh, only Matthew employs the term "to fast" (νηστεύω) in his temptation account (Matt. 4:2), which recalls the distinctive feature of abstaining from food and drink on Yom Kippur, as well as the holy day's famous moniker, "the Fast" (ἡ νηστεία). Eighth, Matthew's choice to extend Jesus's quotation of Deut. 8:3 (Matt. 4:4) highlights the motifs of heavenly manna and Israel's desert afflictions, which are linked to the Day of Atonement in certain Second Temple traditions.

In light of these parallels, it seems likely that Matthew has constructed a goat for Yahweh and goat for Azazel typology in his baptism-temptation narrative, which foreshadows Jesus's typological designation as both goats in the Barabbas and Roman-abuse episodes, respectively (Matt. 27:15–26, 27–31)

In chapter 3, I concluded that the Day of Atonement has informed Luke or, more likely, Luke's special material from which he seems to have composed the Nazareth synagogue and expulsion episodes (Luke 4:18–19, 29).

Though the Gospel of Luke may not evince a sustained Jubilee typology, the allusion to Lev. 25:10 LXX in Jesus's reading from the Isaianic scroll (Luke 4:18–19//Isa. 58:6; 61:1–2) is quite clear, especially in light of the Jubilary evocations in Isa. 61:1–2 and the genealogy of Jesus (Luke 3:23–38). However, the Jubilary motif does not explain Jesus's citation of Isa. 58:6. Yet, the Day of Atonement supplies much of the imagery contained in Isaiah 58, especially the phrase, "to afflict yourself" (Isa. 58:3, 5; Lev. 16:29, 31; 23:27, 29, 32; Num. 29:7), and the motif of fasting (Isa. 58:1–7). Jesus's combination of Isa. 58:6 and 61:1–2 LXX appears to be best explained not only with reference to the Jubilee year but in connection to the forgiveness of sins associated with the Day of Atonement, on which the Jubilee began (Lev. 25:9). The repetition of ἄφεσις and ἀποστέλλω in the combined Isaianic citation—two important terms in Leviticus 16 LXX—suggests that the Day of Atonement was an impetus for this scriptural conflation. 11QMelchizedek supports this reading, which interprets the Jubilary "liberty" of Isa. 61:1 in terms of the elect's release from "all their iniquities," escalating in an eschatological Yom Kippur (11Q13 II, 6–7).

While the Delphian's execution of Aesop by lethal plummet in the *Life of Aesop* parallels the attempted execution of Jesus in Luke 4:29, this parallel is best explained by the common cultural trope of elimination rituals in the ancient world. In light of the echo of Yom Kippur in Luke 4:18–19, the townspeople's expulsion of Jesus and attempt to hurl him down a cliff recalls the scapegoat's banishment from the city (Lev. 16:10, 21–22) and descent down an abyss (Philo, *Plant.* 61; m. Yoma 6:6; Tg. Ps.-J. Lev. 16:22; cf. 1 En. 10.4–5; 88.1; Apoc. Ab. 14.5). From a literary perspective, the attempted expulsion of Jesus from Nazareth foreshadows Jesus's ultimate banishment from Jerusalem, which begins a series of events culminating in the forgiveness of sins (Luke 1:77; 3:3; 24:47; Acts 2:38; 5:31; 10:43; 13:38; 26:18).

Chapter 4 argued that ancient elimination rituals and Second Temple scapegoat traditions have influenced the Gerasene/Gadarene pericope in all three Synoptic accounts to varying degrees. Jesus transfers an evil onto a vehicle for disposal, which then eliminates that evil in an uninhabitable realm, leading to the restoration of the demoniac(s). The destruction of the pigs, then, is not a bizarre sign of the exorcism's effectiveness, but rather part of the cure for the demon-possessed man. In light of the echoes of the

Watchers tradition, the expulsion of the demon(s) mimics that of Asael/ Azazel and anticipates God's eschatological judgment of the Devil/Satan and his associates.

Often in ancient expulsion rituals, the impure object of elimination is disposed in a body of water, as is the case in the exorcism story. In the Gerasene/ Gadarene pericope, an evil (the impure spirits) is transferred from a subject (the demoniac) onto an object (the swine) and disposed in an uninhabitable realm (the sea), resulting in a positive outcome (the man is healed). Matthew and Luke retain the basic elements of this template, though Matthew does not narrate the healing of the demoniacs. The most famous Jewish elimination rite was the scapegoat ritual, which received an apocalyptic reworking in the mythology of Asael/Azazel and the fallen angels' punishment. Five parallels between early Jewish Day of Atonement traditions and the Markan Gerasene narrative suggest that the Second Evangelist has molded this pericope with Yom Kippur motifs in view: (a) the transference of evil/impurity onto the scapegoat, (b) the descent of the scapegoat unto its demise, (c) the command to "afflict yourselves" on Yom Kippur, (d) the physical and verbal abuse of the scapegoat, and (e) the eschatological restoration associated with the scapegoat's demise. The apocalyptic scapegoat tradition has impacted Mark's Gerasene narrative most noticeably, though Matthew and Luke also seem to be aware of it.

For Mark, Jesus's scapegoat-like expulsion of Legion signals God's banishment of hostile cosmic powers from their positions of authority over the nations (cf. Mark 3:27) and portends God's kingdom reign, in which Gentiles are released from bondage to these powers and welcomed into the family of God (Mark 3:13–19, 31–35). Luke's version tells a similar tale, correlating the "deserts" into which the demons would drive the demoniac (Luke 8:29) with the "abyss" into which they are finally sent (Luke 8:31), arguably making the scapegoat-Asael/Azazel typology stronger. While Matthew greatly abridges the exorcism account, the expulsion scene now becomes explicitly eschatological and is the focal point of the story, adumbrating the Son of Man's victory over "the Devil and all his angels" (Matt. 25:41). The presence of two demoniacs possibly foreshadows the two scapegoats that later appear in Matthew's passion narrative.

Chapter 5 explored the possible impact of Yom Kippur on John's resurrection narrative, particularly John 20:11–23. I concluded that John's description of the "two angels in white, sitting where the body of Jesus had been lying, one at the head and the other at the feet" (John 20:12) most probably alludes to the image of the cherubim situated at either end of the mercy seat or atonement slate, "one cherub at one end, and one cherub at the other" (Ezek. 25:19). Though this verse contains the only real "echo" of the Day of Atonement in the resurrection narrative, it seems that the cultic imagery associated with Yom Kippur has indirectly contributed to other aspects of the story.

In particular, the clustering of the following concepts suggests that Yom Kippur was an available conceptual matrix that the fourth-gospel writer drew upon in composing his resurrection account: (a) the presence of arboreal imagery (John 19:41; 20:15), (b) the performance of weeping or mourning (20:11, 13, 15), (c) ascension into the heavenly realm (20:17), (d) beholding a vision of God (20:18, 20, 25, 28), and (e) the pardoning of sin (20:22). Granted that John's resurrection narrative is also effectively an ascension narrative, the allusion to the cherubim and mercy seat in John 20:12 may suggest that Jesus's atoning work is only complete upon his ascension to the Father in heaven (20:17).

## THE IMPACT OF YOM KIPPUR ON THE GOSPELS

Though scholars have conducted various individual case studies on the subject, previous scholarship has neglected to consider the impact of Yom Kippur on the gospels as a collective. This analysis paints a nuanced and variegated portrait of the influence of Leviticus 16 and its associated traditions on the four gospels of the New Testament. On the whole, it must be admitted that the imprint of the Day of Atonement on the gospels is modest and, in some instances, it is hardly recognizable without a detailed knowledge of the Yom Kippur ritual and its sundry Second Temple traditions.

The Day of Atonement has made the greatest impact on the Gospel of Matthew, which is no surprise, given the author's robust familiarity with Jewish traditions. As I have laid out in detail elsewhere, Matthew composes two sets of Yom Kippur typologies in his passion narrative.[1] He depicts Jesus Barabbas (27:16–17) as a released scapegoat and Jesus the Messiah (27:17, 22) as the sacrificial goat, though he extends the scapegoat typology to the sin-bearing crowd as well (Matt. 27:24–25).[2] He then portrays Jesus as a king who himself bears and carries away the moral impurities of the world as a typological fulfillment of the scapegoat in the following episode (Matt. 27:27–31).[3] Matthew thereby completes his Christological goat typology, so that Jesus fulfills the role of both immolated goat and scapegoat. Finally, Jesus's destiny as goat for Yahweh is arguably fulfilled when Jesus releases his life force ($\pi\nu\epsilon\hat{\upsilon}\mu\alpha$) and the sanctuary curtain is torn in two (Matt. 27:50–51a), and Jesus's destiny as goat for Azazel is arguably fulfilled when Jesus is presumed to have descended into the underworld (Matt. 27:51b–53).[4]

The present investigation lends further support for Matthew's Christological goat typology in the passion narrative by way of the criterion of recurrence. First, Jesus's role as goat for Yahweh is foreshadowed at his baptism. In an environment where all of Israel's sins are being confessed (Matt. 3:5–6), Jesus's sacrificial vocation is evoked by the voice of the deity (3:17), who reveals himself to Jesus behind the heavenly veil (3:16b). Second, Jesus's role as goat for Azazel is adumbrated at his temptation. Having identified with the sinful people by means of the priestly baptizer's rite of elimination (Matt. 3:16a), Jesus is sent into the wilderness (4:1a), where he encounters a nefarious deity (4:1b). Notably, Jesus's encounter with God and reception of the Spirit (Matt. 3:16–17) parallels the release of Jesus's spirit and the rending of the veil (27:50–51a), and Jesus's encounter with the Devil in the desert (Matt. 4:1–11) parallels Jesus's descent into the cosmic wilderness (27:51b–53; cf. 12:40).

While he identifies only Jesus with the goat for Yahweh in his gospel, Matthew identifies multiple fulfillments of the scapegoat figure in his gospel. We raised the question as to why Matthew would apply a scapegoat typology to both the unrighteous at the Final Judgment (Matt. 22:13; 25:41) and to Jesus in the passion narrative (Matt. 26:28; 27:28, 31). Does this not create a contradiction? The answer seems to be that Matthew applies a scapegoat typology to multiple figures in the gospel, because he favors a conception of sin as an object requiring physical removal or elimination, and the scapegoat's principal function was to do just this: physically eliminate iniquity. While Jesus's death "for the release of sins" (Matt. 26:28) is central to the Matthean storyline, the conclusion to the drama of moral impurity in the First Gospel involves the Son of Man's purgation of iniquity from the cosmos in a manner reminiscent of the scapegoat ritual.

Turning to the Gospel of Mark, it is much more ambiguous whether the evangelist employs a Christological goat typology in his Barabbas (Mark 15:6–15) and Roman-abuse episodes (15:16–20).[5] Mark probably understands the rending of the veil (Mark 15:38) against the background of Leviticus 16, though this is not certain.[6] Nevertheless, the gospel writer seems to be aware of Second Temple scapegoat traditions, as seen in our analysis of Mark 5:1–20. His interest in Jesus's eschatological battle with Satan seems to have inspired Mark to draw freely from what he knew of the Watchers and Azazel traditions, applying such traditions to Jesus's inimitable foe in the Gerasene exorcism story. But why does Mark not evince a strong scapegoat Christology like his Matthean counterpart? It is possible that, without the same (Jewish) notion of sin as an object in need of removal as found in Matthew, Mark could not easily apply a scapegoat typology to more than one figure in his gospel; and so, given the strong association between Azazel and the scapegoat, he applies it only to the demonic entity instead of Jesus. Indeed, more remains to be explored regarding the role of the Azazel myth in Mark's overall gospel narrative and demonological schema.

The Gospel of Luke contains no certain Yom Kippur typology, though it betrays relatively strong evidence of the Day of Atonement's influence on certain material within the gospel. Namely, Yom Kippur seems to be the impetus behind the scriptural conflation of Isa. 61:1–2 and 58:6 LXX in Luke 4:18–19, and it appears to underlie the tradition of the townspeople's attempt to hurl Jesus off the cliff in Luke 4:29. Yet given the lack of an explicit theology of atonement vis-à-vis the temple cult in the Third Gospel, these echoes of the Day of Atonement probably derive from a Jewish source within Luke's special material. This source may be closely related to the source underlying the Lukan genealogy (Luke 3:23–38), which also employs Jubilary motifs.

Again, Yom Kippur appears to have exercised an effect on Luke's Gerasene exorcism story (Luke 8:26–40), which is most evident in the evangelist's additions in Luke 8:29 ("into the deserts") and 8:31 ("into the abyss"). Yet these additions are not characteristically Lukan, and neither the Day of Atonement nor Enochic Judaism appears to have significantly impacted Luke-Acts. Thus, it seems prudent to credit the Yom Kippur echoes to one of Luke's Jewish sources. This is, however, still an open question, and it could be that Luke heard all the echoes of Scripture and tradition in his Jewish sources. At least now the role of the Day of Atonement in the Gospel of Luke can be included in scholarly discourse.

Finally, the Gospel of John, as with the Third Gospel, does not possess a clear Day of Atonement typology. Nevertheless, traditions pertaining to this Jewish holy day seem to have borne some influence on the evangelist's resurrection narrative. This influence is most direct in John 20:12, which evokes the image of the cherubim and atonement slate stationed in the Holy of Holies, though there seems to be faint traces of the Yom Kippur *imaginaire* elsewhere in John 20:11–23. Given that John's resurrection narrative is also, in effect, an ascension narrative, it may be that John's theology of atonement diverges from the Synoptic tradition and aligns more closely with the author of the Epistle to the Hebrews, who conceives the ascended Jesus as a high priest who makes atonement before God in the heavenly sanctuary. This thesis may read more into John 20:12 and its surrounding narrative than was intended by the Fourth Evangelist, but the possibility ought to be further investigated.

## NOTES

1. The Yom Kippur typologies in the Barabbas episode (Matt. 27:15–26) and Roman-abuse scene (Matt. 27:27–31) have quite a long reception history, dating back to the early fathers, and numerous contemporary scholars have accepted them (see Moscicke, *New Day of Atonement*, 7–29, 90–7, esp. 8 n. 5, 27 n. 94, 140 n. 4).

2. Ibid., 99–138.

3. Ibid., 139–80.

4. Ibid., 181–230.

5. Berenson Maclean thinks he does ("Barabbas, the Scapegoat Ritual," 321–24), but Stökl Ben Ezra doubts this ("Fasting with Jews," 179). See my analysis in Hans M. Moscicke, "Jesus as Goat of the Day of Atonement in Recent Synoptic Gospels Research," *CBR* 17 (2018): 59–85.

6. Hengel, *Atonement*, 42; Berenson Maclean, "Barabbas, the Scapegoat Ritual," 331; An, "Baptism and Temptation," 14–17.

# Bibliography

*Abbreviations follow the general style guidelines of the Society of Biblical Literature.

Aalen, Sverre. "St. Luke's Gospel and the Last Chapters of 1 Enoch." *NTS* 13 (1966): 1–13.

Adrados, Francisco R. "The 'Life of Aesop' and the Origins of Novel in Antiquity." *QUCC* 1 (1979): 93–112.

Allegro, John M. *Qumran Cave 4. Vol. 1: (4Q158–4Q186)*. DJD 5. Oxford: Clarendon, 1968.

Allison, Dale C. *The New Moses: A Matthean Typology*. Minneapolis: Fortress, 1993.

An, Hannah S. "Reading Matthew's Account of the Baptism and Temptation of Jesus (Matt 3:5–4:1) with the Scapegoat Rite on the Day of Atonement (Lev 16:20–22)." *Canon & Culture* 12 (2018): 5–31.

Angel, Joseph L. "Enoch, Jesus, and Priestly Tradition." Pages 285–316 in *Enoch and the Synoptic Gospels: Reminiscences, Allusions, Intertextuality*. Edited by Loren T. Stuckenbruck and Gabriele Boccaccini. EJL 44. Atlanta: Scholars, 2016.

Aune, David. *Revelation 17–22*. WBC 52. Nashville: Thomas Nelson, 1998.

Baillet, Maurice. *Qumran Cave 4. Vol. 3: (4Q482–4Q520)*. DJD 7. Oxford: Clarendon, 1982.

Barker, Margaret. *King of the Jews: Temple Theology in John's Gospel*. London: SPCK, 2014.

———. "The Time is Fulfilled: Jesus and the Jubilee." *SJT* 53 (2000): 22–32.

Barkley, Gary Wayne. *Origen: Homilies on Leviticus 1–16*, FC 83. Washington, DC: Catholic University of America Press, 1990.

Barrett, C. K. *The Gospel According to St. John*. 2nd ed. Philadelphia: Westminster, 1978.

Barthélemy, D. and J. T. Milik. *Qumran Cave 1*. DJD 1. Oxford: Clarendon, 1955.

Bauckham, Richard, ed. "The Lukan Genealogy of Jesus." Pages 315–73 in *Jude and the Relatives of Jesus in the Early Church*. London: T&T Clark, 1990.

Bautch, Kelley Coblentz. "The Fall and Fate of Renegade Angels: The Intersection of Watchers Traditions and the Book of Revelation." Pages 69–93 in *The Fallen Angels Traditions: Second Temple Developments and Reception History*. Edited by Angela Kim Harkins, Kelley Coblentz Bautch, and John C. Endres S.J. CBQMS 53. Washington, DC: Catholic Biblical Association of America, 2014.

Baynes, Leslie. "The Parables of Enoch and Luke's Parable of the Rich Man and Lazarus." Pages 129–52 in *Enoch and the Synoptic Gospels: Reminiscences, Allusions, Intertextuality*. Edited by Loren T. Stuckenbruck and Gabriele Boccaccini. EJL 44. Atlanta: Scholars, 2016.

Beale, G. K. *The Temple and the Church's Mission: A Biblical Theology of the Dwelling Place of God*. NSBT. Downers Grove, IL: InterVarsity, 2004.

Beasley-Murray, George R. *John*. WBC 36. Waco, TX: Word, 1987.

Berenson Maclean, Jennifer K. "Barabbas, the Scapegoat Ritual, and the Development of the Passion Narrative." *HTR* 100 (2007): 309–34.

Berman, Joshua. *The Temple: Its Symbolism and Meaning Then and Now*. Northvale, NJ: J. Aronson, 1995.

Betz, Otto. "Jesus and Isaiah 53." Pages 70–87 in *Jesus and the Suffering Servant: Isaiah 53 and Christian Origins*. Edited by William H. Bellinger and William R. Farmer. Harrisburg, PA: Trinity Press International, 1998.

Black, Matthew, and Albert-Marie Denis, eds. *Apocalypsis Henochi Graece*. FPQSG. Leiden: Brill, 1970.

Blinzler, Josef. "The Jewish Punishment of Stoning in the New Testament Period." Pages 147–61 in *The Trial of Jesus: Cambridge Studies in Honour of C.F.D. Moule*. Edited by E. Bammel, SBT 2. London: SCM, 1970.

Blocher, Henri. "Zacharie 3: Josué et le Grand Jour des Expiations." *ETR* 54 (1979): 264–70.

Blosser, Donald W. "Jesus and the Jubilee: The Year of Jubilee and Its Significance in the Gospel of Luke." PhD diss. The University of St. Andrews, 1979.

Boccaccini, Gabriele, ed. *Enoch and the Messiah Son of Man*. Grand Rapids: Eerdmans, 2007.

Bock, Darrell L. *Luke*. 2 vols. BECNT. Grand Rapids: Baker Academic, 1994–1996.

Boda, Mark J. *Haggai, Zechariah*. Grand Rapids: Zondervan, 2004.

Bonner, Campbell. "Additions and Corrections." *HTR* 37 (1944): 333–39.

———. "Technique of Exorcism." *HTR* 36 (1943): 39–49.

Bottéro, Jean. "The Substitute King and His Fate." Pages 138–55 in *Mesopotamia: Writing, Reasoning, and the Gods*. Translated by Zainab Bahrani and Marc van de Mieroop. Chicago: University of Chicago Press, 1992.

Bovon, François. *A Commentary on the Gospel of Luke*. 3 vols. Translated by Christine Thomas, Donald Deer, and James Couch. Hermeneia. Minneapolis: Fortress, 2002–2013.

Boyce, Richard N. *Leviticus and Numbers*. Louisville, KY: Westminster John Knox Press, 2008.

Brand, Miryam T. *Evil Within and Without: The Source of Sin and Its Nature as Portrayed in Second Temple Literature*. JAJS 9. Göttingen: Vandenhoeck & Ruprecht, 2013.

Bremmer, Jan N. "The Scapegoat between Northern Syria, Hittites, Israelites, Greeks and Early Christians." Pages 169–214 in *Greek Religion and Culture, the Bible and the Ancient Near East*. By idem. JSRC 8. Leiden: Brill, 2008.

———. "Scapegoat Rituals in Ancient Greece." Pages 271–93 in *Oxford Readings in Greek Religion*. Edited by Richard Buxton. Oxford: Oxford University Press, 2000.

Brooke, George J. "Shared Intertextual Interpretations in the Dead Sea Scrolls and the New Testament." Pages 35–57 in *Biblical Perspectives: Early Use and Interpretation of the Bible in Light of the Dead Sea Scrolls*. Edited by Michael E. Stone and Esther G. Chazon. STDJ 28. Leiden: Brill, 1998.

Brown, Raymond E. *The Birth of the Messiah*. New York: Doubleday, 1993.

———. *The Gospel According to John*. 2 vols. AB. Garden City, NY: Doubleday, 1966–1970.

Bruno, Christopher. "Jesus is our Jubilee … But How? The OT Background and Lukan Fulfillment of the Ethics of Jubilee." *JETS* 53 (2010): 81–101.

Bryan, Steven M. "The Eschatological Temple in John 14." *BBR* 15 (2005): 187–98.

Bultmann, Rudolf. *The History of the Synoptic Tradition*. Translated by John Marsh. New York: Harper & Row, 1963 (1921).

Burkert, Walter. "Transformations of the Scapegoat." Pages 59–77 in *Structure and History in Greek Mythology and Ritual*. By idem. Berkley: University of California Press, 1979.

Carey, George L. "The Lamb of God and Atonement Theories." *TynBul* 32 (1981): 97–122.

Carson, Donald A. "Matthew." Pages 3–599 in *The Expositor's Bible Commentary*. Edited by F. E. Gaebelein. Vol. 8. Grand Rapids: Zondervan, 1984.

Casey, Maurice. *Son of Man: The Interpretation and Influence of Daniel 7*. London: SPCK, 1979.

Catchpole, David R. "The Poor on Earth and the Son of Man in Heaven: A Re-appraisal of Matthew 12:31–46." *BJRL* 61 (1979): 378–83.

Charles, R. H. *The Book of Enoch or I Enoch*. Oxford: Clarendon, 1912.

Charlesworth, James H., ed. "The Date and Provenience of the Parables of Enoch." Pages 37–57 in *Parables of Enoch: A Paradigm Shift*. Edited by James H. Charlesworth and Darrell L. Bock. London: Bloomsbury, 2013.

———. *Old Testament Pseudepigrapha*. 2 vols. New York: Doubleday, 1983, 1985.

Childs, Brevard S. *Isaiah*. OTL. Louisville, KY: Westminster John Knox, 2001.

Collins, Adela Yarbro. "Finding Meaning in the Death of Jesus." *JR* 78 (1998): 175–96.

———. *Mark: A Commentary*. Hermeneia. Minneapolis: Fortress, 2007.

———. "The Secret Son of Man in the Parables of Enoch and the Gospel of Mark: A Response to Leslie Walck." Pages 338–51 in *Enoch and the Messiah Son of Man*. Edited by Gabriele Boccaccini. Grand Rapids: Eerdmans, 2007.

Collins, John J. *The Apocalyptic Imagination: An Introduction to Jewish Apocalyptic Literature*. 2nd ed. Grand Rapids: Eerdmans, 1998.

Coloe, Mary L. *God Dwells with Us: Temple Symbolism in the Fourth Gospel*. Collegeville, MN: Liturgical, 2001.

———. "Temple Imagery in John." *Int* 63 (2009): 368–81.

Crossan, John Dominic. *The Cross that Spoke: The Origins of the Passion Narrative.* San Francisco: Harper & Row, 1988.

Cullmann, Oscar. *The Christology of the New Testament.* Translated by Shirley C. Guthrie and Charles A. M. Hall. London: SCM, 1959.

Curtis, Byron G. *Up the Steep and Stony Road: The Book of Zechariah in Social Location Trajectory Analysis.* AcBib 25. Atlanta: SBL, 2006.

Dalmn, Gustaf. *Arbeit und Sitte in Palästina: Band VI.* Hildesheim: Georg Olms Verlagsbuchhandlung, 1964 (1939).

Danby, Herbert. *The Mishnah: Translated from the Hebrew with Introduction and Brief Explanatory Notes.* Oxford: Oxford University Press, 1933.

Danker, Frederick W., Walter Bauer, William F. Arndt, and F. Wilbur Gingrich. *Greek-English Lexicon of the New Testament and Other Early Christian Literature.* 3rd ed. Chicago: University of Chicago Press, 2000.

Davies, W. D., and Dale C. Allison. *The Gospel According to Matthew.* ICC. 3 vols. Edinburgh: T&T Clark, 1988–1997.

Dawson, David. *Flesh Becomes Word: A Lexicography of the Scapegoat or, the History of an Idea.* East Lansing, MI: Michigan State University Press, 2013.

DeMaris, Richard E. "Jesus Jettisoned." Pages 91–111 in *The New Testament in its Ritual World.* By idem. London: Routledge, 2008.

Derrett, J. Duncan M. "Contributions to the Study of the Gerasene Demoniac." *JSNT* 3 (1979): 2–17.

Dibelius, Martin. *From Tradition to Gospel.* Translated by Bertram Lee Woolf. New York: Scribner, 1965 (1919).

Dimant, Devorah. "1 Enoch 6–11: A Methodological Perspective." *SBLSP* (1978): 323–39.

Donahue, John R., and Daniel J. Harrington. *The Gospel of Mark.* SP 2. Collegeville, MN: Liturgical, 2002.

Dorman, Anke. "'Commit Injustice and Shed Innocent Blood': Motives Behind the Institution of the Day of Atonement in the Book of Jubilees." Pages 49–62 in *The Day of Atonement: Its Interpretation in Early Jewish and Christian Traditions.* Edited by Thomas Hieke and Tobias Nicklas. Leiden: Brill, 2012.

Douglas, Alex. "The Garden of Eden, the Ancient Temple, and Receiving a New Name." Pages 36–47 in *Ascending the Mountain of the Lord: Temple, Praise, and Worship in the Old Testament.* Edited by Jeffrey R. Chadwick, Matthew J. Grey, and David Rolph Seely. Provo, UT: Brigham Young University, 2013.

Draper, Jonathan A. "Temple, Tabernacle, and Mystical Experience in John." *Neot* 31 (1997): 263–88.

Eberhart, Christian A. "To Atone or Not to Atone: Remarks on the Day of Atonement Rituals According to Leviticus 16 and the Meaning of Atonement." Pages 197–231 in *Sacrifice, Cult, and Atonement in Early Judaism and Christianity.* Edited by Henrietta L. Wiley and Christian A. Eberhart. Atlanta: SBL, 2017.

Elder, Nicholas A. "Of Porcine and Polluted Spirits: Reading the Gerasene Demoniac (Mark 5:1–20) with the Book of Watchers (*1 Enoch* 1–36)." *CBQ* 78 (2016): 430–46.

Epstein, Isidore. *The Babylonian Talmud.* London: Soncino, 1935–1952.

Eubank, Nathan. *Wages of Cross-Bearing and Debt of Sin: The Economy of Heaven in Matthew's Gospel.* BZNW 196. Berlin: De Gruyter, 2013.

Evans, Ernest. *Tertullian: Adversus Marcionem: Books 1–3.* Oxford: Clarendon, 1972.

Falk, Daniel K. *Daily, Sabbath, and Festival Prayers in the Dead Sea Scrolls.* STDJ 27. Leiden: Brill, 1998.

———. "Moses, Texts of." Pages 2:577–81 in *Encyclopedia of the Dead Sea Scrolls.* Edited by Lawrence H. Schiffman and James C. VanderKam. 2 vols. Oxford: Oxford University Press, 2000.

Falls, Thomas B. *St. Justin Martyr: Dialogue with Trypho.* Revised by Thomas P. Halton. Edited by Michael Slusser. SFC 3. Washington, DC: Catholic University of America Press, 2003.

Finlan, Stephen. "Curse Transmission Rituals and Paul's Imagery." Pages 73–121 in *The Background and Content of Paul's Cultic Atonement Metaphors.* By idem. Atlanta: SBL, 2004.

Fishbane, Michael. *Biblical Interpretation in Ancient Israel.* Oxford: Clarendon, 1985.

Fitzmyer, Joseph A. *The Gospel According to Luke.* 2 vols. AB 28. Garden City, NY: Doubleday, 1981–1985.

Fletcher-Louis, Crispin H. T. "Enoch, Levi, and Peter: Recipients of Revelation in Upper Galilee." *JBL* 100 (1981): 575–600.

———. "Jesus as the High Priestly Messiah: Part 1." *JSHJ* 4 (2006): 155–75.

———. "Jesus as the High Priestly Messiah: Part 2." *JSHJ* 5 (2007): 57–79.

———. "The Revelation of the Sacral Son of Man: The Genre, History of Religions Context and the Meaning of the Transfiguration." Pages 247–98 in *Auferstehung—Resurrection. The Fourth Durham-Tübingen-Symposium: Resurrection, Exaltation, and Transformation in Old Testament, Ancient Judaism, and Early Christianity.* Edited by Friedrich Avemarie and Hermann Lichtenberger. WUNT 1:135. Tübingen: Mohr Siebeck, 2001.

France, R. T. *The Gospel of Mark. A Commentary on the Greek Text.* NIGTC. Grand Rapids: Eerdmans, 2002.

———. *The Gospel of Matthew.* NICNT. Grand Rapids: Eerdmans, 2007.

Friedrich, Johannes. *Gott im Bruder?* CTM 7. Germany: Calwer Verlag Stuttgart, 1977.

Froelich, Margaret, and Thomas E. Phillips. "Throw the Blasphemer off a Cliff: Luke 4.16–30 in Light of the *Life of Aesop.*" *NTS* 65 (2019): 21–32.

Gane, Roy. *Cult and Character: Purification Offerings, Day of Atonement, and Theodicy.* Winona Lake, IN: Eisenbrauns, 2005.

Gibbs, Jeffery A. "Israel Standing with Israel: The Baptism of Jesus in Matthew's Gospel (Matt 3:13–17)." *CBQ* 64 (2002): 511–26.

Gilders, William K. "The Day of Atonement in the Dead Sea Scrolls." Pages 63–74 in *The Day of Atonement: Its Interpretation in Early Jewish and Christian Traditions.* Edited by Thomas Hieke and Tobias Nicklas. Leiden: Brill, 2012.

Grabbe, Lester L. "The Scapegoat Tradition: A Study in early Jewish Interpretation." *JSJ* 18 (1987): 152–67.

Grappe, Christian. "Les deux anges de Jean 20:12: Signes de la présence mystérieuse du Logos (à la lumière du targum d'Ex 25:22)?" *RHPR* 89 (2009): 169–77.

Gray, Sherman W. *The Least of My Brothers, Matthew 25:31–46: A History of Interpretation.* SBLDS 114. Atlanta: Scholars, 1989.

Green, Joel B. *The Gospel of Luke.* NICNT. Grand Rapids: Eerdmans, 1997.

Greenfield, Jonas C., and Michael E. Stone. "The Enochic Pentateuch and the Date of the Similitudes." *HTR* 70 (1977): 51–65.

Grigsby, Bruce H. "The Cross as an Expiatory Sacrifice in the Fourth Gospel." *JSNT* 15 (1982): 51–80.

Guelich, Robert A. *Mark 1-8:26.* WBC 34A. Dallas: Word Books, 1989.

Gundry, Robert H. *Mark: A Commentary on His Apology for the Cross.* Grand Rapids: Eerdmans, 1993.

———. *Matthew: A Commentary on His Handbook for a Mixed Church under Persecution.* 2nd ed. Grand Rapids: Eerdmans, 1994.

Gurtner, Daniel M. *The Torn Veil: Matthew's Exposition of the Death of Jesus.* SNTSMS 139. Cambridge: Cambridge University Press, 2007.

Ha, KyeSang. "Cultic Allusions in the Suffering Servant Poem (Isaiah 52:13–53:12)." PhD diss. Andrews University, 2009.

Halperin, David J. *The Faces of the Chariot: Early Jewish Responses to Ezekiel's Vision.* TSAJ 6. Tübingen: Mohr Siebeck, 1988.

Hamilton, Catherine Sider. *The Death of Jesus in Matthew: Innocent Blood and the End of Exile.* SNTSMS 167. Cambridge: Cambridge University Press, 2017.

Hare, Douglas R. A. *The Solution to the "Son of Man" Problem.* London: T&T Clark International, 2007.

———. *The Son of Man Tradition.* Minneapolis: Fortress, 1991.

Harkins, Angela Kim, Kelley Coblentz Bautch, and John C. Endres S.J., eds. *The Watchers in Jewish and Christian Traditions.* Minneapolis: Fortress, 2014.

Hays, Richard B. *The Conversion of the Imagination: Paul as Interpreter of Israel's Scripture.* Grand Rapids: Eerdmans, 2005.

———. *Echoes of Scripture in the Letters of Paul.* New Haven: Yale University Press, 1989.

Hengel, Martin. *The Atonement: The Origins and the Doctrine in the New Testament.* Philadelphia: Fortress, 1981.

Herbert, Arthur Sumner. *The Book of the Prophet Isaiah, Chapters 40–66.* CBC. Cambridge: Cambridge University Press, 1975.

Hertig, Paul. "The Jubilee Mission of Jesus in the Gospel of Luke: Reversals of Fortunes." *Missiology* 26 (1998): 167–79.

Hieke, Thomas and Tobias Nicklas, eds. *The Day of Atonement: Its Interpretation in Early Jewish and Christian Traditions.* Leiden: Brill, 2012.

Himmelfarb, Martha. *Ascent to Heaven in Jewish and Christian Apocalypses.* New York: Oxford University Press, 1993.

Hindley, J. C. "Towards a Date for the Similitudes of Enoch." *NTS* 14 (1968): 551–65.

Hooker, Morna. "Did the Use of Isaiah 53 to Interpret his Mission Begin with Jesus?" Pages 88–103 in *Jesus and the Suffering Servant: Isaiah 53 and Christian Origins*. Edited by W. H. Bellinger and William R. Farmer. Harrisburg, PA: Trinity Press International, 1998.

―――. *Jesus and the Servant: Influence of the Servant Concept of Deutero-Isaiah in the New Testament*. London: SPCK, 1959.

―――. "Response to Mikael Parsons." Pages 120–24 in *Jesus and the Suffering Servant: Isaiah 53 and Christian Origins*. Edited by W. H. Bellinger and William R. Farmer. Harrisburg, PA: Trinity Press International, 1998.

Hoskins, Paul M. *Jesus as the Fulfillment of the Temple in the Gospel of John*. Eugene, OR: Wipf and Stock, 2007.

Hrobon, Bohdan. *Ethical Dimensions of Cult in the Book of Isaiah*. BZAW 418. Berlin: De Gruyter, 2010.

Hughes, Dennis D. "The Pharmakos and Related Rites." Pages 97–114 in *Human Sacrifice in Ancient Greece*. By idem. Repr. London: Routledge, 2010.

Huizenga, Leroy A. *The New Isaac: Tradition and Intertextuality in the Gospel of Matthew*, NovTSup 131. Leiden: Brill, 2009.

Hulster, Izaak J. de. "The Two Angels of John 20:12: The Old Testament Background." *BN* 162 (2014): 97–120.

Janowski, Bernd. "Azazel." Pages 128–31 in *Dictionary of Deities and Demons in the Bible*. Edited by Karel van der Toorn, Bob Becking, and Pieter W. van der Horst. 2nd ed. Leiden: Brill, 1999.

―――. "He Bore Our Sins: Isaiah 53 and the Drama of Taking Another's Place." Pages 48–74 in *The Suffering Servant: Isaiah 53 in Jewish and Christian Sources*. Edited by Bernd Janowski and Peter Stuhlmacher. Translated by Daniel P. Bailey. Grand Rapids: Eerdmans, 2004.

Janowski, Bernd, and Gernot Wilhelm. "Der Bock, der die Sünden hinausträgt." Pages 109–69 in *Religionsgeschichtliche Beziehungen zwischen Kleinasien, Nordsyrien und dem Alten Testament*. Edited by Bernd Janowski et al. OBO 129. Göttingen: Vandenhoeck & Ruprecht / Fribourg: Universitätsverlag, 1993.

Jeremias, Joachim. *The Eucharistic Words of Jesus*. 3rd ed. Translated by Norman Perrin. New York: Charles Scribner's Sons, 1966.

Johnson, Luke Timothy. *The Gospel of Luke*. SP 3. Collegeville, MN: Liturgical, 1991.

Keener, Craig S. *A Commentary on the Gospel of Matthew*. Grand Rapids: Eerdmans, 1999.

―――. *The Gospel of John: A Commentary*. 2 vols. Grand Rapids: Baker Academic, 2003.

Kerr, Alan. *The Temple of Jesus's Body: The Temple Theme in the Gospel of John*. LNTS 220. London: T&T Clark, 2006.

Kinzer, Mark. "Temple Christology in the Gospel of John." SBLSP. Atlanta: Scholars, 1998, 447–64.

Kittel, Gerhard, and Gerhard Friedrich, eds. *Theological Dictionary of the New Testament*. Translated by Geoffrey W. Bromiley. 10 vols. Grand Rapids: Eerdmans, 1964–1976.

Klawans, Jonathan. *Impurity and Sin in Ancient Judaism*. Oxford: Oxford University Press, 2000.

Kleinig, John. *Leviticus*. ConC. Saint Louis: Concordia, 2003.

Klutz, Todd. *The Exorcism Stories in Luke-Acts: A Sociostylistic Reading*. Cambridge: Cambridge University Press, 2004.

Knibb, Michael A. "The Date of the Parables of Enoch: A Critical Review." *NTS* 25 (1978–1979): 344–59.

Koester, Helmut. *Ancient Christian Gospels: Their History and Development*. London: SCM, 1990.

Kosmala, Hans. "Form and Structure of Isaiah 58." *ASTI* 5 (1967): 69–81.

Kulik, Alexander. *Retroverting Slavonic Pseudepigrapha: Toward the Original of the Apocalypse of Abraham*. Leiden: Brill, 2005.

Kümmel, Hans Martin. "Ersatzkönig und Sündenbock." *ZAW* 80 (1968): 289–318.

Kurke, Leslie. *Aesopic Conversations: Popular Tradition, Cultural Dialogue, and the Invention of Greek Prose*. Princeton: Princeton University Press, 2011.

Lambrecht, Jan. *Out of the Treasure: The Parables in the Gospel of Matthew*. Louvain: Peeters, 1991.

Lau, Markus. "Die *Legio X Fretensis* und der Besessene von Gerasa: Anmerkungen zur Zahlenangabe 'ungefähr Zweitausend' (Mk 5,13)." *Bib* 88 (2007): 351–64.

Léon-Dufour, Xavier. *Lecture de l'Évangile selon Jean: Tome IV: L'heure de la glorification (chapitres 18–21)*. Paris: Seuil, 1996.

Levenson, Jon D. *Resurrection and the Restoration of Israel: The Ultimate Victory of the God of Life*. New Haven: Yale University Press, 2008.

Levine, Amy-Jill, and Ben Witherington III. *The Gospel of Luke*. NCB. Cambridge: Cambridge University Press, 2018.

Levine, Baruch A. *Leviticus*. JPSTC. Philadelphia: Jewish Publication Society, 1989.

Liddell, Henry George, Robert Scott, and Henry Stuart Jones. *A Greek-English Lexicon*. 9th ed. with revised supplement. Oxford: Clarendon, 1996.

Lindars, Barnabas. *The Gospel of John*. NCBC. Grand Rapids: Eerdmans, 1972.

Lunn, Nicholas P. "Jesus, the Ark, and the Day of Atonement: Intertextual Echoes in John 19:38–20:18." *JETS* 52 (2009): 731–46.

Luthy, James. *Rethinking the Acceptable Year: The Jubilee and the Basileia in Luke 4 and Beyond*. Eugene, OR: Wipf and Stock, 2019.

Luz, Ulrich. "The Final Judgment (Matt 25:31–46): An Exercise in 'History of Influence' Exegesis." Pages 271–310 in *Treasures New and Old: Contributions to Matthean Studies*. Edited by David R. Bauer and Mark Allen Powell. Atlanta: Scholars Press, 1996.

———. *Matthew: A Commentary*. Translated by James E. Crouch. 3 vols. Hermeneia. Minneapolis: Fortress, 2001–2007.

Marcovich, Miroslav. *Iustini Martyris: Dialogus cum Tryphone*. PTS 47. Berlin: De Gruyter, 1997.

Marcus, Joel. *Mark: A New Translation with Introduction and Commentary*. AB 27–27A. New York: Doubleday, 2002–2008.

Marshall, I. Howard. *The Gospel of Luke: A Commentary on the Greek Text*. NIGTC. Exeter, UK: Paternoster, 1978.

Martínez, Florentino García, and Eibert J. C. Tigchelaar, eds. *The Dead Sea Scrolls Study Edition.* 2 vols. Leiden: Brill, 1997–1998.

McCaffrey, James. *The House with Many Rooms: The Temple Theme of Jn 14.2–3.* AnBib 114. Rome: Pontifical Biblical Institute, 1988.

McEnerney, John I. *St. Cyril of Alexandria: Letters 1–50*, FC 76. Washington, DC: Catholic University of America Press, 1987.

McKnight, Scot. *Jesus and His Death: Historiography, the Historical Jesus, and Atonement Theory.* Waco, TX: Baylor University Press, 2005.

McLean, Bradley H. "Apotropaeic Rituals." Pages 65–104 in *The Cursed Christ: Mediterranean Expulsion Rituals and Pauline Soteriology.* By idem. JSNTSup 126. Sheffield: Sheffield Academic, 1996.

McNamara, Martin, Robert Hayward, and Michael Maher. *Targum Neofiti 1: Leviticus. Targum Pseudo-Jonathan: Leviticus.* ArBib 3. Collegeville, MN: Liturgical, 1994.

Mearns, Christopher L. "Dating the Similitudes of Enoch." *NTS* 25 (1978–1979): 360–69.

Meier, John P. *Matthew.* NTM 3. Wilmington, DE: Michael Glazier, 1980.

Mettinger, T. N. D. "Cherubim." Pages 189–92 in *Dictionary of Deities and Demons in the Bible.* Edited by Karel van der Toorn, Bob Becking, and Pieter W. van der Horst. 2nd ed. Leiden: Brill, 1999.

Milgrom, Jacob. "Israel's Sanctuary: The Priestly 'Picture of Dorian Gray.'" *RB* 83 (1976): 390–99.

———. *Leviticus: A New Translation with Introduction and Commentary.* AB. 3 vols. New York: Doubleday: 1991–2001.

Milik, J. T. *The Books of Enoch: Aramaic Fragments of Qumrân Cave 4.* Oxford: Clarendon, 1976.

Miller, Merrill P. "The Function of Isa 61:1–2 in 11QMelchizedek." *JBL* 88 (1969): 467–69.

Moffitt, David M. *Atonement and the Logic of Resurrection in the Epistle to the Hebrews.* NovTSup. Leiden: Brill, 2011.

Moore, Stephen D. *Empire and Apocalypse: Postcolonialism and the New Testament.* BMW 12. Sheffield: Sheffield Phoenix, 2006.

Morales, L. Michael. *Who Shall Ascend the Mountain of the Lord? A Biblical Theology of the Book of Leviticus.* Downers Grove, IL: IVP Academic, 2015.

Morgenstern, Julian. "Two Prophecies from the Fourth Century B.C. and the Evolution of Yom Kippur." *HUCA* 24 (1952–1953): 1–71.

Moscicke, Hans M. "The Gerasene Exorcism and Jesus's Eschatological Expulsion of Cosmic Powers: Echoes of Second Temple Scapegoat Traditions in Mark 5:1–10." *JSNT* 41 (2019): 363–83.

———. "Jesus, Barabbas, and the Crowd as Figures in Matthew's Day of Atonement Typology (Matt 27:15–26)." *JBL* 139 (2020): 125–53.

———. "Jesus as Goat of the Day of Atonement in Recent Synoptic Gospels Research." *CurBR* 17 (2018): 59–85.

———. "Jesus as Scapegoat in Matthew's Roman-abuse Scene (Matt 27:27–31)." *NovT* 62 (2020): 229–56.

———. *The New Day of Atonement: A Matthean Typology*. WUNT 2:517. Tübingen: Mohr Siebeck, 2020.

Motyer, Stephen. "The Rending of the Veil: A Markan Pentecost." *NTS* 33 (1987): 155–57.

Murcia, Thierry. "La question du fond historique des récits évangéliques. Deux guérisons un jour de Kippour: l'hémorroïsse et la résurrection de la fille de Jaïre et le possédé de Gérasa/Gadara." *Judaïsme Ancien* 4 (2016): 123–64.

Myers, Ched. *Binding the Strong Man: A Political Reading of Mark's Story of Jesus*. Maryknoll, NY: Orbis, 2008 (1988).

Nagy, Gregory. *The Best of the Achaeans: Concepts of the Hero in Archaic Greek Poetry*. Baltimore: John Hopkins University Press, 1979.

Nel, Marius J. "The Conceptualisation of Sin in the Gospel of Matthew." *In die Skriflig/In LuceVerbi* 51 (2017): 1–8.

Nickelsburg, G. W. E. *1 Enoch 1: A Commentary on the Book of 1 Enoch, Chapters 1–36; 81–108*. Hermeneia. Minneapolis: Fortress, 2001.

———. *Resurrection, Immortality and Eternal Life in Intertestamental Judaism*. Cambridge: 1972.

———. "Revisiting the Rich and the Poor in 1 Enoch 92–105 and the Gospel according to Luke." Pages 2:547–71 in *George W. E. Nickelsburg in Perspective: An Ongoing Dialogue of Learning*. Edited by Jacob Neusner and Alan J. Avery-Peck. 2 vols. JSJSup 80. Leiden: Brill, 2003.

Nickelsburg, G. W. E., and James C. VanderKam, eds. *1 Enoch: The Hermeneia Translation*. Minneapolis: Fortress, 2012.

Nielson, Jesper Tang. "The Lamb of God: The Cognitive Structure of a Johannine Metaphor." Pages 217–56 in *Imagery in the Gospel of John: Terms, Forms, Themes, and Theology of Johannine Figurative Language*. Edited by Jörg Frey, Jan G. van der Watt, and Ruben Zimmermann. Tübingen: Mohr Siebeck, 2006.

Nolland, John. *The Gospel of Matthew: A Commentary on the Greek Text*. NIGTC. Grand Rapids: Eerdmans, 2005.

———. *Luke*. WBC 35A–C. Dallas: Word Books, 1989–1993.

Olson, Daniel. *Enoch. A New Translation: The Ethiopic Book of Enoch, or 1 Enoch*. North Richland Hills, TX: Bibal, 2004.

Orlov, Andrei A. *Dark Mirrors: Azazel and Satanael in Early Jewish Demonology*. Albany, NY: State University of New York, 2011.

———. *Demons of Change: Antagonism and Apotheosis in Jewish and Christian Apocalypticism*. Albany, NY: State University of New York, 2020.

———. *Divine Scapegoats: Demonic Mimesis in Early Jewish Mysticism*. Albany, NY: State University of New York, 2015.

———. *The Glory of the Invisible God: Two Powers in Heaven Traditions and Early Christology*. JCTCRS 31. London: T&T Clark, 2019.

Pao, David W., and Eckhard J. Schnabel. "Luke." Pages 251–414 in *Commentary on the New Testament Use of the Old Testament*. Edited by G. K. Beale and D. A. Carson. Grand Rapids: Baker, 2007.

Papaioannou, Kim. *The Geography of Hell in the Teaching of Jesus: Gehenna, Hades, the Abyss, the Outer Darkness Where There is Weeping and Gnashing of Teeth*. Eugene, OR: Wipf and Stock, 2013.

Perrin, Nicholas. *Jesus the Priest.* Grand Rapids: Baker, 2018.

―――. *Jesus the Temple.* Grand Rapids: Baker Academic, 2010.

Perrot, Charles. *La Lecture de la Bible dans la Synagogue: Les anciennes lectures palestiniennes du Shabbat et des fêtes.* Hildesheim: Gerstenberg, 1973.

Pinker, Aron. "A Goat to Go to Azazel." *JHebS* 7 (2007): 2–25.

Pola, Thomas. *Das Priestertum bei Sacharja: Historische und traditionsgeschichtliche Untersuchung zur frühnachexilischen Herrschererwartung.* Tübingen: Mohr Siebeck, 2003.

Rahlfs, Alfred. *Septuaginta.* 2 vols. Stuttgart: Deutsche Bibelgesellschaft, 1935, 1979.

Reed, Annette Yoshiko. *Fallen Angels and the History of Judaism and Christianity: The Reception of Enochic Literature.* Cambridge: Cambridge University Press, 2005.

Ridderbos, Herman N. *The Gospel according to John: A Theological Commentary.* Translated by John Vriend. Grand Rapids: Eerdmans, 1997.

Riley, G. J. "The Devil." Pages 244–49 *Dictionary of Deities and Demons in the Bible.* Edited by Karel van der Toorn, Bob Becking, and Pieter W. van der Horst. 2nd ed. Leiden: Brill, 1999.

Ringe, Sharon H. "The Jubilee Proclamation in the Ministry and Teaching of Jesus: A Tradition-Critical Study in the Synoptic Gospels and Acts." PhD diss. Union Theological Seminary, 1981.

Roitto, Rikard. "The Two Cognitive Frames of Forgiveness in the Synoptic Gospels." *NovT* 57 (2015): 136–58.

Rubinkiewicz, Ryszard. *Die Eschatologie von Henoch 9–11 und das Neue Testament.* Translated by Herbert Ulrich. ÖBS 6. Klosterneuburg: Österreichisches Katholisches Bibelwerk, 1984.

Runesson, Anders. "Purity, Holiness, and the Kingdom of Heaven in Matthew's Narrative World." Pages 144–80 in *Purity and Holiness in Judaism and Christianity: Essays in Memory of Susan Haber.* Edited by Carl Ehrlich, Anders Runesson, and Eileen Schuller. Tübingen: Mohr Siebeck, 2013.

Rutledge, Fleming. *The Crucifixion: Understanding the Death of Jesus.* Grand Rapids: Eerdmans, 2015.

Sacchi, Paolo. "The 2005 Camaldoli Seminar on the Parables of Enoch." Pages 499–512 in *Enoch and the Messiah Son of Man.* Edited by Gabriele Boccaccini. Grand Rapids: Eerdmans, 2007.

Sanders, James A. "Isaiah in Luke." Pages 14–25 in *Luke and Scripture: The Function of Sacred Tradition in Luke-Acts.* Edited by Craig A. Evans and James A. Sanders. Eugene, OR: Wipf and Stock, 1989.

Schwartz, Baruch. "The Bearing of Sin in the Priestly Literature." Pages 3–22 in *Pomegranates and Golden Bells: Studies in Biblical, Jewish, and Near Eastern Ritual, Law, and Literature in Honor of Jacob Milgrom.* Edited by David P. Wright, David Noel Freedman, and Avi Hurvitz. Winona Lake, IN: Eisenbrauns, 1995.

Schweizer, Eduard. *The Good News according to Mark.* Translated by Donald H. Madvig. Richmond: John Knox, 1970.

Senior, Donald. *Matthew.* ANTC. Nashville: Abingdon, 1998.

Shepherd, Jerry. *Leviticus*. SGBC. Edited by Tremper Longman III and Scot McKnight. Grand Rapids: Zondervan (forthcoming).

Shively, Elizabeth E. *Apocalyptic Imagination in the Gospel of Mark: The Literary and Theological Role of Mark 3:22–30*. Berlin: Walter de Gruyter, 2012.

Sim, David C. *Apocalyptic Eschatology in the Gospel of Matthew*. SNTMS 88. Cambridge: Cambridge University Press, 1996.

———. "Matthew 22.13a and 1 Enoch 10.4a: A Case of Literary Dependence?" *JSNT* 47 (1992): 3–19.

Simenel, Philippe. "Les 2 anges de Jean 20:11–12." *ETR* 67 (1992): 71–76.

Sloan, Robert B. *The Favorable Year of the Lord: A Study of Jubilary Theology in the Gospel of Luke*. Austin, TX: Scholars, 1977.

Stanton, Graham. *A Gospel for a New People: Studies in Matthew*. Edinburgh: T&T Clark, 1992.

Stead, Michael R. *The Intertextuality of Zechariah 1–8*. LHBOTS 506. London: T&T Clark, 2009.

Stökl Ben Ezra, Daniel. "The Biblical Yom Kippur: The Jewish Fast of the Day of Atonement and the Church Fathers." *SP* 34 (2002): 493–502.

———. "Fasting with Jews, Thinking with Scapegoats: Some Remarks on Yom Kippur in Early Judaism and Christianity, in Particular, 4Q541, Barnabas 7, Matthew 27 and Acts 27." Pages 165–88 in *The Day of Atonement: Its Interpretation in Early Jewish and Christian Traditions*. Edited by Thomas Hieke and Tobias Nicklas. Leiden: Brill, 2012.

———. *The Impact of Yom Kippur on Early Christianity: The Day of Atonement from Second Temple Judaism to the Fifth Century*. WUNT 1:163. Tübingen: Mohr Siebeck, 2003.

———. "Yom Kippur in the Apocalyptic Imaginaire and the Roots of Jesus's High Priesthood." Pages 349–66 in *Transformations of the Inner Self in Ancient Religions*. Edited by Jan Assmann and Guy Stroumsa. Leiden: Brill, 1999.

Strobel, A. "Die Ausrufung des Jobeljahrs in der Nazarethpredigt Jesu: Zur apokalyptischen Tradition Lc 4,16–30." Pages 38–50 in *Jesus in Nazareth*. Edited by W. Eltester. BZNW 40. Berlin: De Gruyter, 1972.

Stuckenbruck, Loren T. "The Book of Enoch: Its Reception in Second Temple Jewish and in Christian Tradition." *EC* (2013): 7–40.

———. *The Book of Giants from Qumran: Texts, Translation, and Commentary*. Tübingen: Mohr Siebeck, 1997.

Sweeney, M. A. *The Twelve Prophets: Vol. 2*. Collegeville, MN: Liturgical, 2000.

Tannehill, Robert T. *Luke*. ANTC. Nashville: Abingdon, 1996.

Tawil, Hayim. "Azazel, the Prince of the Steepe: A Comparative Study." *ZAW* 92 (1980): 43–59.

Theisohn, Johannes. *Der auserwählte Richter*. SUNT 12. Göttingen: Vandenhoeck & Ruprecht, 1975.

Theissen, Gerd. *The Miracle Stories of the Early Christian Tradition*. Translated by Fancis McDonagh. Philadelphia: Fortress, 1983.

Tiemeyer, Lena-Sofia. "The Guilty Priesthood (Zech 3)." Pages 1–19 in *The Book of Zechariah and its Influence*. Edited by Christopher Tuckett. Burlington, VT: Ashgate, 2003.

————. *Priestly Rites and Prophetic Rage: Post-Exilic Prophetic Critique of the Priesthood.* Tübingen: Mohr Siebeck, 2006.

Tiller, Patrick A. *A Commentary on the Animal Apocalypse of 1 Enoch.* EJL 4. Atlanta: Scholars, 1993.

Tödt, Heinz Eduard. *The Son of Man in the Synoptic Tradition.* Translation by Dorothea M. Barton. London: SCM, 1965.

Trevaskis, Leigh M. *Holiness, Ethics and Ritual in Leviticus.* Sheffield: Sheffield Phoenix, 2011.

Twelftree, Graham H. *Jesus the Exorcist: A Contribution to the Study of the Historical Jesus.* WUNT 2:54. Tübingen: Mohr Siebeck, 1993.

Ulansey, David. "The Heavenly Veil Torn: Mark's Cosmic *Inclusio*." *JBL* 110 (1991): 123–25.

Um, Stephen T. *The Theme of Temple Christology in John's Gospel.* LNTS 312. London: T&T Clark, 2006.

VanderKam, James C. *The Book of Jubilees: Translated.* CSCO 511. Louvain: Peeters, 1989.

————. *Enoch: A Man for all Generations.* Columbia, SC: University of South Carolina Press, 1995.

Walck, Leslie W. *The Son of Man in the Parables of Enoch and in Matthew.* London: T&T Clark, 2011.

————. "The Son of Man in the Parables of Enoch and the Gospels." Pages 299–337 in *Enoch and the Messiah Son of Man.* Edited by Gabriele Boccaccini. Grand Rapids: Eerdmans, 2007.

Washburn, David L. *A Catalogue of Biblical Passages in the Dead Sea Scrolls.* TCSt 2. Leiden: Brill, 2003.

Weber, Kathleen. "The Image of the Sheep and the Goats in Matthew 25:31–46." *CBQ* 59 (1997): 657–78.

Wenham, Gordon J. "Sanctuary Symbolism in the Garden of Eden Story." Pages 399–404 in *I Studied Inscriptions before the Flood.* Winona Lake, IN: Eisenbrauns, 1994.

Wevers, John William. *Leviticus. Septuaginta.* VTG 2:2. Göttingen: Vandenhoeck & Ruprecht, 1986.

Wiechers, Anton. *Aesop in Delphi.* Beiträge zur Klassischen Philologie 2. Meisenheim: Anton Hain K. G., 1961.

Williams, J. T. "Cultic Elements in the Fourth Gospel." *Stud Bib* (1978): 339–50.

Wills, Lawrence M. *The Quest for the Historical Gospel: Mark, John, and the Origins of the Gospel Genre.* London: Routledge, 1997.

Wilson, Benjamin R. *The Saving Cross of the Suffering Christ: The Death of Jesus in Lukan Soteriology.* BZNW 223. Berlin: De Gruyter, 2016.

Wratislaw, Albert Henry. *Notes and Dissertations: Principally on Difficulties in the Scriptures of the New Covenant.* London: Bell and Daldy, 1863.

————. "The Scapegoat-Barabbas." *ExpTim* 3 (1891–1892): 400–03.

Wright, Archie. "The Demonology of 1 Enoch and the New Testament Gospels." Pages 215–44 in *Enoch and the Synoptic Gospels: Reminiscences, Allusions, Intertextuality.* Edited by Loren T. Stuckenbruck and Gabriele Boccaccini. EJL 44. Atlanta: Scholars, 2016.

————. *The Origin of Evil Spirits: The Reception of Genesis 6:1–4 in Early Jewish Literature*. Tübingen: Mohr Siebeck, 2005.

Wright, David P. "Deuteronomy 21:1–9 as a Rite of Elimination." *CBQ* 49 (1987): 387–403.

————. *The Disposal of Impurity: Elimination Rites in the Bible and in Hittite and Mesopotamian Literature*. SBLDS 101. Atlanta: Scholars, 1987.

Yoder, John Howard. *The Politics of Jesus*. 2nd ed. Grand Rapids: Eerdmans, 1994 (1972).

Ziegler, Joseph, ed. *Isaias*. 3rd ed. Septuaginta. VTG 14. Göttingen: Vandenhoeck & Ruprecht, 1983.

# Name and Subject

Aaron, 16, 33, 37, 113
Abraham, 11, 13, 15, 17, 83, 84, 86
Adam, 60
Adrados, Francisco, 66
Aesop, 65, 66, 69, 81, 124
Akedah, 35
*Allegorical Interpretation* (Philo), 43
Allison, Dale, 3, 31, 34, 40, 89
Amoraic traditions, 62
An, Hannah, 38
ancient elimination rituals, 2, 66, 69, 78, 80–82, 92, 124–25
angel Raphael, 14, 83, 86, 87
angel Yahoel, 83
Animal Apocalypse, 16, 67, 84, 88
antithetical destination, 6, 9, 15–17, 19
Apocalypse of Abraham, 3n4, 13, 17, 41, 67, 84, 85, 92, 113
apocalyptic dimensions, 77, 82, 84–86, 90, 92, 108, 113, 115, 125
Apollos, 65, 66, 67, 81
Aquila, 109
*Arbeit und Sitte in Palästina* (Dalman), 11
Athens, 66
atonement, 17–19, 44, 57, 68, 85, 92, 105, 107–9, 111–16, 125, 128
Azazel, 1, 2, 6, 13–17, 19, 21n5, 39–40, 44, 45, 67, 77–85, 87–93, 121–23, 125–27; portrayed as

scapegoat, 12; traditions impact on Matt. 25:31–46, 6–8

Babylonian Talmud, 13, 44
baptism-temptation narrative, 31–33, 35–38, 40, 43, 45, 46, 123, 124
Barabbas, 1, 2, 17, 31, 46, 124, 127
"Barabbas, the Scapegoat Ritual, and the Development of the Passion Narrative," (Berenson Maclean), 31
Barthélemy, D., 44
Bauckham, Richard, 60
Berenson Maclean, Jennifer K., 31
blasphemy, 65–67
Bock, Darrell, 59, 60
bodily cleansing, 36, 45, 123
Bogomil influence, 13
Bovon, François, 63, 88
Brand, Miryam, 11
Brooke, George, 60
Brown, Raymond, 112, 113

Catchpole, David, 6
Christ, 42
Collins, Yarbro, 84, 85
Coloe, Mary, 106
cosmic powers, 86, 92, 125
cosmos, 6, 19, 82, 109, 123, 127
crucifixion, 13, 57, 112, 113

# Ancient Sources

## OLD TESTAMENT

*Genesis*: 1:2, 87; 2–3 LXX, 109; 2:10–
14, 118n10; 3:1 LXX, 109; 3:24,
108; 6:1–4, 78; 7:11, 87; 8:2, 87;
15:9, 26n24; 22, 35, 45, 123; 22:2,
34, 49n26, 49n27; 22:3, 49n27; 22:6,
49n27; 22:11, 49n26; 22:12, 34,
49n26; 22:13, 49n27; 22:15, 49n26;
22:16, 49n26; 22:16 LXX, 34; 27:9,
25n23; 27:16, 25n23; 28:12, 106;
28:22, 106; 32:14–15, 26n24; 37:31,
10, 25n23; 37 LXX, 10; 38:17,
25n23, 27n32; 38:20, 25n23, 27n32;
38:23, 25n23, 27n32

*Exodus*: 12:5, 23n23; 21:2, 71n10;
24:18, 40; 25:14, 116n2; 25:17–22,
107, 108, 118n22; 25:19, 118n17;
25:20, 108; 25:22, 113, 116n2;
30:19, 50n37; 30:26, 116n2; 31:15,
72n38; 34:28, 40; 37:6–9, 118n22;
37:7–9, 107, 108; 40:2–3, 116n2;
40:3, 116n2; 40:5–6, 116n2; 40:21,
116n2; 40:22, 116n2; 40:24, 116n2;
40:26, 116n2; 40:29, 116n2; 40:34–
35, 106, 113

*Leviticus*: 1:4, 47n9; 1:10, 25n23,
27n32; 3:2, 47n9; 4:4, 47n9; 4:24,
47n9; 9:23, 106; 16, 1, 3n4, 5, 6, 8,
19, 30n75, 31, 33, 35, 38, 39, 52n58,
67, 77, 82, 87, 89, 92, 114, 121,
126, 127; 16:1, 61, 62; 16:2, 113;
16:2–4, 36; 16:3, 29n47; 16:4, 36,
45, 123; 16:5, 29n47; 16:5–22, 5,
9, 45; 16:7–8, 11; 16:7–10, 11, 45,
66, 90, 123; 16:7 LXX, 51n54; 16:8,
10, 14, 16, 21n5, 39, 45, 52n56, 77,
81, 96n59, 122, 123; 16:8–10, 9, 14;
16:8–10, 36, 54n95, 122; 16:10, 10,
14, 16, 21n5, 39, 45, 51n49, 68, 69,
73n53, 77, 81, 87, 91, 96n59, 122,
123, 124; 16:10 LXX, 74n54, 74n56,
99n105; 16:11–17, 36, 112; 16:15,
9; 16:15–16, 37; 16:15–17, 45, 123;
16:15–19, 26n28, 32, 33; 16:15–22,
45, 123; 16:16, 47–48n11, 61, 62;
16:18, 9; 16:20–22, 9, 66; 16:20–22,
33, 46–47n5, 77, 90; 16:21, 10, 37,
45, 47n11, 61, 62, 68, 74n55, 80,
95n48, 123; 16:21–22, 6, 14, 15, 17,
26n28, 39, 45, 69, 74n54, 81, 83, 84,
87, 98n85, 99n105, 121, 123, 124;
16:21 LXX, 33, 47–48n11; 16:22,
10, 14, 37, 44, 68, 74n55, 80; 16:26,
21n5, 30n71, 39, 45, 68, 73n53,
74n54, 96n59, 98n85, 123; 16:26–27,

## NEW TESTAMENT

## APOCRYPHA AND PSEUDEPIGRAPHA

# DEAD SEA SCROLLS

# PHILO

# JOSEPHUS

# RABBINIC LITERATURE

# EARLY CHRISTIAN LITERATURE

# GRECO-ROMAN LITERATURE

*Lib. Hist.:* 2.55, 95n43

Herodotus
*Hist.:* 2.39, 95n42; 4.103, 97n61

Leo
*Sermon:* 92.2, 73n42

Plutarch
*Mor.:* 363b, 95n43

Strabo
*Geogr.:* 10.2.9, 75n71

Tzetzes
*Child.:* 5.728–45, 95n41

# About the Author

Hans M. Moscicke received his PhD from Marquette University in 2019, in Judaism and Christianity in Antiquity. He is the author of *The New Day of Atonement: A Matthean Typology* (2020) and numerous articles published in journals such as *Journal of Biblical Literature, Novum Testamentum, New Testament Studies, Journal for the Study of the New Testament,* and *Journal of Early Christian Studies.* He is currently an instructor at Saint Louis University.